Service Management and Marketing Principles

This book explores the service economy and challenges that all organizations face as goods and services make way for a world where customers (B2C) and businesses (B2B) seek seamless, thoughtful, and exceptional experiences. This book introduces readers to a range of interrelated topics and the application of service management and marketing theories which are fundamentally critical to the success of all enterprises seeking competitive advantage through enhanced customer experience.

This book analyses management and marketing challenges in the service and experience economy and provides insights into how marketers and managers can strike a balance between supply, demand, price, and quality and leverage technology for operational efficiency and to better manage customer service and expectations. Through the coverage of critical foundational topics, from how value is created; the evolution of global economies from goods, services to experiences; foundations of customer-centric management; managing service workers; integrating human touch with high-tech service; and many others, the authors provide a holistic understanding of management in a complex, globally interconnected world.

This book will be useful for students, researchers, and instructors of business management, marketing, commerce, and economics. It will also be of interest to professionals working in healthcare, retail, financial services, government hospitality, leisure, tourism, and other services.

Jay Kandampully is Professor of Service Management and Hospitality in the Department of Human Sciences at the Ohio State University, USA.

David J. Solnet is Professor of Service Management and Service Work at University of Queensland, Business School, Australia.

Service Management and Marketing Principles

Competing in the Service Economy

Jay Kandampully and David J. Solnet

LONDON AND NEW YORK

Designed cover image: © Getty Images / Suriya Phosri

First published 2024
by Routledge
4 Park Square, Milton Park, Abingdon, Oxon OX14 4RN

and by Routledge
605 Third Avenue, New York, NY 10158

Routledge is an imprint of the Taylor & Francis Group, an informa business

© 2024 Jay Kandampully and David J. Solnet

The right of Jay Kandampully and David J. Solnet to be identified as authors of this work has been asserted in accordance with sections 77 and 78 of the Copyright, Designs and Patents Act 1988.

All rights reserved. No part of this book may be reprinted or reproduced or utilised in any form or by any electronic, mechanical, or other means, now known or hereafter invented, including photocopying and recording, or in any information storage or retrieval system, without permission in writing from the publishers.

Trademark notice: Product or corporate names may be trademarks or registered trademarks, and are used only for identification and explanation without intent to infringe.

British Library Cataloguing-in-Publication Data
A catalogue record for this book is available from the British Library

ISBN: 978-1-032-60370-4 (hbk)
ISBN: 978-1-032-74965-5 (pbk)
ISBN: 978-1-003-47037-3 (ebk)

DOI: 10.4324/9781003470373

Typeset in Sabon
by Deanta Global Publishing Services, Chennai, India

Contents

List of Figures		*vi*
List of Tables		*vii*
Acknowledgments		*viii*
	Introduction	1
1	The service economy	3
2	Management and marketing challenges in the service economy	20
3	Management implications for service supply and demand	44
4	Understanding service quality	63
5	Customer centricity in practice	86
6	Translating service vision to action	112
7	Managing customer experience and service failures	135
8	Crafting a culture for service excellence	162
9	Leveraging technology	184
10	Fostering service innovation	207
	Index	227

Figures

1.1	Service as a unified force	6
1.2	GDP composition by sector: Developing countries in Asia	9
2.1	Product-experience continuum	24
3.1	Relationship between service demand and quality	48
4.1	The nonlinear relationship between satisfaction and loyalty	72
4.2	Technical quality and functional quality in service quality	76
4.3	Perceived service quality gap	77
4.4	Relative importance of service dimensions in meeting expectations	80
4.5	ZOT's for outcome and process dimensions	81
6.1	Moments-of-truth 'cascade' in a basic retail setting	128
6.2	Example of a customer journey map	132
7.1	Three stages of service consumption along the value and experience continuum	138
7.2	The service encounter triad	141
8.1	External, internal, and interactive marketing	166
8.2	Levels of organizational culture	172
8.3	The service-profit chain	178
9.1	Different types of service encounters	186
9.2	The 'three realms' of today's integrated servicescape	189
9.3	Types of online platforms	192
10.1	The innovation S-curve	212
10.2	David's Noodle and Hotpot	219

Tables

2.1	Implications of distinctive characteristics of service	28
2.2	An extended marketing mix for services	38
5.1	Product-centric versus customer-centric approaches	90
5.2	Potential challenges and proposed strategies for customer centricity	93
7.1	Common challenges with managing the employee–customer interface	143
7.2	Strategies for managers to overcome challenges in the service encounter	144
9.1	REDTAG's data-driven approach to customer experience	202
9.2	The changing roles of customers and employees in the Service Encounter 2.0	203

Acknowledgments

Writing a textbook requires the support of many – friends, family, and a 'village' of supporting colleagues. As coauthors, we must make a number of specific acknowledgments. This book would not have been possible without our two outstanding writing and research assistants – Siobhan Rees and Dr Maria Golubovskaya – who have worked with us over many years and many projects. Their work is and has always been of the highest quality and absolutely invaluable. They are the detailed eyes and ears for all elements of the book; they asked the hard questions, identified critical gaps in the material, and encouraged us to pursue or further develop some topics. They challenged us, kept us going, and made sure the book was completed on time!

We could never adequately thank Siobhan and Maria enough for their contribution – we are both eternally grateful to them.

In addition, a special thank you must be given to our colleagues from around the world who contributed relevant cases that have helped to bring the service concepts to life throughout the book. We acknowledge the contributions of our colleagues listed below:

Chapter 1

Dr. Aarti Saini, Department of Commerce, Shaheed Bhagat Singh College, University of Delhi, India.

Author of *BYJU's the Learning App*.

Chapter 2

Dr. Senthil Kumaran P, Welcomgroup Graduate School of Hotel Administration, Manipal, India.

Author of *Branded Differentiation: Making the Intangible, 'Tangible'*.

Chapter 3

Dr. Meeta Munshi and Dr. Sandip Trada, Institute of Management, Nirma University, India.

Authors of *Internet Saathi: Empowering Rural Women in India through ICT*.

Dr. Madhavi Ayyagari, Executive Director, Mindsbourg Consulting, UAE.
Dr. Sanjai Parahoo, Hamdan Bin Mohammed Smart University, UAE.
Dr. Joseph Stevens, Murdoch University Dubai, UAE.

Authors of *CAFU: Fuel-on-Demand Powered by AI, IoT and Machine Learning*.

Chapter 4

Dr. Mayank Bhatia and Dr. Samik Shome, Institute of Management, Nirma University, India.

Authors of *Burner India: Excelling through Service Quality*.

Chapter 5

Dr. Mithilesh Pandey, Department of Marketing & Strategy, ICFAI Business School (IBS), Hyderabad, India.

Author of *PayTm Gold: Transforming Product to Service*.

Dr. Vibha Arora, Department of Marketing, ICFAI Business School (IBS) Gurugram, India.
Dr. Ravi Chatterjee, IMT Business School, Dubai, UAE.

Authors of *Customer Centricity at Indian Coffee House*.

Chapter 6

Dr. Ardhendu Shekhar Singh, Symbiosis International (Deemed University), India.
Dr. Sanjai K Parahoo, Hamdan Bin Mohammed Smart University, UAE.
Dr. Madhavi Ayyagari, Executive Director, Mindsbourg Consulting, Dubai, UAE.

Authors of *Nahari: Meeting Needs through a Transformative Service Initiative*.

Dr. Kameshwar Rao V.S. Modekurti, Finance and Accounting, ICFAI Business School (IBS), India.

Author of *Narayana Health: Transformative Leadership in Health Care Service*.

Chapter 7

Ms.Vishakha Kumari, The Ohio State University, USA.

Author of *An Integrated Relationship and Supply Chain: Crimson Cup Coffee & Tea*.

Dr. Malini Majumdar, Army Institute of Management, Kolkata, India.

Author of *Recovery with a Smile: How Zomato Effectively Handles Service Failure*.

Chapter 8

Dr. Rajneesh Choubisa, Birla Institute of Technology & Sciences, India.

Author of *The 'Three Es' at Tata Tele Business Services: Employee Engagement, Empowerment, and Eudaimonia*.

Dr. Bin Wang (Peter), Hilton School of Hospitality, Sichuan Tourism University, China.

Author of *Employee-centricity in Action: A Tale of Dignity, Respect, and Happiness*.

Chapter 9

Dr. Madhavi Ayyagari, Executive Director, Mindsbourg Consulting, Dubai, UAE.
Dr. Sanjai Parahoo, Hamdan Bin Mohammed Smart University, UAE.
Dr. Ravi Chatterjee, IMT Business School, Dubai, UAE.

Authors of *Enhancing Customer Experience through Data-driven Decision-making: The Case of REDTAG*.

Dr. Yupal Shukla, University of Bologna, Italy.

Author of *How Gamification Helped CRED to Transform Customer Experience*.

Chapter 10

Dr. Vidya Patwardhan, Dr. Thirugnanasambantham K, and Dr. Senthil Kumaran P, Welcomgroup Graduate School of Hospitality Administration, Manipal, India.

Authors of *Innovation and Empowerment: The Bombay Canteen – Local Food with Love.*

Dr. Sanjai k Parahoo, Hamdan Bin Mohammed Smart University, UAE.
Dr. Madhavi Ayyagari, Executive Director, Mindsbourg Consulting, Dubai, UAE.
Dr. Ardhendu Shekhar Singh, Symbiosis International (Deemed University), India.

Authors of *iGrab Café: An Innovative Business Model to Compete in a Congested Market.*

Introduction

Our world continues to undergo a dramatic transformation from the days when agriculture and manufacturing drove global economic output and employment. Gone are the days when firms create products then attempt to sell them. *The purpose of this book is to address the fundamental essence of business today, which particularly in service organizations (which this book will explain includes nearly all organizations!) is to solve problems for customers and society.* This concept of a solution orientation has instigated a new mindset and has provided service firms with a unique opportunity to think differently and to operate from an outside–in perspective. In other words, service firms have to shift from a firm (organizational) focus to a customer- and solution-oriented focus.

This model recognizes the importance of the entire ecosystem, with its multiple capabilities inside and outside the firm creating value for the customer. It is this new perspective of networks of capabilities that has helped firms such as Airbnb and Uber to conceive business models that have revolutionized the market. The idea that customers within large networks of relationships provide more long-term value for the firm is also exemplified by firms such as Google, Facebook (Meta), YouTube, and many others. To achieve that, they had to disregard the short-term inside–out business models that focused on increased revenues and move toward value co-creation through networks of relationships which organically convert into revenue growth.

We acknowledge that it is important for the readers of this textbook to gain a specialized understanding of traditional business topics such as management, marketing, operations, finance, and human resources. This book, however, focuses on all these areas but from the perspective of the *service imperative* that has evolved within all industry sectors. We, therefore, introduce the reader to a range of interrelated topics that are critical for the success of all enterprises, including a B2B context. You will notice that some of the topics discussed in this book are not only interconnected but are also closely linked with each other.

DOI: 10.4324/9781003470373-1

Chapter 1 introduces you to the 'service economy' and the transformation from manufacturing to goods to experiences. Chapter 2 presents a range of challenges for managers and marketers as a result of the transformation to a service and experience-based economy. Chapter 3 digs deeply into one of the key challenges in services – variations in supply and demand. Chapter 4 provides insights into how customers perceive quality of service and how this can be measured and managed. Chapter 5 addresses the foundational concept of customer centricity and helps the reader understand how easy it is to say the words but how difficult it is to be truly customer centered. Chapter 6 presents the link between service strategy, vision, and operational needs. Chapter 7 articulates the key stakeholders in service through the service encounter 'triad' and then provides a rich discussion about the inevitability of service failure and how great firms address failures through proactive service recovery strategies. Central to all service enterprises is the need for a service-oriented organizational culture, addressed in Chapter 8. Chapter 9 focuses on technology and some of the important considerations service managers and marketers must take into account to ensure the right balance and motivations for the use of technology. The final chapter, fittingly, addresses innovation and the need for all enterprises to have innovation woven into their DNA, knowing that stagnation does not lead to sustainability. Indeed, all of the elements in this book must be understood as unifying fields of knowledge.

You may have gathered by now that as a service manager you are stepping into a very different role. A role that will require you to recognize and value the contributions of all people around you. To put it bluntly, understanding the core concepts of service management and marketing requires you to adopt a new 'lifestyle,' and a new way of thinking, different from the past. Service leaders thus have the ability to create positive ripples of impact on all stakeholders of the firm and society, and enhance the sustainability of the environment. We as authors of this book have had the chance to work for many years in the service industry. We are very happy to have had the opportunity to adopt this 'lifestyle' that transformed our lives. We hope that you will find this new 'lifestyle' of a service leader equally rewarding and enjoyable.

Jay and David

Chapter 1

The service economy

Study objectives

Having completed this chapter, readers should be able to understand:

- the evolution from a product-based to a service and experience-based economy;
- the importance of service organizations in the modern experience-based economy;
- the concept of service marketing and management and the complex nature of service; and
- the interdependency among service firms in providing customers with desired benefits.

The framework of this chapter

This chapter is set out as follows:

- Introduction
  o The scope of this book
  o Linking service and experience management
- The evolution of global economies
- The growth of the service economy
- Defining service marketing and service management
  o The evolution of thought for a service business
- The nature of 'service'
  o Core services and peripheral services
  o The tangible–intangible continuum
  o What really matters to customers
- Servitization
- Interdependency of service providers
  o Coordinated benefits
  o Service interrelationships

DOI: 10.4324/9781003470373-2

4   The service economy

  o Online, sharing economy, and technology-led interrelationships
- Applying these service theories and concepts
- Summary of chapter
- Review questions
- Suggested readings
- References

Introduction

Technology and global connectivity have brought about many changes and innovations in almost all industry sectors around the globe. These never-ending technological advancements and access to knowledge mean that it is nearly impossible for any organization to compete on product differentiation alone. Rather, an organization's ability to differentiate through service and the way a customer experiences the interactions with the organization has become the key differentiator. It is not unusual for firms now to allocate many of their marketing budgets to increasing service and customer experience – the best way to create repeat business.

Caterpillar, the world's leading manufacturer of construction and mining equipment, is recognized in the market for their initiative in developing 'Customer Experience Champions' in all corners of their company. This strong message of their commitment to customer experience provides a unique sense of reliability to their customers and to their network of stakeholders. Similarly, many companies create roles and positions that are devoted to customer experience (for example, Chief Customer Officer, Customer Experience Officer, and Vice-President of Customer Experience). These also communicate the importance of service and customer experience externally as well as create accountability within the company.

Customers today are simply no longer satisfied with products alone, and they are more discerning and informed than ever before. They expect a wide range of experiences, purchase options, and connections to other brands and services. Businesses often have to collaborate with nontraditional partners (clothing retailers incorporating hairdressers, spas, nail salons, etc.) to offer different blends of experiences to offer uniqueness to their customers. Service and experience have emerged as the new product in today's customer-driven marketplace. For example, Adidas, the shoe company, has been very successful in selling experiences. They blend their shoe offer with a unique experience that connects customers with like-minded communities and instills people with the idea of a healthier lifestyle. Experience has become the new yardstick or even the currency that measures the strengths/longevity of firms to create relationships with customers through personalized experiences.

The concept of service is therefore able to transform the needs of a customer into a solution orientation. This was one of the ways that IBM in the 1990s transformed from a 'computer company' to a 'solutions provider'.

Their solution-oriented business models have the capacity to create unique experiences at all levels of the economy and to form lasting relationships. This holds true for many familiar and successful global businesses (Apple, Google, Amazon, FedEx, Starbucks, and more). Thus, imagining and solving customer unsolved service needs have fueled the growth of the service industry around the globe.

It is therefore imperative for all parts of any business to focus on creating personalized, holistic, and memorable experiences for the customer. Firms today don't have to attract customers; if they are able to offer unique experiences, customers will seek out those firms they consider more valuable. How many of us have seen advertisements from Google? Customers trust the answers provided by Google. It is their accuracy and efficiency that people trust and value. Value and price have very different meanings in today's world. Even at the lower end of the economy, customers are not happy to accept something that is not associated with value or trust. While technology is imperative in today's world, only people – real people! – can effectively create and build a bonding relationship, commonly occurring through the service process. Therefore, it is imperative today more than ever before that service has to be understood and managed from every aspect of business knowledge we have.

The scope of this book

If you were studying business before the early 1990s, it is not likely that you would have focused on the service sector. The idea that the world was transforming into one dominated by services had yet to dawn on practitioners and educators. In the past, the fundamental basis for business was selling products. Although this was a misplaced focus even then, since the service economy was already well-developed in the 1990s, it is more so now. In fact, over 80% of advanced economies in the world today are service-based – and nearly every business creates a customer experience in some way. To most effectively address the challenges of today's global economy, this book draws upon various fields, including marketing, management, operations, human resource management, and others – to introduce the principles of this vitally important subject area, relevant to practically any type of business or organization across all sectors. Understanding the service and experience economy and how leadership and management can be most effective is vital and the main scope of this text.

This book is about management and marketing and the many interrelated key factors that drive success in the service and experience economy. Because of the focus on the customer and the importance of a total organizational approach, the terms management and marketing in a business context are used collectively to create a unified approach. This is because marketing, managing, and leading in a service industry require a firm to have a service 'mindset' in all of its internal and external activities. This book offers principles and insights into how to bring this mindset to life.

Linking service and experience management

A brief history of the evolution from 'product to service' was nicely summarized in a seminal article in 1993 by Fisk, Brown, and Bitner that references the growth and maturity of the field of service marketing, which according to their analysis had reached an element of maturity in the late 1980s. This disciplinary area has undergone constant transformation since then, with a broadening of the area of 'service' to 'customer experience' (CX) or experience management. Nevertheless, it is the foundational service theory that is most critical and instrumental for managers to help them define, innovate, lead, and measure CX. Figure 1.1 illustrates the interconnection of service and experiences to many disciplinary perspectives (e.g., management, marketing, operations, human resources). This book will continually view service through these interdisciplinary lenses (with consistent repeating messages about how certain phenomena might be viewed by a manager, a marketer, or a human resource manager).

Figure 1.1 Service as a unified force

The evolution of global economies

There is a consensus that economic growth, higher disposable income, and technological advances have contributed to the rapid growth of the service sector. Moreover, this growth has not been at the expense of mining, farming, or manufacturing. In fact, the service sector has become an enabling factor in assisting these primary and secondary industries to achieve global competitiveness. They have transformed themselves into truly customer-oriented, service-focused enterprises, irrespective of the products that they actually produce and sell. One of the authors of this book was recently involved in an executive development program for a large mining company based in China. This company mines iron ore and converts this to steel that is used by manufacturers. Does this sound like a service firm? In fact, they have always considered themselves a commodity company competing on price. But increasing competition has put pressure on the company to innovate, and one of the ways they did so was to educate senior executives, transforming the company mindset. A transformative shift occurred whereby the company realized that creating excellent customer experiences (mainly B2B), customer-centered processes, doing small things to create trusting relationships, and working hard to exceed customer expectations could create a competitive advantage so that price would not be the only deciding factor on purchase decisions. This transformation of mindset from a 'mining' mindset to a customer experience and service mindset helped transform company leadership and put the company on a new path to success.

As highlighted above, changes in the business world, such as the rapid advancement of technology and social media, have also meant that organizations have to transform from simply making and selling 'products' to considering the whole customer experience. Companies are no longer just defined by the products they make. Instead, they have to deliver superior value and establish meaningful relationships with customers. This therefore involves creating memorable experiences, which means thinking about how to engage customers across all points of contact (called 'touchpoints', covered in more detail in Chapter 6). Today's business interactions with customers do not occur as a linear process – rather, customers co-create and customize products and services with the firm. Indeed, transformations are occurring across all industry segments and thus represent a new wave of dramatic economic revolution with an intense preoccupation with service and experience.

In order to survive in today's competitive marketplace, companies must be willing and able to transform. Take Marks and Spencer, for example; this retail company was formed in the 1800s, but in the late 1990s, in the face of decline, they underwent a major reinvention. This involved thinking beyond the 'bricks and mortar' of their stores, to focus on how to engage customers across multiple touchpoints – both physical and digital. By making the buying experience easier, creating a seamless online presence, and taking a renewed focus on frontline staff, the company was able to exceed customers' expectations. Overall, their transformation was not about their products, but rather about developing a service focus within the organization to offer a customer-centric experience.

There are many more examples of how the business world is moving from being product-oriented to service- and experience-oriented. But first, let's take a step back and look at how the service sector has evolved and its importance in the global economy.

The growth of the service economy

The service sector plays a significant role in the economic growth of every nation in the world. The national economy of most nations depends heavily on its service infrastructure – including transportation, communication, education, healthcare, and various government services. This growth can be partially attributed to increasing household spending across most countries in the last few decades.

Ernst Engel, a German statistician, showed that prosperity and an increase in service infrastructure go together. More businesses undertake service-oriented activities – offering services either directly to the final customer or to other business operations. The majority of the population within a community subsequently becomes employed in service-related activities. Service thus lies at the very heart of the economic activity of any society.

In the second half of the twentieth century, economically developed nations underwent extensive social and economic transformation accompanied by a significantly increased rate of spending on services. In the early 1950s, service expenditure accounted for approximately one-third of personal consumption expenditure. It now accounts for about one-half of household expenditure and is expected to continue to rise. This trend has been apparent in both developed and developing countries in the past 30 years.

Most developed economies have transformed from being farming, mining, and manufacturing economies into service economies. The service sector today employs more than twice as many people as the manufacturing and agricultural sectors combined. The influence of this growing service sector permeates every part of the economy. The service sector in most of the developed economies contributes more than 70% of the world's gross domestic product (GDP) and offers employment to more than 75% of the population. In the developing economies in Asia, the service sector is also the greatest contributor to national GDP compared to the manufacturing industry and agriculture (see Figure 1.2). A key finding by the Australian Bureau of Statistics (ABS) during that time period was that the service industries overall were the largest contributors to national employment growth (ABS, 2019).

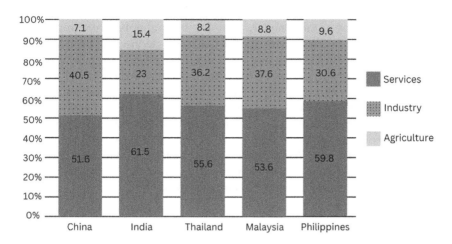

Figure 1.2 GDP composition by sector: Developing countries in Asia (*developed based on statistics from CIA (n.d.)*)

Defining service marketing and service management

Service marketing, like service management, is a comprehensive framework that effective organizations should utilize throughout their entire operations, rather than limiting it to specific departments. Indeed, everyone from management, marketing, operations, HR, and all other areas of an organization is responsible for the quality of service that the firm delivers. Service marketing has a much wider perspective in the service context and therefore is multidisciplinary in focus, contributing to the success of modern organizations.

The term 'service management' was not actually introduced into mainstream scholarship until the early 1980s. One of the earliest, yet still often cited, definitions of service management is that it is "a total organizational approach that makes the quality of service, as perceived by the customer, the primary driving force for the operation of any business..." (Albrecht, 1988, p. 20). The underlying theme of today's service management approach is that service management is a comprehensive framework that emphasizes a mindset throughout the entire organization rather than limiting it to parts of an organization. Ben Schneider (2004), a great advocate of service management from an organizational behavior perspective, defines service management as "a multidisciplinary field of practice and research on service quality that includes services marketing, services operations management, and services human resources management" (p. 144). All of these definitions emphasize the multidisciplinary nature of service management, highlighting the point that, while perhaps not a discipline in its own right, it is clearly a vital aspect of success in service organizations.

The evolution of thought for a service business

As outlined earlier in this chapter, there has been a global shift from product sales-focused marketing to that of managing services and experiences. Accordingly, academic theory and terminology have evolved too. This is clear in the expansion of the traditional four Ps of the 'Marketing Mix' (McCarthy, 1960) – including Product, Price, Place, and Promotion. These Ps were an established formula for marketing products; however, service marketers soon found this mix insufficient due to the unique nature of service. Thus the seven Ps were introduced (or the 'Extended Marketing Mix') – which included the traditional four Ps, plus People, Processes, and Physical Evidence (Booms & Bitner, 1981). The unique nature of service and service marketing will be discussed in more detail later in this book (see Chapter 2).

The nature of 'service'

What exactly does the word 'service' or 'services' mean? Service is often defined as an act or a process (a verb), representing a form of economic exchange. Services (with an 's'), on the other hand, are defined as intangible units of output or activities (a noun) which in a commercial sense are offered for sale or as part of a sale. While the two words are frequently used interchangeably, in this text we adopt the position that it is the managing and marketing of 'service' (i.e., managing the delivery of customer value which includes aspects of both tangible and intangible offerings) which is the primary focus for managers.

Service has been described as a 'deed, act, or performance' or as 'encounters in time, rather than physical objects'. In other words, services are subjective outcomes achieved through time, motion, and emotion – but achieved in the presence of, and with the assistance of, tangible products and information. Similarly, services can be described as various combinations of activities, benefits, and interactions. For example, from a student's perspective, a university's services consist of:

- *activities* – a variety of activities such as lectures, tutorials, extra-curricular clubs, sports, and so on;
- *benefits* – such as the knowledge received in lectures, personalized assistance in tutorials, and social interactions and connections established through the various extracurricular activities; and
- *interactions* – all the interactions that the students are exposed to while participating in the above activities and receiving the listed benefits.

Thus, from the customer's point of view, service can be understood as a total experience. Moreover, it is an experience in which the customer encounters and interacts at an intimate level with the service provider, other guests, the physical environment, and the process of service delivery. On a conceptual level, this experience can be termed as a bundle, a package, or an assemblage.

Core services and peripheral services

Although it is theoretically possible to make a distinction between services and goods, the reality is that most services are associated with some physical items and most products are accompanied by some aspects of service. In theory, each of these components – the intangible service component and the tangible product component – constitutes only one part of the competitive package that the firm offers. But, in reality, from the perspective of the customer, the two components do not exist independently. A service firm offers a 'package' or a 'bundle' that includes a mixture of services, physical items, images, and experiences. Neither services nor goods are marketed on their own. What is marketed is a 'bundle' or package to meet a specific need of the customer.

The service package is the sum total of all the goods, services, and experiences offered to the customer. Most service offerings or service packages consist of:

- a *core service* – the major benefit that the consumer is seeking; and
- *peripheral services* – the little things offered as added bonuses.

The core service is the centerpiece of the service offering – the basic reason for being in business. Without the core service, a business enterprise makes no sense. For example, if you buy a smartphone, the core service is the ability to communicate with your contacts. The peripheral services are a naturally compatible set of goods, services, and experiences which, when combined with the core service, serve to create an impression of high value in the customer's mind. Using the same example from above of a smartphone, peripheral services include access to the Internet, emails, camera, calculator, navigation system, recording, and so forth. However, it should be noted that you would not buy a smartphone only because it has a great camera and other gadgets if it cannot be reliable for making phone calls. This means customers will not compromise on the *core service* offer.

The peripheral service should support, complement, and add value to the core service. The peripheral service, in most cases, is intended to provide the 'leverage' that helps build or enhance the value of the total package in the eyes of the customer. Similarly, the core service of a hotel is a clean and safe place to sleep. But there are many peripheral offerings that most hotels provide, and as the cost increases, expectations about quality and offerings go up as well.

Firms commonly compete in similar markets and offer comparable core services. Scholars and practitioners argue that the highest levels of customer satisfaction come from the peripherals that surround the core service – how the food is served in the restaurant; how the receptionist assists the customer when a credit card is not accepted; and so on. Thus, from a customer satisfaction perspective, the differentiation between core service and peripheral service can be crucial. Core product and/or service differentiation is a challenging task in a competitive market; therefore, in many situations, the only possible difference between competitors lies with these peripherals. The strongest company in the marketplace will often be the one that offers the best-designed package of peripherals (provided their core offering meets customer expectations).

The tangible–intangible continuum

Almost all services and products are offered to customers as a combination of service elements and product elements. There are very few 'pure' services that do not utilize some form of product element in their service offering and, conversely, there are very few 'pure' products that do not require a service element as a component of their offer to the customer. Businesses exist on a continuum – those that have very little tangible product component are at one end of this continuum, and those with a larger tangible element are at the other end.

What really matters to customers

The customer's perception of quality, and the subsequent image (position) gained by the firm in the market, is often influenced more by the intangible elements of the offer than by its tangible elements. In a competitive marketplace, firms find difficulty in maintaining superiority based on the tangible components of their offer alone – because these components are easily replicable by competing firms. However, positive personal interaction with an obliging employee in addition to the various service elements in the package demonstrates a firm's superior service. Competitors have more difficulty emulating this sort of intangible element of service. The importance of 'human touch' to customers is considerably more valuable to the customers than the growing technology-supported service encounters. This aspect is covered in more detail in Chapter 9.

Differentiating and understanding the tangible and intangible elements of the business are important for service managers to identify methods to enhance customers' perception of quality. The nature of service and the differences between goods and services will be discussed further in Chapter 2.

Servitization

The competitive advantage of offering a memorable service experience has become increasingly evident, since there is generally little to differentiate competing products from the customer's perspective. Indeed, service has become an important value-assessment variable in predicting a firm's success in the marketplace. Over the past few decades, we have witnessed more businesses focusing on their service offerings to enhance their core 'product' offerings. This point is expanded further below when we introduce service packages or 'bundles'.

By taking a customer-focused view on providing holistic and long-term engagement, companies have thus incorporated more 'service' components within their offers. This concept was coined 'servitization' (Vandermerwe & Rada, 1988) in the late 1980s, and is now characteristic of most traditional 'product' companies. For example, the computer manufacturer IBM evolved from being a 'computer company' to a service-focused 'solution provider'. By adding value to the overall experience of buying a physical product, companies are able to differentiate from competitors and develop a more meaningful relationship with their customers.

Interdependency of service providers

Coordinated benefits

Ultimately, services or experiences are usually offered in sequences or in 'bundles'. These are of two main types:

- A single service provider might offer a number of services in sequence to any given customer; or
- A single customer might receive additional services from *other* providers before and after the service currently being rendered.

Although each of these services can be seen as an isolated benefit, they must be compatible, complementary, and coordinated.

Let us consider, as an example, a tourist or business traveler staying in a hotel. This traveler might have received services from an airline, a taxi company, a rideshare, or a limousine hire service before arriving at the hotel. After leaving the hotel, the traveler might take an Uber or a tour coach to receive the next service. From the customer's perspective, although these services are experienced separately, they are interrelated. The linkage between them is important if the traveler's itinerary is to run smoothly. The needs of customers can thus extend beyond the capabilities of one company's product or service offering.

Service firms cannot and do not exist in isolation. Through partnerships and collaborations with other firms, bundles of services are offered to satisfy the various needs of individual customers. These partners might or might not be involved in serving the customers directly. The entire system, however, is internally organized by an interactive web of relationships in which the customer participates at various stages – in both the production and consumption of the various services.

Service products are thus often a composite product which, from the perspective of a customer, is viewed as a total experience made up of individual parts. This poses a major challenge in delivering superior service. The overall service 'product' is comprised of a combination of services which, although fundamentally independent, are consumed by customers in a continuous chain, one after the other. Hence, poor performance within one sector, or by one service provider, can affect customers' perception of the other service providers in the chain. For example, a tourist receiving a positive experience at the airline check-in counter may then have a higher perceived experience on their flight and perhaps even influence perceptions about other services that are yet to be received (local transport, accommodation, and so forth). Therefore, a positive initial experience can also influence the tourist's favorable perception of the destination. Conversely, a negative experience may also trigger many successive negative perceptions.

Ultimately, service networks (ecosystems) are intended to benefit both the customer and the firm, and they often extend beyond national boundaries, depending on the firm and what is being offered to the customer. Through global networks, businesses are able to enhance the perceived value of their offer.

Service interrelationships

The concept of *service interrelationships* is critical to leading, managing, and marketing of service firms. It reflects the importance of *all* services involved in the relationship. And it must be understood that service interrelationship applies within a single organization, as well as across collaborating organizations.

Within any service organization, almost all service needs are cross-functional in nature. For example, a customer's request for car repair work is primarily an operational task; however, how the mechanic explains the repair work to the customer is clearly a function linked to the quality and skill of the mechanic which positively impacts the marketing of the firm. Cross-functional *systems* are therefore required within all service firms – that is, systems capable of fulfilling customer needs in a coordinated fashion. Thus, within any service organization, all departments and functional units (for example, the marketing team, the operations team, and the HR team) must be interdependent and coordinated, with their cross-functionality managed and coordinated effectively (for example, if the firm says that customers and customer experience are essential, then this priority must flow through all areas including motivators, performance evaluations, incentives, and the like). Essentially, this means that in any service interface, every employee should be capable of going beyond departmental boundaries to assist the customer. Technically, leading service firms will limit departmental boundaries to empower employees to serve the customer better.

In today's experience-based economy, almost every enterprise is essentially a *service* enterprise. The business must therefore be studied within a service framework, and service theory is required to understand and explain management, marketing, and operations.

Online, sharing economy, and technology-led interrelationships

Despite successful partnerships and collaborations among service firms improving overall value for customers, changing preferences and consumption patterns have disrupted the system. Fueled by the digital networks, ever-growing powerful mobile, and smart technologies, online platforms have altered the face of the service ecosystem and created new business models by connecting consumers with service providers and allowing them to transact directly. In today's sharing economy, these platform businesses provide a viable alternative for customers to receive services such as transport, accommodation, and meals from their peers who are supported by global organizations like Uber and Airbnb. The growth of online platforms and the changing business models around the concept of sharing economy have also given rise to entirely new service offerings, such as the ability to rent designer clothes or share the care for your pet (Wirtz et al., 2019). As this new ecosystem develops, 'traditional' service organizations have no choice but to consider how to position themselves against such competition and harness the unique nature of online platforms to connect multiple service providers to fulfill their customers' different needs.

Another concept that is becoming imperative to the management and marketing of services is Frontline Service Technology (FST) defined as: "any combination of hardware, software, information, and/or networks that supports the co-creation of value between a service provider and customer at the organizational frontline" (De Keyser et al., 2019, p.158). While technology has played a role in service delivery for some time (bank cash machines), the recent rise of smart technologies and connected devices has seen new forms of service encounters emerge and challenged service businesses to rethink how technology can enhance service delivery and customers' experience.

Research by Keyser et al. (2018) highlights how connected smart technologies (e.g., artificial intelligence (AI), extended reality (XR), and blockchain technology) are altering the nature of the service encounter between customers and frontline employees. The authors offer an updated table of FST infusion archetypes, which shows a variety of configurations where FST plays either an augmenting or substituting role in the service encounter. Technology-free encounters are rare in today's smart and connected world, as FSTs have become a dominant force in service experiences. Given the growing use of and demand for technology-supported services by consumers, it is critical for businesses to keep pace with the latest innovations if they want to future-proof their operations and remain relevant in the market. This issue, the interconnection between human and technology in delivering service, is covered in more detail in Chapter 9.

> ### The Story of BYJU'S – The Learning App
>
> By Dr. Aarti Saini, Department of Commerce,
> Shaheed Bhagat Singh College, University of Delhi
>
> Over the past decade, technology has significantly improved India's existing education system. Self-learning platforms have replaced traditional methods and the introduction of technology-based systems, such as 'BYJU'S – The Learning App,' has revolutionized the student experience. The app's founder, Byju Raveendran, was motivated to teach students more effectively and efficiently after his experience managing a busy schedule taking classes in three to four states per day. He identified an opportunity to deliver his lectures differently and saw the utilization of technology as a way to reach more students across the country. BYJU'S was based on the idea of offering an improved service to students by having pre-recorded presentations that would be enhanced by extra graphics and made available at any time or place. The idea gained momentum and with a strong, dedicated team in place, Raveendran launched his online video-based learning app in 2015. This innovation highlights the growing role of technology in traditional face-to-face service industries like education.
>
> India has the largest K-12 education system in the world, with a market size of around 260 million students. It was top of mind for Raveendran that if he really wanted to make an impact on students' learning experience, he needed to let students fall in love with the subject and interact with the content. He also understood that Indian parents liked to be involved in their child's education and thus took a culturally oriented approach in designing the app-based service. In 2011, Raveendran launched Think & Learn Pvt. Ltd. (the parent company of BYJU'S) with a focus on the K-12 segment (school-going students from 4 to12). The learning service was initially delivered via YouTube and Facebook, then expanded to a website, and finally launched as a mobile app in 2015. During the early years, there were only a few million people in India who owned a smartphone, and data prices were high. However, with the proliferation of low-cost handsets over the past decade, millions of people have come online, and demand for their flagship product, BYJU'S, is booming. Having a technology-based service has also allowed Raveendran to reach a broader audience globally, with over 20% of their users now international students.
>
> Raveendran's solid experience in an 'offline' teaching environment helped to motivate parents and students to subscribe to BYJU'S online

learning program. He focused on creating high-quality content and utilized artificial intelligence to design a personalized learning tool known as the 'knowledge graph,' which tracks a student's progress, identifies areas for improvement, and adjusts the learning plans accordingly. Students' learning gaps are addressed using engaging, concept-based videos and tests, which are delivered via the app. In traditional classroom settings, the average teacher-to-student ratio is around 1:35, and learning can be limited due to a lack of access to quality teachers. Accordingly, BYJU'S addressed this market need and gave students a more personalized, fun learning experience.

Many companies today use technology as a key partner to provide valuable services to their customers that have not been previously possible. Raveendran's technology-based innovation has become a key contributor to the success of his company. BYJU'S provides a unique combination of teacher-led interactions alongside fun games and interactive videos that deliver complex concepts in a visual, contextual, and easy-to-understand way. As technology continues to advance, BYJU'S is well-positioned to leverage new ways of delivering their learning experience and enhancing the value of its service to students.

Applying these service theories and concepts

The core philosophy of this book is founded on the basis that the primary function of all businesses and organizations is to provide *service to a customer* (whether this is an external customer, another business, or even an internal customer). For firms that sell physical products, the key to adding value for customers and differentiating from competitors lies in the way that the product is delivered and the full customer experience. It is therefore extremely important that managers (operations, human resources, marketing) and all key organizational functions understand in depth what they are offering, and how it should be offered, to create the best experience for all customers. This perspective of business necessitates a re-examination and readjustment of ideas, concepts, systems, and methods. Fundamentally, this new perspective calls for a better understanding of the nature of a service and the basis for the remaining content in this book.

Summary of chapter

The emerging global economy, and the competitive forces that accompany globalization, are changing the nature of competition in all industries. Because products can be easily replicated, traditional competitive strategies based on product features alone have been rendered inappropriate for firms' sustainable long-term growth. Businesses have therefore been forced to search for new ways to differentiate themselves from competitors, which is where a focus on service excellence and customer experience plays a crucial role.

A market- or customer-oriented perspective is required, by which competition is based on customer value rather than on the quality of products per se. This enables managers to include customers' expectations and perceptions in the design of their offerings, as well as in the design of various collaborations with other firms. The aim is to form a strategic network that can provide customers with a total service experience.

Furthermore, today's business transactions are not a linear process – rather, customers co-create and customize products and services *with* the firm. To enable this, companies must have innovative and effective systems in place to understand how and why customers use their products or services. Indeed, business transformation is occurring across all industry segments, and it's only the beginning of this economic revolution.

The rest of this book explores these basic issues in further detail. The intelligent application of service management and marketing theory is essential to success in the modern competitive marketplace.

Review questions

1. What key evidence is there of the evolution from a product-based to a service and experience-based economy?
2. What is the importance of networking in service industries? Why do service firms need to collaborate with other firms?
3. Identify at least three core services and peripheral services within university/studying settings from a student's point of view.
4. Briefly describe the concept of service packaging. Why is it important, and how might managers manipulate the different elements of a service package to gain a competitive advantage?
5. Describe the evolution of the service economy, and what challenges/major forces does it face today.

Suggested readings

This is a list of suggested further reading on topics covered in this chapter. For a separate list of full reference citations quoted in this chapter, see the 'References' section at the end of this chapter.

Bitner, M. J., & Brown, S. W. (2006). The evolution and discovery of services science in business schools. *Communications of the ACM*, 49(7), 73–78.

Grönroos, C. (1994). From scientific management to service management. *International Journal of Service Industry Management*, 5(1), 5–20.

Ostrom, A. L., Parasuraman, A., Bowen, D. E., Patricio, L., Voss, C. A., & Lemon, K. (2015). Service research priorities in a rapidly changing context. *Journal of Service Research*, 18(2), 127–159.

Solnet, D., & Kandampully, J. (2008). How some service firms have become part of "service excellence" folklore: An exploratory study. *Managing Service Quality*, 18(2), 179–193.

Vargo, S. L., & Lusch, R. F. (2008a). Service-dominant logic: Continuing the evolution. *Journal of the Academy of Marketing Science*, 36, 1–10.

Vargo, S. L., & Lusch, R. F. (2008b). Why 'service'? *Journal of the Academy of Marketing Science*, 36, 25–38.

References

Albrecht, K. (1988). *At America's service: How your company can join the customer service revolution*. New York, NY: Warner Books.

Albrecht, K., & Zemke, R. (1985). *Service America: Doing business in the new economy*. Homewood, IL: Dow Jones-Irwin.

Australian Bureau of Statistics. (2019). *Australian industry*. Retrieved from https://www.abs.gov.au/ausstats/abs@.nsf/0/48791677FF5B2814CA256A1D0001FECD?Opendocument

Booms, B. H., & Bitner, M. J. (1981). *Marketing strategies and organizational structures for service firms*. Chicago, IL: American Marketing Association.

Central Intelligence Agency. (n.d.). Field listing. *The world Facebook*. Retrieved from https://www.cia.gov/library/publications/resources/the-world-factbook/fields/214.html

De Keyser, A., Köcher, S., Alkire (née Nasr), L., Verbeeck, C., & Kandampully, J. (2019). Frontline service technology infusion: Conceptual archetypes and future research directions. *Journal of Service Management*, 30(1), 156–183.

Engel, E. (1857). Die production - Und Consumptionsverhaltnisse des Konigreichs Sachsen. In *Zeitschrift der Statistischen Bureaus des Koniglich Sachsischen Ministerium des Inneren*.

Fisk, R. P., Brown, S. W., & Bitner, M. J. (1993). Tracking the evolution of the services marketing literature. *Journal of Retailing*, 69(1), 61–103.

McCarthy, E. J. (1960). *Basic marketing*. Homewood, IL: Irwin.

Normann, R. (2000). *Service management*. West Sussex: Wiley.

Schneider, B. (2004). Research briefs: Welcome to the world of services management. *Academy of Management Executive*, 18(2), 144–150.

Shostack, G. L. (1977). Breaking free from product marketing. *Journal of Marketing*, 41, April, 73–80.

Vandermerwe, S., & Rada, J. (1988). Servitization of business: Adding value by adding services. *European Management Journal*, 6(4), 314–324.

Vargo, S. L., & Akaka, M. A. (2009). Service-dominant logic as a foundation for service science: Clarifications. *Service Science*, 1(1), 32–41.

Wirtz, J., So, K. K.F., Mody, M. A., Liu, S. Q., & Chun, H. H. (2019). Platforms in the peer-to-peer sharing economy. *Journal of Service Management*, 30(4), 452–483.

Chapter 2

Management and marketing challenges in the service economy

Study objectives

Having completed this chapter, readers should be able to:

- describe the characteristics of service and the implications for service organizations;
- identify what makes service different from a marketing perspective by defining the extended marketing mix (seven Ps); and
- understand the principles of service-dominant logic and a total organizational approach, and how these can be useful for managing customer experience (CX).

The framework of this chapter

This chapter is set out as follows:

- Introduction
- Challenges in managing and marketing services
  o Intangibility
  o Heterogeneity
  o Inseparability
  o Perishability
- Implications for managers and marketers
  o Managing intangibility
    - Difficulty in discriminating between one service offering from another
    - Risk perceptions with service purchases
    - Seeking personal information regarding the reliability of service
    - Assessing the quality of service before consumption
  o Managing heterogeneity
    - Variability according to the time, day, and service provider
    - Variability in brand standards at different locations

o Managing inseparability
        • Customers' role in quality control
        • 'Multiple consumption' settings
        • The process of value 'co-creation'
    o Managing perishability
- Implications for marketing services
    o Beyond the traditional 'four Ps' marketing mix
- Toward a new paradigm
    o The importance of a *total organizational approach*
    o Service-dominant logic
- Summary of chapter
- Review questions
- Suggested readings
- References

Introduction

Services are offered by people for people, therefore to a large extent it is a people industry, even when various elements of technology are being more incorporated to aid the interaction between customer and firm. Therefore, service and experience 'offerings' differ from all aspects of physical products in their composition, production process, delivery, and consumption. Management and marketing of services have to consider the appropriate blending of both behavioral and technological aspects to be successful. This blended approach is considerably different from those traditionally used for manufactured goods. The distinctive features of service in the production and delivery of values lead to different consumer perceptions and behaviors—making it difficult for service providers to ensure consistent quality of service, customer satisfaction and to operate within set standards with minimal deviation. It is therefore imperative that service managers and marketers are aware of these and find the best solutions within their specific context to cope with these challenges if they are to compete successfully in a complex and competitive environment.

These qualities also demand a reappraisal of all traditional management and marketing strategies, which were originally developed for the sale of physical goods. Accordingly, traditional theories have been modified and expanded to account for the distinct nature of service. These will be expanded on later in this chapter.

As revealed in Chapter 1, the secret to success for firms today is to offer superior *service to positively influence customers*. Of particular note here is the emergence of thought and practice that nearly every value exchange, be it product, service, or experience, is in fact reliant on a service and experience vision the firm has set as a goal over all other factors. According to this vision, perceived value and loyalty are driven mostly by the full end-to-end experience including all of the points in time where the firm interacts with the customer. Therefore, the lessons in this book, and in this chapter, can be and should be generalized to any business context. Even businesses that sell physical products find that the key to adding value for consumers and differentiating their brand in today's competitive marketplace lies in the service offered and the experience created.

It is therefore important for managers to understand that customers must become the priority of the firm over all other factors to gain a competitive advantage in the market. Think about interactions which you have had with firms which sell 'things' – maybe the purchase of a new or used car. How do car dealers 'differentiate' or work to create an experience beyond the physical nature of the car? You are not really buying a car to look at, but rather you are buying the service of the car (the ability to travel from one place to another). Therefore, your concern is what will happen if the car fails to operate properly. Who will help repair it? Some car dealers and companies understand the concerns of the customer and offer free roadside repair and seamless convenience and care in the service departments. Some offer a loan car for use during repair. These are ways by which service providers communicate the value of service and strength of the unique experience they offer and the focus on the customer's needs. Indeed, the experience becomes more holistic – far more than the physical value of the car. Think about other examples such as appliances and reflect on what you are buying when you have a dishwasher or clothes dryer and what are the factors you take into account in being satisfied with that product?

Challenges in managing and marketing services

As it became clear that earlier management theories, designed for an industrial economy would not be effective in a service context, scholars worked hard to find specific reasons *why* managing a 'service' was different than managing a 'good'. Products are often used, and services are in most cases consumed through interactions with people and/or with technology. This led to the development of what has come to be known as the four 'unique characteristics' of service, affectionately named 'IHIP':

- Intangibility,
- Heterogeneity,
- Inseparability, and
- Perishability.

Addressing service businesses using the same management principles that are used in goods-manufacturing businesses is generally inappropriate or lacking precision. Most services can be assessed only after the service is completed. For example, a haircut can be assessed only after the haircut is completed. This means that the service outcome cannot be pre-examined, thus the service is considered as intangible in nature because of its nonexistence prior to the completion of the service. The service as an outcome therefore is essentially an *activity* conducted by people, for the benefit of people, in their presence. Services, from a managerial perspective, are thus distinctly different from products in their composition, production process, delivery, and consumption. Therefore, managing and marketing services require a different approach from that of products.

There has been much academic research conducted into the unique characteristics of service, and the implications of these differences for management and marketing. Each of these distinctive (or 'particularly challenging') features and the challenges they pose are discussed in the following sections of this chapter. As you review these, reflect not only on how these characteristics impact 'service' but also on how they might impact experiences in a similar way.

Intangibility

Service managers and researchers share agreement that the most distinctive feature is that a service is *intangible*. That is, service cannot be seen, felt, tasted, or touched as a product can be. A service that a customer receives is the result of a deed, a performance, an effort, or an encounter in time. To aid this encounter firms may utilize many combinations of people, technology, and/or machines. A service cannot be displayed, or physically demonstrated, or illustrated. Therefore, assessment of a service prior to consumption is difficult or impossible. Service therefore has few of the characteristics customers often wish to know before purchasing. This means service offers limited benefit for the customer in terms of 'search' qualities, 'experience' qualities, and 'credence' qualities. Specifically, unlike manufactured goods, a service cannot be physically examined ('search' qualities), cannot be checked to see whether the encounter is positive or negative ('experience' qualities), or cannot be tested to find out whether what is being offered is true ('credence' qualities). Furthermore, the quality of service can be judged only by the customer and not by the producer. These unique circumstances in a service context pose many different challenges to service managers.

It was Lynn Shostack, a marketer for a major US bank in 1977 who first brought to the management literature that service is unusual and that university business degrees did not prepare graduates for careers in the service sector. She highlighted *intangibility* as a distinctive characteristic of services, even when the rendering of the service involves some physical goods. Although such services are accompanied by physical objects, these objects cannot be categorized as true product elements. Every business is positioned along a continuum that reflects the degree to which their offering is comprised of tangible and intangible elements (see Figure 2.1). Almost every business offers a combination of

24 Management and marketing challenges

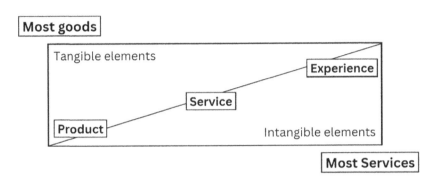

Figure 2.1 Product-experience continuum

both, since services are often delivered as part of a tangible product package to add value to the customer. For example, in the case of a music concert, there are tangible components that all form part of the experience – such as printed tickets, seating, music system, the venue, and merchandise – however, it is the intangible live performance which remains the primary service offering.

(Authors' presentation of a previous idea – adapted from Rushton andCarson (1985)).

Intangibility – the distinctive characteristic of services

Intangibility is *the* distinctive characteristic of services. Although there are four distinctive characteristics of services (intangibility, inseparability, heterogeneity, and perishability), intangibility is considered to be the most critical difference between services and physical goods. In most cases intangibility is the key factor from which all other differences between goods and services emerge.

Heterogeneity

This means variability or diversity. Most services are primarily delivered by people and hence there is the potential for high variability in the performance. Individual performance is subject to fluctuation day in and day out. In other words, identical service is difficult, or impossible, to ensure. Therefore, what the firm has promised to deliver may be entirely different from what the customer receives. Service will also differ in the extent to which it is 'people-based' or 'technology-based'. For example, there is commonly a larger human component involved in providing a restaurant service, whereas in the online retailing context the service could be primarily technology-based.

This distinctive and challenging characteristic of service thus refers to the high level of diversity that exists in a service context. Heterogeneity, or the variability of service performance, can occur at various levels, which leads to challenges such as:

- the quality of service performance varies from one service organization to another (for example, the service at different retail outlets of the same brand will be perceived differently by the customers);
- the quality of service performance varies from one service performer to another (for example, although all employees are trained based on the same standards, each employee's performance will not be uniform); and
- the quality of service performance varies for the same performer on different occasions (for example, employees are unable to maintain consistent standards of service on any one day or time).

For these reasons, service managers have very limited control over the consistency of service that is delivered to customers at any point in time. This means what the firm has promised to deliver (food delivered in 30 minutes) might be quite different from what is being actually delivered to the customer (because of heavy demand and being short staffed the food takes 60 minutes).

Recognizing that heterogeneity is essentially a 'people problem', some service firms have attempted to minimize variation by replacing people with technology. However, this could introduce another form of heterogeneity. For example, the variation between interaction conducted face-to-face ('high-touch') and interaction via the Internet ('high-tech') can be significant, which can have implications for customers' perceptions of the firm's quality of service and the image associated with personalized service and the value. The introduction of technology might 'fix' heterogeneity at one level, but exacerbate it at another level. This is summed up in the common complaint: 'I don't like talking to a machine! I want to talk to a *real* person!'.

Having observed that heterogeneity is all but inevitable in service delivery, it must also be noted that heterogeneity in service is not always a disadvantage. As noted above, some customers prefer receiving service from persons (even if variable) to service from machines/technology (even if more uniform). In a similar way, variation is important to illustrate the firm's commitment to customizing service. In these cases, variability (at least from customer to customer) is an expected element of customer experience.

Inseparability

Typically, goods are produced first, then sold and consumed. Not with a service or an experience! This characteristic means that the production, purchase, and consumption of a service often occur simultaneously – they are inseparable! Since service and experiences are being delivered *as they are being consumed*, it means there is much more complexity and challenges in managing quality and consistency. Imagine going to watch a football match, you are part of the excitement you co-create along with other fans. Fans creating excitement and ambiance can have a positive impact on other fans and even on the players. This is one reason that many teams perform well in front of their home crowd. In almost all service contexts customers contribute considerably to the perception of quality of the service.

Simultaneous production and consumption means that the service provider and customer are often physically present when consumption occurs. For example, a doctor is present when examining a patient who is also present in the hospital (even if in a telehealth context). In almost all service contexts customers have to be in the service 'factory'. On the other hand, imagine how many of us go to a factory to buy a smartphone or car. Although we can, it is not necessary. However, it is difficult to get a haircut without an actual visit to a hair salon (even if the hairdresser came to your home the fact is that the two of you would have to be in the same place to physically interact). Inseparability thus forces the buyer into intimate contact with both the process of production and the process of delivery. In most cases, there is no time lapse between production and consumption. Control of service output thus becomes a difficult and complex issue. In contrast, a physical good, such as a washing machine, might be manufactured in Germany and consumed in London.

The marketing of service is also affected by the inseparability of production and consumption. In the marketing of goods, great emphasis is placed on distributing goods where and when customers desire them —that is the key to goods marketing is to get goods to the *right place* at the *right time*. However, in the case of service, the emphasis shifts to the idea of authenticity of quality of service attempting to ensure that services are produced and delivered (that is, distributed) in the *right way* to meet the needs and expectations of the customer.

The 'inseparability' of services also means that traditional ideas of marketing and quality require radical reappraisal. As the service is often co-created with direct contact and participation of the customer; this means production, consumption, and marketing happen simultaneously thus the judgment of the quality. Therefore, the need for traditionally separate management functions of production, consumption, marketing, and quality control (commonly used in product manufacturing) is not applicable in service business. This critical interconnectedness of service is discussed throughout this chapter and the book because of its implications for managers and marketers.

Perishability

Perishability is another challenging characteristic of service and is closely related to intangibility. Unlike most goods, many services are intangible and cannot be stored for future use and therefore are considered highly perishable. This means services cannot be produced for sale later in time. Examples of perishable items include vacant cinema seats, airline seats, and empty hotel rooms.

Perishability means that service must be produced precisely when needed by a customer. For example, a taxi has to arrive at the right time when you need a ride. An ambulance has to arrive as immediately as possible to help a patient. Demand thus plays a significant role in the production and delivery of services. For example, a fire brigade service is required when there is a fire – not at any other time. Most services have time constraints as to how customers perceive the service. Immediacy and ease of access are thus crucial in most service businesses.

The perishability of service does not pose a problem when demand is steady. In such circumstances, it is relatively easy to predict requirements and arrange for the services to be adequately staffed. This unfortunately is very seldom the case. Almost all service businesses find it challenging to find a balance between demand and supply. When demand fluctuates, service firms encounter many different kinds of problems. High demand for travel services (for example, air travel or train travel) during summer months and holiday season is known to everyone. Although some of these fluctuations are relatively predictable, when the demand is too high or too low it is very challenging for service firms to manage extreme fluctuations.

Perishability (and to some extent intangibility) of service also renders 'ownership' nearly impossible – by either the producer or the customer. Essentially, there is no 'owner' of a service. When purchasing physical goods, buyers acquire a title to the goods. However, when a service is performed, there is no corresponding transfer of ownership. This means resale of service after use is not possible as it is with selling your old clothes or books at a secondhand store. Buyers of service are buying only the *right to a service* – and then only at a designated time. This has implications for both businesses and customers. For businesses, service cannot be patented in the way that physical goods can be, and there is always a possibility that service can be copied by competitors. Although copying is very prevalent, clever firms do not copy from other firms but seek to make it better than the original. This in fact brings a positive impact in the market. This means everyone who copies continues to improve from the original and hence the greater chance of innovation. For consumers, the lack of 'ownership' increases the perception of 'risk' in purchasing service. At the end of the transaction, the consumer does not actually 'possess' anything. This means customers are not able to return a service even if they do not like the services. In marketing service, managers must be aware of this heightened perception of risk among their customers. Therefore, reducing the perceived risk of service is one of the most effective marketing strategies in services.

Implications for managers and marketers

The distinct challenges of service (as compared with physical products or goods), formalized as 'IHIP', present many challenges to managers. Some of these challenges have been mentioned above. Let us now examine these in more detail. Table 2.1 (below) summarizes some of the challenges encountered by service managers and suggestions of possible solutions.

Table 2.1 Implications of distinctive characteristics of service

Distinctive characteristics of service	Implications for service managers and marketers	Possible means to manage the effects
Heterogeneity	• standard of service is dependent on the service provider, the time of the day, and the day of the week • consistent quality of service is difficult to ensure	• careful personnel selection and training • ensure standards are monitored • prepackaged service • quality control
Intangibility	• difficult to calculate the cost or price • no patents possible • customer has access to service but has no ownership of activity or facility • customers have difficulty discriminating between one service offering and another • customers perceive the service purchase as involving high levels of risk • customers seek personal information regarding the reliability of service	• focus on benefits • increase tangibility of service (for example, physical representations of the service) • use of brand names • use personalities to personalize service
Inseparability	• requires the presence of the producer • most service depends on direct sale • limited scale of operation • value is co-created	• train more competent service providers • learn to work in large groups • work faster at one location by one server
Perishability	• cannot be stored • service volume is dependent on demand • managing demand fluctuates • the lack of 'ownership'	• match supply and demand • manage demand as opposed to supply • unbundle back-office operations

Managing intangibility

From the customers' perspective, the intangibility of service is an especially significant problem, and managers must be sensitive to this. Intangibility means that:

- customers are not able to judge the quality of one service offering over another;
- customers perceive the service purchase as involving high levels of risk, because they cannot pre-examine them, or it is hard to return them;
- customers seek personal information regarding the reliability of service; and
- customers have difficulty assessing the quality of service before consumption—meaning that assessment is frequently price-based.

Each of these is discussed below.

Difficulty in discriminating between one service offering from another

Because customers have difficulty in judging one service offering over another, managers have to identify and develop means of offering 'cues' with which customers are able to prejudge the benefits prior to purchase. This will require service firms to offer benefits that communicate reliability and trust to the customers. For example, some service firms offer service guarantees that help the firms reinforce the service promise for the benefit of the customer.

Additionally, some service firms effectively communicate to the customer various types of packages. For example, a hotel can offer special packages to a business traveler inclusive of air travel, taxi service, and access to an executive lounge. These recognizable benefits assist the customer to evaluate the benefits before consumption.

Risk perceptions with service purchases

Reducing customers' perceived risk is one of the most effective ways in which a service firm can communicate its superiority to the customer. This is particularly pertinent in the case of new offerings, or if customers are availing themselves of an organization's service for the first time.

Detailed information about the service and the benefits that customers are entitled to receive also reduces the perceived risk. There are many tools managers and marketers can employ to overcome some of the challenges of the perceived risk of services. We will address 'guarantees' and their effective use in a service context in Chapter 7.

Seeking personal information regarding the reliability of service

Service is an intangible experience that cannot be prejudged prior to purchase. Therefore, word-of-mouth recommendation from other consumers is one of the most effective and trustworthy means of comparing and judging a service. Therefore, potential customers rely heavily on word-of-mouth (or social media) communication much more than the advertisement messages from the service firm. Customer reviews and recommendations have been proven to be far more impactful than other kinds of advertisements and marketing.

Service managers therefore have to design systems and approaches to enhance customer reviews and word-of-mouth information about the service. Offering superior service to existing customers is the most effective mechanism to enhance word-of-mouth recommendation. Moreover, over the long terms, customers will value consistent superior service more than short-term discounting. Therefore, many customers see discounted products and services as inferior in quality. Once customers perceive the quality of a brand to be low, it will prove to be very difficult for the firm to change that perception.

Assessing the quality of service before consumption

In manufacturing, price is often used by marketers as a guide to the quality that consumers might expect. It is a general feeling among consumers that a lower-priced product indicates lower quality and higher price indicates better quality. However, in the case of service, the situation is more complex since using price to differentiate the quality of service might not be appropriate in most cases. For example, in healthcare an expensive hospital may not necessarily produce a high patient evaluation of the healthcare experience. Rather, the evaluation of quality is intensely personal and depends less on price and more on the needs of the patients and their perception of the interactions they had with the doctors and other caregivers. This means that expectations, and perceptions, together with an assessment of the numerous service providers (medical professionals) with whom the patients and their family interact.

Service managers thus have the difficult challenge of trying to control not only the quality of service offered but also the *customers' assessments* of that quality. It is important to understand that only the customer is in a position to judge the quality of a service and not the managers (more on this in Chapter 4). Controlling both the quality of service *and* the customer's assessment of quality is difficult to manage. The focus should therefore extend beyond the quality of service offered to encompass the enhancement of value of the final result and the overall experience as perceived by the customer. Value can be added through many facets of the service that are more controllable than quality alone. The little 'touches' that enhance satisfaction (a kind word to recognize the need of the customer, showing compassion and feelings for the need of the customer, spending additional time with the customer to explain things to them are far more important and valuable to the memories of the experience). Therefore, in most services price discounts have very limited advantages in a service context as opposed to personalized service and care and hence are particularly important in managing and marketing services.

> **Branded Differentiation: Making the Intangible, 'Tangible'**
>
> By Dr. Senthil Kumaran P, Welcomgroup Graduate School of Hotel Administration, Manipal Academy of Higher Education
>
> Service organizations face a unique challenge in their effort to market their offering because what they are essentially selling is intangible; in other words, it cannot be touched, tasted, seen, or smelt, unlike a tangible product. This characteristic of service often means that customers have difficulty determining the value and quality of the offering before purchase, which can result in a high level of perceived risk. Customers look for 'cues' in their assessment of value, thus service marketers use place, people, signage, location, employees, and price as indicators of quality and to make the intangible more 'tangible'.
>
> Many hotel brands include a portfolio of properties serving different market segments, ranging from price-sensitive backpackers to experience-seeking luxury connoisseurs. Commonly, hotels are differentiated based on their level of service by using a rating scale of stars, diamonds, or letters. However, the actual level of service offered by similarly rated hotels can vary widely due to the inconsistent nature of evaluation criteria used by different countries.
>
> To overcome the issues of intangibility and differentiation, some international hotel companies utilize 'branded differentiation', which is common among product manufacturing companies. David Aaker (2004) proposed that 'branding the differentiator' can create an everlasting point of distinction and includes four forms: branded features, branded service, branded ingredients, and branded programs. To resonate with the target market, a branded differentiator must be meaningful, pertinent, and more than just a name.
>
> An example of a branded differentiator is the Heavenly® Bed, which is a uniquely designed bed by the Westin hotel group that is offered at all their properties and carries the promise of ensuring a sound sleep. Since its introduction, this branded differentiator has helped the Westin to increase both customer satisfaction and room occupancy, and has also been extended to include another branded differentiator: the 'Heavenly Bath line'. Today, the Marriott International hotel chain owns the highest number of branded differentiators, including Ritz Kids®, Marriott

Bonvoy®, Marriott Rewards®, The Ritz-Carlton Rewards® and SPG®, The Ritz-Carlton Club®, Family By JW™, Spa by JW®, AWAY® Spa, WET® BAR, W Hotels Music Festival®, Wake Up Call®, WET Deck®, Bonvoy Boundless®, and Marriott Bonvoy Moments®.

To successfully compete, brands must have a unique selling point; in other words, a compelling reason why a customer should purchase the service. However, creating and maintaining a point of difference is challenging for service organizations, since aggressive competitors often attempt to copy the differentiating features and thus dilute their appeal. Branded differentiators act as 'cues' of value and uniqueness that bring a long-lasting competitive advantage and also enable service providers to make their intangible offerings more 'tangible'.

Managing heterogeneity

There are many management challenges associated with heterogeneity, such as:

- the same customer can experience the same service provider differently, depending on many factors, including the time, day, their emotional state (angry, rushed, impatient); and
- variability can also be caused because many different employees are involved in delivering services. This means maintaining brand standards at different service locations is very difficult.

Each of these challenges is discussed below.

Variability according to the time, day, and service provider

In a service business, many employees are required to perform similar services in a similar manner. The very fact that many employees are involved in providing service means that no one service provider can be identical to another However, customers commonly expect consistent service from all employees and all outlets of the same brand. This unfortunately is a big challenge for service managers. Management needs to establish training that facilitates consistency in the service offering and that supports the delivery process. While training is important, identifying and recruiting employees who fit in with the values and vision of the firm is imperative. For example, imagine what prompts you to visit a particular branch of your bank and not other branches. 'People' often create the most reliable, trustworthy, and unique difference in a service firm from the customer's point of view. Of course, in addition to specific training of employees, service procedures and systems can help streamline and reduce variability in task performance.

However, in some situations, variability can present many opportunities for personalized or authentic service. This is particularly pertinent in professional service where professionals from different disciplines are involved to meet a customer's various needs. In these cases, variability constitutes an asset to the organization. In some other cases variability also allows the firm to project the authenticity of the service. Can you think of an example where your service may have been altered 'on the spot' via a highly engaging service provider or where they might have had more time to serve than usual? (What about your food being delivered to your table when you were expecting to have to go to the counter to collect it? Think about the positive and negative implications of this too).

Variability in brand standards at different locations

In large service organizations where there are multiple outlets, services are offered at different locations by different employees. Maintaining a comparable service standard at all outlets is not an easy task for service managers. The delivery of service is highly influenced by individual service providers' personalities and attitudes at different points in time. Therefore, consistency in service interactions at different sites is extremely difficult to maintain. Many exemplar firms focus on the recruitment of like-minded people into the organization, with the hope that behaviors are more stable in many circumstances. Therefore, creating a company-wide culture to maintain standards has been successfully adopted by many leading service organizations. A good example is Singapore Airlines and its company-wide culture of service, portrayed by 'Singapore Girl'. This requires a carefully constructed company policy by which all staff members are not only aware of the 'customer-centric' philosophy of the firm but also trained and empowered to implement it.

This is further exacerbated in international contexts when one company operates the same brand in countries with quite different national cultures. For example, multinational retail firms (IKEA, Walmart, Carrefour, Aldi) and hospitality firms (Marriott, Hilton, Starbucks, McDonald's, Dominos) have to adjust their product (type of meat, spices, alcohol) and services (days and times of operation) to match the expectations of the national culture where these firms operate. Blending company culture and national culture is not an easy task, but international firms often give more importance to national cultures over and above company culture.

Managing inseparability

The inseparability of the simultaneous sale, consumption, and production of service creates significant challenges for service managers, such as:

- quality control is embedded in service delivery with vital and difficult-to-control roles played by the customer (this is primarily because customers can positively or negatively influence the service provider during the production process);
- service is delivered in a setting of 'multiple consumption' (given the nature of multiple consumption, customer-to-customer interactions can positively or negatively influence the outcome of the service); and
- employees and customers interact very closely and hence they are 'co-responsible' for creating value. Value thus collectively created helps nurture the relationship between the customer and service provider which ultimately leads to enhanced memories of experiences.

Each of these are discussed below.

Customers' role in quality control

Since service relies on interaction between the service provider and customer, quality and service delivery are inextricably linked. Service providers are therefore simultaneously responsible for production, marketing, and quality control. Service providers are also referred to as 'part-time marketers' since they are the key variable that is able to communicate value to the customer. In comparison to managing tangible products, where quality control is often performed on a management level prior to the customer's involvement, in service delivery this role is usually performed by frontline staff who represent the firm and all other employees to the customer and actually deliver the service. This has a number of implications for managers including training employees and also empowering them in case of customer dissatisfaction (this is further discussed in Chapter 7).

The inseparable nature of service also means that customers are involved in quality control. Service customers participate in a more or less active fashion, cooperating in the process of production and delivery, and therefore participating in determining the quality of the service received. For example, in medical services, the patient assists the doctor's diagnosis by providing information about symptoms. Similarly, having a haircut requires the customer to share their vision and to give feedback during the process. In both cases, the input from the recipient of the service is crucial to the quality of the service. This has implications for the overall question of quality control in service – a subject considered in more detail in Chapter 4.

'Multiple consumption' settings

Another effect of the inseparability of production and consumption is that service is often delivered in a setting of 'multiple consumption' – that is, the service is consumed by more than one person simultaneously. A typical example is a music concert, in which each member of the audience enjoys the music in the presence of others, but without having to 'share' the service with others. Although the music is not 'shared' (in the sense of any one consumer not receiving all of the 'product'), the presence of others *does* influence the perception of the quality of the service. In such cases, the perception of quality is influenced by two types of interaction – the interaction between the customer and the service provider, and the interactions among customers. Depending on the type of service offered, firms must manage multiple consumption contexts very effectively to create the best customer-perceived impact leading to enhanced memory of experience.

Although there is less control over interactions among customers within service delivery, service managers must account for multiple consumptions in the way it's designed. For instance, the setting in which the service experience takes place, the 'servicescape', (or 'experiencescape') is an important tool to influence the customer's interaction with various aspects of the service environment. The physical aspects of service design and delivery can provide tangible cues to help customers navigate the service process and their role in creating service experience for all customers.

Therefore, co-consumption of service by multiple consumers is the key to enhancing shared experience that has many possibilities to enhance customer perceptions. Service managers have to pre-plan both the production process and the 'multiple consumption' stage if the desired effect is to be achieved.

The process of value 'co-creation'

The concept of value 'co-creation' implies that not only are service production and consumption closely connected, but also that value is not created by the firm as previously thought instead firms and customers not only co-create but also share the benefit of the value thus created. Service managers benefit from recognizing the role of customers as co-creators of experiences and that they can become a new source of competence for the organization. Technology may also serve as an ideal tool for firms to engage and facilitate customers in the value co-creation process. For example, Nike is a good example of a firm which employed an efficient co-creation of value strategy by empowering consumers to be involved with the design process and allowing them to personalize their own shoes from various styles and colors. According to Nike, this strategy helped them to substantially increase sales. Their online customization service is one of the main revenue generators.

The benefits of co-creation extend beyond just value enhancement to also experience and relationship building. The fact that consumers take an active role in the service production process is an excellent opportunity for the firm

36 Management and marketing challenges

and its employees to develop personal relationships with their customers and also gain insights from customers that can influence innovations. There are many good examples of how service firms co-create value and drive innovation with the active participation of customers. For example, in early 2018, IKEA launched 'Co-create IKEA', a digital platform to engage customers and fans to develop new products.

Managing perishability

There are many management challenges associated with perishability, such as:

- inability to store services and/or use them at a later time;
- creating marketing strategy that does not result in overdemand; and
- the inability to 'possess' service which leads to ownership and control issues.

Each of these is discussed below; however, the challenges congruent with perishability is so significant and important that this book allocates much of a full chapter to this topic in Chapter 3.

The perishability of service is one of the most obvious management challenges. The problem with perishability is not an inability to offer the service at all, but an inability to offer the service *when required by the customer*. Perishability of service, coupled with their intangibility, results in the inability to store a service (unlike physical goods which can be kept in a storeroom and sold the next day). Service 'disappears' as quickly as it is delivered. This has important implications for managers and marketers.

The main purpose of marketing is to increase demand and therefore grow firm revenue and profit. This strategy is not always ideal in many service contexts where supply is fixed or has limited flexibility. For example, the number of seats in a flight cannot be increased because there is high demand on a particular day or time (although more flights can be added). Similarly, a doctor cannot treat many patients on any given day although there is high demand because of an accident or outbreak of a virus. This is because most services cannot be pre-produced and stored. Given that supply (the opportunity to offer service) is fixed or has very limited flexibility, the focus in service must be on managing demand—as opposed to managing supply. In fact, the successful management of demand must be the guiding principle in the design of any system or process in the service industry. (Strategies that can be utilized to manage demand fluctuations are discussed in more detail in Chapter 3.)

Another implication of perishability (and intangibility) is the inability to 'possess' or own a service. It is difficult to own and control products that 'disappear' as quickly as they are delivered. This issue forces service managers to reappraise the ideas of ownership and control of their products and has led to the transformative streaming-type services (Netflix, Apple Music) where a service is available on demand but still not 'owned' by the customer.

The challenges presented by 'IHIP' have led to transformative changes in traditional thinking about marketing. Some of these changes are addressed in the next section

Implications for marketing services

Beyond the traditional 'four Ps' marketing mix

There are a set of challenges that render managing service different from the management of physical goods, some of which have been detailed above. Accordingly, the marketing of service is also different from that of product marketing. It should thus be apparent that the traditional elements of the marketing mix (the ' four Ps': *product, price, place,* and *promotion*) do not adequately serve the needs of modern service organizations – there are many gaps! There are numerous reasons for this, linked mainly to some of the challenges of service and experience management highlighted above, as well as the interrelationships of marketing, operations, and human resources in the delivery of service and experiences.

The combination of these two factors means that a new formulation is required. As a result, an extended marketing mix of 'seven Ps' was developed for effective use in a service context. This extended service marketing mix consists of the traditional four 'Ps', together with three new 'Ps', as follows:

- product;
- place;
- price;
- promotion;
- people;
- physical evidence; and
- process.

Each of these 'seven Ps' is examined in more detail in Table 2.2.

The discussions so far have covered the increasing economic importance of the service and experience economy and some of the particular challenges facing managers and marketers in this context. Service researchers have highlighted the need for a different approach to management and marketing, which has led to the development of a new body of knowledge that aims to improve the competitive ability of service firms.

38 Management and marketing challenges

Table 2.2 An extended marketing mix for services *(authors' presentation)*

The 'seven Ps'	Description	Implications for service marketing
Product	A service product is anything – either in isolation or in combination – that a service organization offers to potential customers to satisfy their needs	• In service, the 'product' is a process, not a physical object • The focus is therefore on the customer's personal experience of service delivery, rather than traditional product elements such as design • The product mix is often conveyed as 'service bundles' (see Chapter 1)
Place	Place is the physical space that a customer enters to receive a service.	• It is imperative that the physical location of the service is accessible, appealing, and customer-friendly
Price	The price of a service offering is the monetary amount an organization attributes to the intangible process, based on the customer's perception of value	• Intangibility causes difficulties in pricing a service – it is difficult to justify the cost when customers cannot see it or examine it in the same way as physical goods • The price of a service can influence, in advance, the perceptions of quality and value • Successful pricing depends on recognizing the value that a customer places on a service and pricing it accordingly • Price discrimination – or price cutting – is more likely to occur within service markets than goods markets (see section above regarding managing capacity and demand)
Promotion	Promotion includes the methods that firms employ to attract the attention of existing and potential customers, and to inform them of the firm's service offerings.	• Word-of-mouth promotion is considered the most effective and impactful for service firms • The inseparability of service allows the promotion of production skills – for example, restaurants with 'open kitchens' allow customers to see the skilled chefs at work • Intangibility means that Image is crucially important as it influences customers' perceptions of the service offered
People	People – both customers and employees – are intrinsic to service. In fact, from a customer's perspective, contact employees can represent the service product and even the organization itself.	• The emotions, attitudes, and appearance of contact employees influence customer's perceptions of the service • Employees can provide cues to customers regarding the nature of the service • Other customers in the service environment can also provide such cues • Customer-to-customer interactions also affect perceptions of service • Customers frequently have to share service products and experiences

(Continued)

Management and marketing challenges   39

Table 2.2   (Continued)

The 'seven Ps'	Description	Implications for service marketing
Physical evidence	This service setting or 'servicescape' is the physical surroundings of the service, which provides a setting for the performance and conveys the values of the organization and the ideals it aspires to achieve	• The objects and cues play a critical role in making an intangible service somewhat tangible, helping customers during their assessment of the quality and nature of the service performed • Physical evidence provides excellent opportunities for a service firm to send clear and consistent marketing messages by coordinating all tangible elements • Visible elements of a service must be designed as carefully as the service offering itself to ensure that it represents quality, value, and the desired image to the customer
Process	Service is made up of processes – it is the end result of deeds, acts, performances, and activities performed by the firm's employees in cooperation with the customer.	• From a customer's perspective, the service process provides vital evidence of both the quality of the service and the range of services offered • Processes must be customer-centric – the ease and friendliness of the service process are crucial to the customer's assessment of quality • Processes can be customized to give customers personalized attention and have their specific needs met in a tailored way

The Evolution of Customer Experience from a Marketing Perspective

Professor Ruth Bolton, a leading academic in the fields of marketing and service management, was interviewed by one of the authors of this book and asked to describe the evolution of customer experience. She proposed that this evolution involved four key stages. Originally, customers were regarded with a very narrow notion around attitudes, preferences, and behavior. Then in the 1990s, marketers began to expand their thinking about customers and focus more on satisfaction and loyalty – in other words, they began to care more about customers' *emotions*.

The third phase in the post-2000 period was marked by the advent of digital and social media, during which time marketers broadened their consideration of customer engagement even further to encompass non-purchase behaviors (since customers could now connect with brands in new ways – like blogging about the brand or sharing videos about the brand – all of which help to build a relationship but aren't directly associated with purchasing).

Finally, where we are now with customer experience is the broadest conception yet, with service marketers thinking about three key dimensions: physical, digital, and social. In other words, to deliver a positive customer experience it is important to consider customers' offline and online behavior (wherever that might be), as well as their social behaviors among others.

Toward a new paradigm

The importance of a total organizational approach

The nature of service means that marketing is not an independent function of the service organization, but an *interrelated holistic concept encompassing every activity within the organization with a particular focus on people, operations that are able of delivering customer value, incorporation of technology to support firms with end-to-end customer journey, and the critical importance of creating and developing customer relationships.*

Every service enterprise strives to satisfy its customers. Indeed, making a return on investment (ROI) is totally dependent on customer satisfaction. In keeping with this, the primary focus of successful service firms today more than ever before is squarely on the customer first. Once the customer perceives higher value from a firm's offer and is satisfied with the experience, profit can become an automatic byproduct. This new realization has brought about many new changes in the way service businesses are managed and how they compete in the marketplace.

In the past 20 years or so, this quantum shift in focus has caused leading service organizations to concentrate their energies on improving the total experience of the customer in an effort to create positive memories of experience. Moving away from a departmentalized approach, successful service providers *unify* their efforts through cross-functional strategies that bring together marketing, operations, technology, and human resources as a collaborative function created to leave lasting memories of experiences for the customer.

Thus, this new approach to bring all internal capabilities of the firm (marketing, operations, technology, human resources) together to create lasting memories and relationships with the customer is at the forefront of service leadership and success. For example, a large integrated resort company, Crown Resorts, located in Australia, recently implemented a significant new customer experience system called Medallia and now has dashboards to understand customer experience at thousands of touchpoints across their properties (hotels, gaming, food, and beverage). These dashboards are used by marketers (to understand customer preferences), by operations (to understand how well customers perceive their experience at each touchpoint), and for management to develop customer-focused incentives (remuneration linked to customer experience scores by business segment). Management conversations across the company are centered on the customer experience and all of the metrics and data. Similarly, this system includes an 'employee experience' element that continually pulses employee attitudes and perceptions, another critical element in the custom experience (covered further in Chapters 7 and 8). Indeed, Crown Resorts has come to understand that the customer experience is not the sole responsibility of frontline employees. The whole firm must live and breathe customer experience such that it permeates all activities. That is a total organizational approach!

Service-dominant logic

As the challenges of managing and marketing in the experience economy service became widely acknowledged and accepted, service management began to 'stand on its own' – clearly distinct from managing and selling physical products. The development of 'IHIP' paved the way for a movement known as *service management*, creating a new lens through which to view all organizational practices and developing new ways to approach all organizational functions and academic disciplines in a service context.

While service management had indeed solidified itself as a vital and foundational paradigm for service organizational success, Vargo and Lusch (2004) argued that it was not accurate or useful to see goods and services as distinctive. Their concern was that business language was predominately based on 'goods' vocabulary (selling 'things' that can be held, stored, sold later, consumed later). They called this old language 'goods-dominant' logic and published a seminal paper espousing their ideas in the *Journal of Marketing* in 2004. Vargo and Lusch proposed service-dominant (S-D) logic – a metatheoretical framework that identifies service, rather than goods, as the fundamental basis of economic (and social) exchange.

At the core of this S-D logic is the idea that all economic exchange can be viewed in terms of service-for-service exchange. The focus is on service (rather than 'services') steers attention to the process, patterns, and benefits of exchange, rather than units of output that are exchanged (e.g,. goods). In S-D logic, goods are simply mechanisms or in simple words, an enabler, in an exchange. Further, according to S-D logic, all industries are service industries.

S-D logic can be an important guiding concept to leading and managing service firms and customer experience (CX) – where value is co-created with multiple actors over time. No longer can management paradigms developed in the industrial revolution (where the focus is on the firm) be effective. New thinking says that in service and CX contexts, organizations engage *together* with customers through a journey – co-creating value.

A good example of SD-Logic in action can be illustrated through a global public transport organization (founded in France – UTIP – Union Internationale des Transports Publics). This organization has helped advance the messages globally about urban mobility. As an organization, they do not engage directly in public transport. Rather, they integrate many resources and stakeholders, championing the exchange of ideas and knowledge to further the development and advancement of public transport policy, planning, and operations across many countries. This organization's aim is to nurture public transport communities through the facilitation of local, national, and international networking events and knowledge-sharing opportunities. They co-create value by bringing together government departments, public transport operators, the service and supply industry, as well as research institutions, academics, and consultants with the aim of developing public transport policies and promoting shared learning and best practice on a range of topics associated with public transport innovation and operations. This type of process of integrating resources and working collectively across stakeholders is the co-creation of value in action!

Summary of chapter

Ultimately, the main objective of service organizations (or nearly any organization for that matter!) is or should be to provide customers with outstanding service. It is thus imperative that managers understand the nature of their service offerings and be able to ensure customer satisfaction with service, rather than with the technical features of whatever products they may also be offering.

The four acknowledged challenges between service offerings and manufactured goods—intangibility, inseparability, heterogeneity, and perishability—are well established in the literature. The four characteristics are well established, but the ramifications of these characteristics are complicated and form the basis of this chapter.

Management and marketing of service products have been significantly influenced by theories from the manufacturing sector and/or by the intuitive judgments of individual service managers. This has proven to be challenging and ineffective, as theory generated from the manufacturing sector is inappropriate for service sector organizations, and a reliance on such approaches can lead to decreased customer satisfaction and thereby affect overall business performance.

In addition to the introduction of IHIP as critical challenge for service managers and marketers, this chapter has also elucidated other important elements or challenges, including the marketing mix, moving from four 'original' Ps to the expanded group of seven; the emerging field of service-dominant logic that transforms thinking in all business contexts, basing all marketing and management on service rather than goods; and finally the importance of a holistic integrated approach across business areas to most effectively manage and market service. Managers must be able to design and implement appropriate strategies to overcome the challenges and thus maximize the potential for competitive advantage.

Review questions

1. Briefly describe the four distinctive characteristics of services and why they are of particular concern to service managers and marketers.
2. Briefly describe one managerial implication for each of the characteristics described above.
3. How are the additional "Ps" of the marketing mix relevant to a service marketer?
4. Why has it become necessary for successful service firms to adopt a more 'integrated approach' in their management and organizational structure?
5. Describe the way SD-Logic proposes a new way to consider value exchange and the separation of service and goods.

Suggested readings

This is a list of suggested further reading on topics covered in this chapter. For a separate list of full reference citations quoted in the chapter, see the 'References' section at the end of this chapter.

Bowen, J., & Ford, R. C. (2002). Managing service organizations: Does having a "thing" make a difference? *Journal of Management*, 28(3), 447–469.

Bowen, D. E. (2020). Lessons for all when service scholarship and management practice come together. *Organizational Dynamics*, 49(3), 1–10.

References

Aaker, D. (2003). The power of the branded differentiator. *Sloan Management Review*, October. Retrieved from https://sloanreview.mit.edu/article/the-power-of-the-branded-differentiator/

Bitner, M. J., & Zeithaml, V. A. (1987). *Fundamentals in services marketing: Add value to your service* (C. Surprenant, Ed.). Chicago, IL: AMA Services Marketing Conference Proceedings.

Booms, B. H., & Bitner, M. J. (1981). *Marketing strategies and organizational structures for service firms*. Chicago, IL: American Marketing Association.

Marriott International. (2019). *2019 Annual report*. Retrieved from https://marriott.gcs-web.com/static-files/178683c9-c9d9-47b0-b115-726588f43130

Rushton, A. M., & Carson, D. J. (1985). The marketing of services: Managing the intangibles. *European Journal of Marketing*, 19(3), 19–40.

Shostack, G. L. (1977). Breaking free from product marketing. *Journal of Marketing*, 41, April, 73–80.

Vargo, S., & Lusch, R. (2004). Evolving to a new dominant logic for marketing. *Journal of Marketing*, 68(1), 1–17.

Westin Store. (2021). *The Westin heavenly bed*. Marriott International, Inc. Retrieved from https://europe.westinstore.com/en/?___store=hbeu_en

Chapter 3

Management implications for service supply and demand

Study objectives

Having completed this chapter, readers should be able to understand:

- the interplay between supply, demand, quality, and price;
- strategies and tools for managing service capacity;
- strategies and tools to manage service demand;
- how demand pricing has developed and impacted many services;
- why managing real and perceived wait times is important (and the relevance of the psychology of waiting);
- the growth of on-demand service models; and
- how to balance capacity and demand to achieve operational efficiency and compete successfully.

The framework of this chapter

This chapter is set out as follows:

- Introduction
- Services cannot be stored
- Challenges associated with service capacity (supply) and demand
- Balancing capacity and demand
    o Managing capacity (supply) to fit demand?
    o Change demand to fit capacity?
    o Change both together?
- Managing service capacity
    o Capacity and quality
    o Maximum capacity and optimum capacity
    o Online platforms and the sharing economy
- Managing service demand
    o Understanding the causes of the variations in demand
    o The relationship between demand and service quality

- o Waiting and the psychology of waiting
  - o Queuing strategies
  - o Strategies for managing demand
  - o Pricing and revenue (demand pricing/yield management)
  - o Leveraging 'place' (on-demand service models)
- Summary of chapter
- Review questions
- Suggested readings
- References

Introduction

In the context of service offerings, marketing, and operations are often undertaken simultaneously and by the same employees (as discussed in Chapter 2). This means that in a service context there is an inextricable connection between marketing, operations, and human resources. This connection between these three functional areas is not only evident conceptually but in fact more clearly in the practical context. For example, customers perceive the quality of service based on the performance of the employee in terms of his/her efficiency in dealing with a customer's request. Additionally, the quality of service is perceived by the customers based on the employee's behavior and his/her willingness to listen, respond to a customer's queries, and so forth. This means customers highly value employee's behavioral performance as part of the service. In fact, these two (operational and human) factors effectively serve as the marketing message of a service firm. Thus, marketing assumes a more holistic function in services rather than the narrow function of increasing sales in the product industry.

The interrelationship between operations, human resources, and marketing is critical given that services have to be produced instantaneously when and where customers are in need of a service. This means that, from a customer's point of view, receiving service on time communicates quality. In many service contexts, immediate delivery can be so critical that customers will be unwilling to compromise. Take the ambulance service or fire brigade service for example. Although these are extreme examples, let us take a very mundane example of a taxi service. Will customers value a taxi that arrives 30 minutes late? As discussed in Chapter 2, perishability of service (the inability to store service for future use) poses considerable challenges for service managers to match both demand and supply. The following sections will outline some of the challenges demand fluctuation causes and suggest some possible solutions.

Services cannot be stored

As outlined in Chapter 2, the nature of service presents a range of challenges for managers and marketers, different from selling physical goods.

The four distinct challenges – intangibility, heterogeneity, inseparability, and perishability (i.e., 'IHIP') – provide a roadmap to understanding the nature of service. While each of these presents many considerations and various opportunities for service managers and marketers, it is perishability in particular that presents a different set of challenges. Given that a service cannot be stored for future use, a service has to be produced when the customer requires it. This means managing the supply of service must match the demand for the service to render the service firm to be well functioning. Unfortunately, perfectly matching supply and demand is one of the biggest challenges in most service contexts. While some service demands can be predictable, for example, retailers serve more customers during weekends, holidays, or in the evenings. In other cases it is not possible to predict the demand for some services, for example, ambulance services. Although not all cases will fall into these two categories, there are ways in which we can adopt many strategies to help bring supply and demand to a manageable level.

In fact, the success of business models created by Airbnb and Uber is a clear illustration of the utilization of supply and demand challenges in the accommodation service and taxi service industries. Airbnb recognized that there is an unused supply of bedrooms in private homes which they could match with people who are looking for accommodation. Similarly, Uber recognized that there are both cars and drivers whose service has not been used although there are many people who were in need of rides. Of course, technology and the Internet play key factors contributing to the success of these business models. These two firms made use of the demand and supply challenge in the respective service sector and converted it into a successful business. Think about the huge success of computer firms such as Infosys and Wipro in India serving businesses around the world making use of the time differences and the supply of services overnight for businesses in Europe and North America.

Challenges associated with service capacity (supply) and demand

Due to the perishable nature of service (meaning that it cannot be stored for future use or sale), demand plays a particularly significant role in the production and delivery of a service. *Demand* refers to the need for a service at a given price, place, and time. Capacity or *supply* refers to the availability of a specific service at a given price, place, and time. The word 'supply' has been adopted from the product industry marketing context and hence it really does not communicate the right message in service. Supply may communicate the message that something has been stored for future supply. This of course is not possible in service. From a service manager's perspective it may be better to focus on 'capacity' which is what is important for a service firm. Capacity may communicate more clearly the real challenge of service firms (for example, capacity of an airplane, capacity of a concert hall, capacity of a hospital), and will also communicate service firms' ability to fulfill customers' demands immediately.

Reliability and timing are important in service

Reliability and timing are important issues for service consumers. Consider the following scenarios:

- A hotel, motel, or Airbnb must be available exactly when the traveler wants it. A vacant room tomorrow is useless to a traveler who wants accommodation tonight.
- Food delivery service firms such as Zomato and Swiggy must be able to collect the food when it is ready and efficiently transport it to the customer while it is still fresh.
- A taxi or Uber needs to be available when someone needs a ride. There is no use for a driver when the need for the ride is no longer there.

As highlighted by the examples above, goods consumption can often be delayed, but service is usually produced and consumed almost simultaneously. And more often than not, this must be when the customer requests the service, not before or after. These differences between a product and a service mean that the delivery system used in the goods industry is inappropriate for service organizations. Service managers are thus required to consider alternative systems for the efficient management of demand and supply. Despite the various technological advancements and mobile apps that can be utilized to enhance the service-delivery system, balancing capacity and demand still presents a real challenge. The success of service firms is dependent heavily on their ability to manage or match supply and demand.

An imbalance between supply and demand in the manufacturing sector can be dealt with as an irregular and temporary phenomenon. However, in the case of the service sector, the fact that many services cannot be stored for future use is a problem for service managers if there are significant variations in demand. In many service organizations increasing the capacity to match demand is not possible. For example, an airplane cannot increase the number of seats on the plane to meet the high demand of passengers to fly that plane at that time. On the other hand, when demand is low, productive capacity is wasted; but when demand is high, potential business is lost due to the inability to supply the service in accordance with that demand, which constitutes an irrecoverable revenue loss (refer to Figure 3.1).

48 Service supply and demand

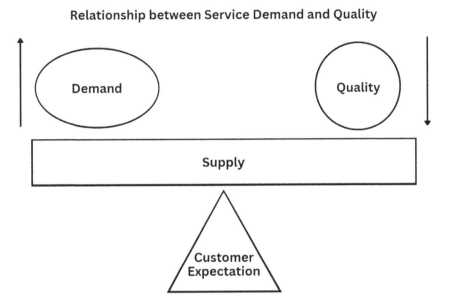

Figure 3.1 Relationship between service demand and quality *(Adapted – authors' representation)*

Balancing capacity and demand

Managing capacity (supply) to fit demand?

Faced with the challenge of limited flexibility to change capacity, service firms often face considerable pressure when there are demand fluctuations (high or low demand at any point in time). Although demand fluctuation causes many problems, service managers have identified some possible options to tailor capacity to meet variations in demand.

During periods of high demand service managers can try to alter the capacity using some strategies. These are termed 'chase demand strategies'. To increase capacity to serve customers during peak periods (periods of high demand) service managers could make use of the following strategies:

- **Employing part-time employees**: this strategy can be effectively used in service firms where an additional number of employees may help to serve more customers during peak demand periods (for example, part-time employees at retail stores during weekends or during the holiday season);
- **Maximizing efficiently:** this strategy can be used to serve a greater number of customers in a short period of time (for example, self- or web- or app-check-in at airports or self-service check-outs at retail or grocery stores

can very effectively serve a greater number of customers in a very short period of time with limited involvement of employees). Enhanced service design can effectively increase workflow and process flow to increase both efficiency and customer perception of the service;
- **Renting additional facilities or sharing capacity**: this strategy is used by many service firms that rent vehicles and equipment for use during times of need. They also share resources, for example, airlines share passengers referred to as 'codeshare', and two or more hotels in proximity often share complimentary airport shuttle services.

Reduction in capacity during periods of low demand might be achieved by:

- reducing employees' hours or scheduling their leave during low-demand seasons;
- renting-out of surplus equipment and facilities during off-peak period; or
- removing surplus equipment and facilities for periodic maintenance and renovation.

Many service companies have found it is more efficient to handle demand whenever it occurs, rather than attempting to smooth out the peaks in demand. The peaks vary according to the type of business. Revenue or yield management software can help service managers to understand when peaks are likely to occur, so they can augment their usual workforce with part-time assistance, rearrange the layout of the service-delivery system to maximize productivity, or even share capacity with another business for mutual benefit. Often managers will employ a mixture of these measures to safeguard the consistency and quality of service.

However, service managers rarely find that these straightforward measures are sufficient to maintain high efficiency. The question then arises as to whether the opposite strategy might be tried – changing demand to fit capacity.

Change demand to fit capacity?

A more effective solution might be achieved by altering the demand for a service. This is clearly a marketing question. That is, can strategic marketing techniques be used to manipulate demand to match available capacity?

In fact, this approach has proven to be very successful in many service sectors. A simple example is when cinemas offer cheaper movie tickets on specific days throughout the week to entice customers to come at particular times and to stay away at peak demand days and times. There are more sophisticated techniques available (such as revenue or yield management that alters price based on predicted demand), but the simple example of strategic price differentiation demonstrates that the manipulation of demand to suit capacity is certainly an option for service managers and marketers. There are also innovative ways that service firms can collaborate to reach new target markets and increase demand to match available capacity, for example, in the case of Internet Saathi outlined below.

> **Internet Saathi: Empowering Rural Women in India through ICT**
>
> By Dr. Meeta Munshi and Dr. Sandip Trada,
> Institute of Management, Nirma University
>
> 'Internet Saathi' is a digital literacy initiative undertaken in 2015 by Tata Trusts and Google India, with the aim of empowering women in rural India by connecting them to the online world. Women accounted for less than 30 percent of Internet users in India in 2015, which was significantly lower than other emerging economies. In rural India specifically, which comprised 68 percent of the country's population, the proportion of women Internet users was only 12 percent. Although women are the backbone of rural India, they face several hurdles in gaining access to health, education, and technology due to the vast gender disparity among rural Internet users. Tata Trusts and Google India recognized this issue and decided to address it by launching Internet Saathi. This program is thus an example of how organizations can collaborate to develop a new service offering that meets the needs of an underserved customer segment, while increasing the demand for an existing service to match available capacity.
>
> Tata Trusts and Google India have used an innovative model for the Internet Saathi program. In this collaboration, Tata Trusts is responsible for implementing the initiative on the ground by reaching out to villages and teaming up with local not-for-profit organizations and 'self-help groups' to deliver internet training to rural women, while Google India provides technical knowledge and resources for the training.
>
> After receiving sufficient training about using the Internet and digital technologies, these selected rural women become 'Saathis' (meaning 'Partners' in English) and are assigned to clusters of villages where they educate other rural women about the Internet, its benefits, and how to embrace it in their daily lives. The Saathis are provided necessary resources like training materials, Internet cycle cart, data, smartphones, tablets, and power backups by Google India, while their daily stipend and other expenses are funded by Tata Trusts. The local stakeholders provide a community space for women to convene and interact with the Saathis. Once the Saathis are confident that the rural women can independently use the Internet and smartphones to improve their livelihoods, they move to the next village of interested women.

In order to make Internet accessible to rural women after the Saathis leave the village, Tata Trusts and Google India collaborate with local stakeholders to establish several 'common centers' at school and self-help group premises. These centers are equipped with smartphones, computers, tablets, and good Internet connection. Some of the trained rural women act as volunteers to impart digital training as well as providing support at the common center, thus making this program both sustainable and empowering.

The Internet Saathi program has had a huge influence on the lives of rural women, who were previously precluded from using the Internet and mobile phones due to low digital literacy rates and cultural rigidity. As a result of this program, many rural women are now able to avail the benefits of the Internet in numerous areas. Furthermore, digital literacy has significantly improved the social and economic lives of many rural women in the following areas:

- Education and healthcare: acquiring basic education through online courses, learning about current affairs, getting tips for child healthcare and hygiene, and finding medical facilities, especially during pregnancy and after giving birth;
- Agriculture: getting useful information regarding farming, crop management, weather conditions, and the best rates for their produce;
- Skill development: learning different vocational skills like knitting, sewing, weaving, beautician training, making handicraft products, and getting guidance to set up small-scale businesses; and
- Government schemes and services: availing of benefits from several government services such as medical facilities, safety service, skill development programs, employment opportunities, rural banking services, and pensions and widow schemes, to name a few.

By providing the above benefits, Internet Saathi has empowered millions of rural women to take ownership of their lives. For instance, within the first four years of the program, 70,000 Saathis had trained more than 26 million women across 2.6 lakh villages, spanning 20 states of the country. These positive results show how Internet Saathi has boosted the social and economic status of rural women, thus shrinking the gender divide and the gap between rural and urban India. The program is also a successful example of how organizations can change demand to fit capacity, as well as identify opportunities for new services by meeting the unmet needs of a specific customer segment.

Change both together?

Despite the fact that capacity can be manipulated to suit demand, and that demand can be manipulated to suit capacity, it is imperative that service organizations seek to manage both demand and capacity simultaneously – rather than working on either independently. Indeed, the fact that a service is produced and consumed simultaneously means that marketing approaches to capacity and demand are inherently interrelated.

An integrated approach (between marketing, operations, and management) requires a concerted attempt to coordinate capacity and demand. Effective service leaders rigorously apply such an approach.

Managing service capacity

Although capacity and demand must be coordinated and considered in an integrated manner, it is useful to consider them separately in attempting to clarify the important issues involved. After the issues have been clarified in isolation, management is in a better position to consider integrated and coordinated marketing strategies.

When establishing strategies to coordinate demand and capacity in service organizations, it is important to first consider the capacity or 'supply side' of the equation (for example, the number of available rooms). The following aspects of capacity are worthy of note:

- capacity and quality;
- maximum capacity and optimum capacity; and
- online platforms and the sharing economy.

Each of these is considered below.

Capacity and quality

If the fluctuation of demand is rapid and unpredictable (for example, at a retail store), it is extremely difficult for managers to forecast requirements and to develop contingency plans in terms of altering capacity to meet demand. However, simply increasing capacity can be a rather blunt response. Excess capacity not only results in a loss of profit but also can actually decrease the quality of the service experience. For example, although many patrons might say that they like a relatively uncrowded restaurant, a restaurant that has only one table occupied has such an excess of capacity that it fails to offer the desired social ambience to its patrons. In addition, it is more difficult to motivate staff in a very quiet demand period.

Nevertheless, a chronic inability to meet service demand does constitute a serious quality and revenue problem for many service businesses. A demand far in excess of capacity usually leads to dissatisfaction regarding quality among those who are served, and no service at all for those who cannot be accommodated! Taken together this represents a significant loss (both potential and permanent) for the business.

Having said that, it must be noted that there is a subtle distinction between maximum capacity and optimum capacity. In assessing capacity and quality, a distinction must be made between these two concepts of capacity.

Maximum capacity and optimum capacity

There is a difference between maximum capacity and optimum capacity for fixed-capacity service firms. Maximum capacity represents the upper limit that the organization can possibly achieve (for example, restaurant capacity to seat 100 customers), whereas optimum capacity is the desirable level achievable (for example, 80 seats full in a 100-seat restaurant). As shown in Figure 3.1., at any given point in time, a service organization can be faced with one of four conditions:

- demand exceeds maximum available capacity, when potential business can be lost;
- demand exceeds the optimum capacity level, when no one is turned away, but all customers are likely to perceive deterioration in the quality of service delivered;
- demand and supply are well balanced at the level of optimum capacity; or
- demand is below optimum capacity, when productive resources are under-utilized and, in some instances, customers might find the experience disappointing or have doubts about the viability of the service.

When demand exceeds maximum capacity, potential customers can be disappointed when they are turned away, and their business might be lost forever. When demand is operating between optimum and maximum capacity, there is a risk that some customers might receive inferior service, and consequently decide not to return in the future. When demand and supply are well balanced, the optimum level of capacity is achieved; this is likely to vary from one service business to another, and even from one market segment to another.

Online platforms and the sharing economy

Fueled by the growth of the Internet, mobile technologies, advancements in analytics and AI, and changing consumer preferences, online platforms and the sharing economy have emerged as new business models that have addressed some of the challenges service organizations have traditionally faced in balancing supply and demand, and are now viable alternatives to fulfill customers' needs.

There are numerous online platforms and mobile apps today that enable the sharing of capacity-constrained assets (for example, cars and homes, through platforms like Uber or Airbnb) or capacity-unconstrained resources (for example, music, through a platform like Spotify). The online nature of these businesses means that there is almost infinite potential to add more supply to meet consumer demand. However, research has shown that there is still an optimum level of capacity that should be aimed for, since an oversupply of listings on such platforms can create a negative experience for users in the form of search costs.

Ultimately, by harnessing the power of the Internet and advanced analytics, sharing platform businesses are able to facilitate efficient and effective matching of a service offering with customers' unique needs, at any given place or time, thereby efficiently balancing capacity and demand and enhancing value for all stakeholders (Wirtz et al., 2019).

Managing service demand

Understanding the causes of the variations in demand

Service managers recognize that variation in demand is a major challenge in service organizations. To identify strategies to manage variations in demand they should first understand factors that govern the demand for a specific service at a given point in time. Therefore, it is important for service managers to understand some of the factors leading to demand variation. Some of these factors are:

- *Does the level of demand for the service follow a regular predictable cycle?* If so, what are the underlying causes of these predictable variations? (for example, variation in demand because of summer holidays, Christmas and New Year, weekends, and so forth.) These are predictable fluctuations in demand and hence service managers can establish strategies to cope with these demand fluctuations.
- *Are changes in the level of demand largely random in nature?* If so, are there any underlying causes the firm has encountered in the past? If this is the case, how did they manage in the past during similar situations? Can they replicate similar strategies used in the past to cope with random changes in demand?

Technological advancements mean that there are now powerful digital tools that allow service managers to collect and analyze a wealth of data, which helps them to answer these questions from a position of accuracy, rather than guesswork. Empowered with this data, service managers and marketers can then identify patterns and subsequently make informed forecasts and decisions on how to best manage demand.

When demand for a service fluctuates widely in the short term, but follows a predictable pattern over a known cycle, it might be economically worthwhile to develop marketing strategies designed to smooth out major fluctuations over time. Regular fluctuations in demand – such as seasonal cycles – can be influenced, to a large extent, by creative marketing. However, no strategy is likely to succeed unless it is based on an understanding of why customers seek to use the service when they do.

In contrast, marketing efforts can do little to smooth out random fluctuations in demand over time – because these are usually the result of factors outside human control. Examples include pandemics, natural calamities, political events, economic crises, and so on.

In searching for strategies to coordinate demand and capacity in services, let us now consider the 'demand side' of the equation. The following aspects of demand are worthy of note:

- the relationship between demand and service quality;
- waiting and the psychology of waiting;
- queuing strategies;
- strategies for managing demand; and
- pricing and revenue (demand pricing).

Each of these are considered below.

The relationship between demand and service quality

Demand significantly affects quality in service organizations. Customers expect a firm's quality of service to be consistent – whatever the current level of demand is (for example, during the weekend at dinner time customers will expect the same level of good service and good quality of food). To gain customer confidence, maintain image, and engender customer loyalty, quality must be delivered consistently. It is imperative that service managers design strategies that assist them to manage demand and quality simultaneously. Although this is a challenging task, if the firm wants to attract high demand, service managers have to identify various strategies to maintain quality (for example, at a restaurant, recruiting more employees to work during peak periods, offering a short menu that is easy to make or pre-prepare, or offering buffet service rather than an a la carte menu).

In general (but not invariably), increased demand tends to decrease quality. Personal service is less likely to be as attentive and comfortable if there is a crowd of people to be looked after. However, if a firm has adequate quality-improvement programs in place, the drop-off in quality in these circumstances can be minimized.

There are circumstances in which increased demand actually improves quality as perceived by consumers. For example, a crowded dance floor in a nightclub might engender a desirable 'party atmosphere', and a sporting contest with a large crowd cheering enthusiastically might be experienced as a more exciting and stimulating event. Despite these exceptions, it is generally the case that increased demand threatens quality.

Waiting and the psychology of waiting

Another key consideration when it comes to quality is the impact that waiting can have on a customer's experience when demand exceeds capacity. One useful way to approach customer waiting is to think about it as the organization is 'charging' the customers in 'time' currency. So, saving a customer's time is one of the quickest ways to increase the value of the service experience. The challenge for service managers is to make waiting, or more importantly, 'perceived waiting' less painful or less uncomfortable.

Waiting for a service often causes a misperception of the amount of time a person was waiting. This concept is called the 'psychology of waiting' and there are many different conditions that affect a person's perception of wait times. Some of these include:

- unoccupied time feels longer than occupied time;
- anxious, sad, and angry waits feel longer than relaxed ones;
- waits of uncertain length feel longer than certain ones;
- unexplained waits feel longer than explained ones;
- uncomfortable waits feel longer than comfortable ones; and
- unfair waits feel longer than fair ones.

It is important for service managers and marketers to understand the psychological impact that waiting has on customers. Many successful service firms now take advantage of technology and mobile apps to reduce the wait or wait perception. For instance, the 'virtual queue' concept eliminates physical waiting by allowing customers to register their place in line and then spend that time doing other activities.

Queuing strategies

To minimize the negative impacts that waiting can have on a customer's experience when demand exceeds capacity, service organizations can utilize various queuing strategies to inventory demand, provide predictability, and give customers the assurance that they are being treated fairly.

There are several different queue configurations, such as single or parallel lines leading to one or multiple serving stations where customers need to be physically present, or virtual queues (as referred to above) that allow customers to remain occupied elsewhere until it is their turn to be served. It is important for service managers to work closely with the operations department to ensure that the most suitable type of queue is selected and implemented.

After selecting the type of queue that best matches the service process, service managers and marketers need to ensure that a customer's time spent in a queue is as 'painless' as possible. Many leading service organizations today are utilizing digital technologies and smartphone apps to keep customers entertained during their wait and to provide greater transparency about wait times. For example, real-time maps are used on apps like Uber and Deliveroo that show customers how far away their ride or meal delivery is to provide more certainty regarding the expected time of arrival.

Furthermore, service managers should take customer market segments into account and tailor queuing systems accordingly. When prioritizing how different customers will be served, the factors to consider here include:

- urgency (for example, in a hospital setting the most critical patients should be treated first);
- price (for example, providing faster or more personalized service to customers who have paid more); and
- importance (for example, giving preferential treatment to members of an organization's loyalty program).

Strategies for managing demand

There are many different strategies for managing demand available to service organizations, including but not limited to:

- the 'chase-and-level' strategy – whereby a firm 'chases' demand by altering the marketing mix and going after a new target market, while simultaneously 'leveling' capacity using any combination of the aforementioned strategies;
- yield management – which is used to alter demand by careful forecasting, overbooking, choosing high-yield customers, and so on; and
- product variation, time-and-location variation, queuing theory, and pricing theory.

Apart from the above (often complex) strategies, the following 'demand-leveling' options are especially useful for many service marketers to consider in accordance with the 'seven Ps':

- Product – developing complementary services;
- Price – applying differential pricing schemes;
- Place – broadening access to a service through digital channels;
- Promotion – developing nonpeak demand through promotions;
- People – utilizing virtual assistants or chatbots to provide online customer service;

- Process – creating digital reservation systems to inventory demand; and
- Physical evidence – utilizing VR, AR, or XR to overcome physical limits.

Each of the above-discussed service marketing elements offers many different possibilities to manage demand in different service sectors. Based on the reader's interest they should undertake further research to examine and understand different opportunities that are possible to manage demand in any particular service sector. Two elements are worthy of note though, given their evolving role and significance to service managers and marketers, being Price and Place.

Pricing and revenue (demand pricing/yield management)

While every element of the marketing mix can be used to manage demand, as outlined above, 'price' is perhaps the most frequently used variable by service managers and marketers to either stimulate or shift demand to match capacity. After all, who hasn't noticed that hotels in business destinations have much lower pricing on weekends than weekdays, or that prices for flights can vary dramatically even on the same day (for example, a 5 pm flight could cost three times as much as a 10 pm flight).

Demand pricing (sometimes also referred to as 'dynamic pricing') describes the strategy of setting different prices for different market segments based on the demand for a service at different times. More recently, Uber has normalized the use of 'surge pricing' to increase fares during periods of peak demand. This strategy has the effect of attracting more drivers to the road during those times (i.e., increasing capacity) while encouraging price-sensitive customers to travel during off-peak times (i.e., tempering demand). As the use of smartphones and Internet connectivity continues to grow, and the collection and application of real-time data becomes easier, it is likely that more service businesses will begin to apply this strategy to balance supply and demand while maximizing their profit margin. Advances in algorithm-based technology mean that what used to be a difficult and arduous mathematical process to determine pricing changes can now be done quite easily. The benefits to organizations of high-demand pricing are astounding, and in some cases, can even be seen as price gouging – an ethical question that many firms must consider in their demand pricing strategy.

In applying a dynamic pricing strategy, service organizations become attuned to the price sensitivity of particular market segments at particular times. To determine what price a customer may be willing to pay for a service at a particular point in time, most service organizations today utilize a revenue management system that collects relevant historical data for analysis and forecasting. This can be quite an intricate process that requires strong analytical skills; thus, a whole new field of study has emerged alongside a professional occupation (revenue managers) to study this area and understand how to best use algorithms to improve service firms' financial performance. In using this data, revenue managers can define the demand curve and adjust their prices accordingly among market segments.

Ultimately, pricing and revenue management are effective strategies to deal with service perishability and swings in demand, and as digital capabilities continue to advance these practices are likely to become ever more sophisticated and widespread across service organizations.

Leveraging 'place' (on-demand service models)

Another key element of the service marketing mix that has evolved due to technological developments is the third 'P' mentioned above – Place – as many services are now able to be delivered through both physical and digital channels. By leveraging digital service delivery, organizations can increase their available capacity and thus better meet increases in demand. A simple example may be online banking services using an app or website, rather than going to a bank. Many banks have fewer and smaller on-site locations now because of this, reducing costs but still having that face-to-face option available for some customers and some situations (for example, people are more likely to want to see a person to receive financial advice or borrow money).

Alongside advances in technology, customer expectations have also evolved. As services can now be accessed almost anywhere, customers also expect to be able to access them at any time. Thus, speed and convenience are important factors driving the growth of on-demand service models. Research has shown that on-demand services are distinct from other services according to three key characteristics: availability, responsiveness, and scalability (van der Burg et al., 2019). Well-known examples of such business models include Spotify and Netflix, which provide customers with 24/7 access to a comprehensive library of music and films. Think about how different this is from only a few years ago when you had to either go to the cinema or perhaps watch a movie at home using a DVD or watch on a network or cable channel.

Customers' expectation of immediacy has several implications for service managers and marketers, most notably here being the challenge of eliminating the time between order and fulfillment (i.e., demand and supply). In this context, service firms must find a way to balance on-demand service delivery with reasonable prices/costs and levels of standardization/customization, which requires the application of innovative technologies and algorithms. Organizations that are able to find a way to deliver on-demand services while maintaining an acceptable margin will establish a competitive advantage in the 'on-demand economy'.

CAFU: Fuel-on-Demand Powered by AI, IoT, and Machine Learning

By Dr. Madhavi Ayyagari, Mindsbourg Consulting,
Dr. Sanjai Parahoo, Hamdan Bin Mohammed Smart University, and
Dr. Joseph Stevens, Murdoch University Dubai

The COVID-19 pandemic and subsequent lockdowns in many countries led to the 'great online migration'. Businesses and consumers were forced to pivot and adapt; meetings became virtual and those who had never ordered groceries online started doing so. Getting things delivered at home has now become part of everyday life for millions of people around the world. However, have you heard of home delivery of petrol (or gasoline, as it is called in some places)? A Dubai-based startup, CAFU, has developed an application (app) that enables on-demand delivery of fuel to cars, motorbikes, and even boats. And in a region where high summer temperatures make the queuing and purchase process at fuel stations uncomfortable and inconvenient, the advantage of home refueling cannot be over-emphasized.

The founder, Rashid Al Ghurair, claims that this intelligent app launched in 2018 is probably the most disruptive innovation since the introduction of the combustion engine in the 1800s – as effectively conveyed in its advertisements. The aim is to free people from their errands so that they can utilize their time more productively. The company leverages artificial intelligence (AI), the Internet of Things (IoT), and machine learning capabilities that enable app users to get petrol delivered promptly to any location – home, office, gym, and even the beach. A customer specifies the location of the vehicle for fuel delivery using GPS technology embedded in the app, which enables the system to map the shortest route to the delivery site. On the operations side, embedded AI in the app leverages customer data to estimate fuel demand and optimize the matching of drivers to orders received for fuel delivery. Furthermore, machine learning is used to establish a baseline of normal activity and to monitor the fuel delivery process including temperature and pressure in the refueling tanks, while IoT sensors monitor in real-time the exact volume of fuel pumped into a customer's car.

This judicious utilization of new technologies (AI, IoT, and machine learning) enables CAFU to respond to a customer's order safely, quickly, and with a high level of dependability, thereby providing an easy and efficient service process and an enjoyable customer experience. The 'CAFU Pilots' run the fleet of distinctly branded delivery trucks to fuel customers' vehicles at any time of the day or night; for instance, a customer can book the 2:00 am to 3:00 am delivery time slot before going to bed and wake up to a full tank in the morning. The contactless service is complemented by 'CAFU Ambassadors' who attend to customer queries from 8:00am to 12:00am seven days a week, even on public holidays. The price of the fuel is on par with the prices charged by petrol stations. Subscribers can opt for a monthly subscription for about $7 or choose the pay-as-you-go option. The company adopted a charge per delivery model in the first two years but shifted to a free-delivery model in 2020 to support consumers further throughout the COVID pandemic.

The company is now exploring the potential for replicating its business model – which is based on a technology-driven service design to transform routine tasks into a new type of experience for the customer – for product and market development. CAFU's expansion is driven by new offerings like an on-demand car wash service and entry into new markets like Oman. Central to CAFU's success is the way the company uses technology to design a service that delivers a unique customer experience. CAFU leverages state-of-the-art technology like IoT and AI to free their customers from mundane tasks. The assurance of timely availability of fuel at any location also brings peace of mind and helps consumers save time. And importantly, throughout the COVID-19 pandemic, the company transformed fuel recharge into a contactless service that reduces the risk of exposure to unavoidable tasks. Testament to the company's success, CAFU won two awards in 2019 including the 'Best Platform Using AI in the Energy Sector' at the Ai Everything Brave Awards by the Government of Dubai, as well as the 'App of the Year' at the Enterprise Agility Awards by Entrepreneur Middle East.

Summary of chapter

One key aim of this book is to help managers first understand the many complexities that exist in the service and experience economy, and then become aware of some of the ways managers can overcome these complexities. Among these challenges and complexities are the perishability of service and the many implications for the simple fact that service can rarely be 'stored' for later use. This chapter presents a more detailed overview of one of the four stated service challenges (IHIP) and presents a set of concepts and principles necessary for service managers. These include ways to affect supply and demand, either separately or concomitantly; the interrelationships between supply, demand, price, and quality; and ways managers can better cope with inevitable waiting through the concept known as 'the psychology of waiting'.

Review questions

1. Why is fluctuation in demand a particular challenge for service managers?
2. What is service 'supply' and how is this a different challenge for service managers than supply of goods?
3. How can managers manipulate supply? And demand?
4. What are the impacts of supply and demand changes on service quality?
5. How is the 'psychology of waiting' so important to service managers, and why is 'perceived waiting' more important than actual waiting times?
6. Describe 'on-demand' service models and how this is transforming many service offerings.

Suggested readings

Buell, R. W., & Norton, M. I. (2011). Think customers hate waiting? Not so fast… *Harvard Business Review*, 89(5), 34.

Dickson, D., Ford, R. C., & Laval, B. (2005). Managing real and virtual waits in hospitality and service organizations. *Cornell Hotel and Restaurant Administration Quarterly*, 46(1), 52–68.

Mollenkopf, D. A., Ozanne, L. K., & Stolze, H. J. (2021). A transformative supply chain response to COVID-19. *Journal of Service Management*, 32(2), 190–202.

Noone, B. M., & Coulter, R. C. (2012). Applying modern robotics technologies to demand prediction and production management in the quick-service restaurant sector. *Cornell Hospitality Quarterly*, 53(2), 122–133.

Sasser, W. E. (1976). Match supply and demand in service industries. *Harvard Business Review*, November–December, 133–140.

van der Burg, R.-J., Ahaus, K., Wortmann, H., & Huitema, G. B. (2019). Investigating the on-demand service characteristics: An empirical study. *Journal of Service Management*, 30(6), 739–765.

Wirtz, J., So, K. K. F., Mody, M. A., Liu, S. Q., & Chun, H. H. (2019). Platforms in the peer-to-peer sharing economy. *Journal of Service Management*, 30(4), 452–483.

References

CAFU. (2022). *Petrol and diesel delivery in the UAE*. Retrieved from https://www.cafu.com

van der Burg, R.-J., Ahaus, K., Wortmann, H., & Huitema, G. B. (2019). Investigating the on-demand service characteristics: An empirical study. *Journal of Service Management*, 30(6), 739–765.

Wirtz, J., So, K. K. F., Mody, M. A., Liu, S. Q., & Chun, H. H. (2019). Platforms in the peer-to-peer sharing economy. *Journal of Service Management*, 30(4), 452–483.

Chapter 4

Understanding service quality

Study objectives

Having completed this chapter, readers should be able to:

- Understand the basic concepts of quality management and service excellence;
- Understand the need for, and challenges of, quality measurement and management; and
- Have a thorough understanding of the various service quality models and their application in both a B2C and B2B context.

The framework of this chapter

This chapter is set out as follows:

- Introduction
- The development of quality management
  o The early days of quality control
  o The emergence of quality management in Asia
  o Quality as a management philosophy
- The TQM movement
- The service quality movement
  o The emergence of service quality
- Service quality theory
  o Defining service quality
    - The confirmation/disconfirmation paradigm
    - Understanding expectations
    - Aim to exceed expectations
- The importance of quality
  o Product differentiation and competitive advantage
  o Customer satisfaction and loyalty

DOI: 10.4324/9781003470373-5

- Linking satisfaction and loyalty
  - Customer delig
- Service quality approaches
  - A variety of approaches
  - The Nordic approach
  - The 'Gaps' principle
    - The Gaps model
  - SERVQUAL
    - Zone of tolerance
  - Service quality in the digital age
- Summary of chapter
- Review questions
- Suggested readings
- References

Introduction

The concept of quality management has become the recognized guiding strategy for almost all firms around the world. Quality ultimately gives firms a competitive advantage and customer acceptance. This emphasis has been felt across all lines of business, whether profit-making or nonprofit-making, including public services.

As we discovered in Chapter 2, service and experiences are often characterized by distinctive challenges not generally found with either buying or selling manufactured products (notwithstanding the delivery aspect of purchasing products). Service (hitherto also referring to experiences) quality can be assessed only by the customer and hence it has little similarity with product quality. This means that quality of service has to be managed differently by managers. For example, the performance of every service provided varies and hence managers have limited opportunity to control the quality of service before it is delivered. Although service quality is difficult to define and difficult to control, scholars have identified some measures to improve the quality of service. Ultimately, it is solely the *expectations and perceptions of customers* that matter, and which are the only valid approach to assessing service quality.

Both service scholars and managers have identified the need to define service quality and to effectively manage it, with the view to gain a sustainable competitive advantage in the market. This chapter begins with a brief outline of the history and evolution of quality management and the contribution of quality 'gurus', to provide us with the foundation of formation and promotion of quality control principles. We then present some of the most significant quality management theories, together with their implications for managers.

The development of quality management
The early days of quality control

Quality control was first introduced in the manufacturing context by engineers and statisticians during the 1920s. The primary focus was on the physical production of goods and the associated internal measurements of the production and assembly line processes. Quality control was originally established to maintain consistency among the parts produced by different sections of a single company so that parts could be interchanged with confidence.

At first this was achieved by having an inspection process for 100% of all outputs. In those days it was relatively common for engineers to design the products, for manufacturing people to build them, and for quality personnel to inspect them as they came off the production line. If a problem existed, manufacturing was expected to correct it.

A breakthrough occurred with the introduction of the concept of *statistical* quality control – the idea that only a random sample of output warranted inspection to ensure an acceptable quality level. Modern quality control began in the 1930s when Walter Shewhart, a physicist employed at Bell Labs, invented *process control*, using control charts and the 'Plan–Do–Check–Act' cycle of continuous improvement.

The emergence of quality management in Asia

In the early decades after World War II, Japan produced goods which had an international reputation for 'shoddy mimicry'. Today, however, goods from Japan have a well-deserved reputation for delighting the customer with excellence. So what has changed? The answer is *quality* – or, more specifically, the elevation of *quality management* to being a matter of the highest priority. Japan faced up to its industrial shortcomings and committed itself to the production of quality goods.

In July 1950, the Union of Japanese Scientists and Engineers (JUSE) invited an American statistician, Dr W. Edwards Deming, to Japan. Deming held a series of lectures during which he taught the basic principles of statistical quality control to Japanese executives, managers, and engineers. His teachings made a deep impression and provided great impetus to the implementation of quality control in Japan. This continued through the 1980s and beyond and led to significant improvements in the quality of Japanese products.

Quality as a management philosophy

A confusing array of terms and acronyms had developed to describe various aspects of the general idea of quality control. The translation of terms from English to Japanese, and back again, produced shades of meaning and variations in usage. But these variations actually reflected a real difference in philosophy and attitude.

In the Japanese language, the word 'control' has a similar connotation to that of the word 'management' in English – that is, a more general concept of 'overseeing', rather than a more narrow idea of 'checking'. Consequently, the Japanese definition of 'quality control' was far removed from the traditional Western interpretation.

The Japanese understanding was more akin to a general management philosophy, whereas the Western idea had a narrower emphasis on 'inspection'. The Japanese idea of 'control' as a management philosophy was markedly pervasive in Japanese culture. Indeed, by 1954, 'quality control' had gone beyond being a major theme in Japanese management thinking, to have become a national preoccupation exalted in the time-honored Japanese fashion with slogans and festivals which celebrated November as 'National Quality Month'.

The TQM movement

Total quality management (TQM) is an overall management philosophy which has been influenced by numerous academics and practitioners since the term 'total quality control' was first introduced by Feigenbaum in 1956. Some of the more influential figures in this 'TQM movement' have been, among others, Deming, Juran, Crosby, Ishikawa, Kano, Imai, and Mizuno.

Because this movement has had input from many people over several decades, and because the idea is difficult to define with any precision, there is little consensus in the literature regarding the core ideas of TQM. Everyone seems to have a different set of essential principles. However, the core belief is that if firms focus on continually improving quality, profitability in the short and long term is a natural outcome.

The following points (based on Marchese (1991)) provide a useful guide to the sorts of 'core ideas' often put forward in an attempt to describe the essence of TQM:

1. *Customer-driven* – excellence is achieved by customer-driven organizations that systematically integrate customer feedback into their strategic planning and into the delivery of products and services;
2. *Focus on quality* – customer-driven organizations have a strong focus on quality, with quality being defined both in terms of the measurable objective qualities of products and services and in terms of the perceptions of customers;
3. *Continuous improvement in systems* – continuous improvement results from such a focus on quality, and continuous improvement requires fundamental changes to manufacturing or service processes;

4. *Collaboration* – TQM requires a change to existing mindsets, involving a paradigm shift in which organizational and individual success is perceived to be a result of collaboration rather than competition;
5. *Objectivity* – decisions should be objective and data-driven; that is, previous experiences need to be systematically documented and analyzed to achieve continuous improvement;
6. *Teamwork* – teamwork is the practical application of collaboration; so to be effective, teams must be trained in creative and analytical problem-solving techniques;
7. *Empowerment* – people should be empowered; that is, they should have real input and decision-making power in job design and organizational policies that affect them;
8. *Education and training* – education and training are essential; indeed, according to another author, Ishikawa, TQM begins and ends with education;
9. *Shared vision* – a shared vision must be known and embraced by all employees and managers; this is the key to any organization's unified direction and avoids wasteful duplication of efforts and infighting; and
10. *Leadership* – organizational change is possible only through effective leadership by example; empty promises and speeches only make existing problems worse.

Other authors prefer to express the core ideas of TQM in different terms, and the above list is certainly not presented as being the 'last word' on the subject. However, the points do give a good guide to the essential elements of TQM.

A perusal of the above ten points reveals certain recurring themes. Whichever words are chosen by different authors, and whichever points are emphasized, there are certain *general recurring themes* of TQM, including:

- TQM is customer-centric and customer-driven;
- TQM has a conscious philosophy of continual systemic improvement;
- TQM requires empowered employees involved in collaborative action; and
- TQM requires committed management showing inspiring leadership.

While TQM is a useful managerial concept, still used by many organizations today, it is fundamentally a product-based concept, designed to reduce errors and seek continuous improvement. Despite efforts to modernize TQM more toward a customer view of quality, a new movement emerged in the 1980s, that of 'service quality', being a new and distinct approach to quality aligned with the growing service sector and the importance of service in delivering value.

The service quality movement

The emergence of service quality

Early definitions of service quality were driven by management and were only incrementally different from existing product quality approaches. That is, initially, there was minimal reference to an overall *philosophy* of quality; little was said about *concepts* of quality or *management models* of quality. Rather, as had occurred in the very early days with manufactured goods – when quality had been traditionally equated with 'quality checking' of completed goods at the end of an assembly line – service quality was more or less treated as another possible variable but with limited importance. Indeed, this is a situation which still unfortunately applies in many areas of service management.

As they attempted to develop an appropriate philosophy of service quality, service researchers and practitioners alike recognized that the characteristics of services were not the same as physical goods (see Chapter 2). Whereas goods quality could be measured objectively by such indicators as durability and the number of defects, there were no objective measures to assess the quality of intangible services. It was clear that many of the 'quality strategies' available to managers were inappropriate for service firms.

Because of these historical and conceptual factors, ideas of service quality had to be developed very much 'from scratch'. Instead of using quality concepts from the manufactured goods industry, service management researchers developed their own concepts of service quality. In drawing up these 'service-specific' models, they turned from an emphasis on manufacturing design to an emphasis on *consumer behavior*. The consumers' ideas of quality became the benchmark.

The consumer became central in these deliberations because, as many authors have noted, people evaluate services in a fundamentally different way from that in which they evaluate goods. Service is a *performance*, usually conducted in the presence of the customer, and service quality is therefore very much a function of subjective perception of an experience rather than objective examination of a physical object.

The service quality literature has thus been firmly based on the notion that service quality is defined by the *customer* – as opposed to the situation in manufactured goods, where quality tends to be defined by designers, inspectors, or operations managers.

Service quality theory

Defining service quality

Quality of service as perceived by customers has become a great differentiator among service providers. As noted above, it is the most powerful competitive weapon that many leading service organizations possess. Business survival and success are dependent on the delivery of superior quality of service. However, even though it is well accepted that service quality is a crucial element in the success of any service organization, there is no single universal definition of service quality.

According to Parasuraman (1985), service quality is an abstract and elusive concept due to the distinctive features of services – intangibility, heterogeneity, inseparability, and perishability (see Chapter 2). Because of these features, definitions of quality can vary from person to person and from situation to situation. Furthermore, experiences are incidents in time, and the critical time to be considered is difficult to define and control – it falls in the variable one-to-one personal interactions that occur between the consumer and the provider.

In developing an understanding of service quality, it is therefore important to understand what *customers* are looking for, and what *they* deem to be quality in services. According to Grönroos (1982b), such an understanding requires two distinct elements:

- how customers *perceive* the quality of a service and
- how service quality can be *managed* (i.e., how such service quality is influenced, and which resources and activities affect service quality*)*.

The confirmation/disconfirmation paradigm

According to theories of consumer behavior, the subjective evaluation of various experiences associated with consumption is based on what is technically called a 'confirmation/disconfirmation paradigm' – that is, consumers compare their *prior expectations* of product performance with the *actual performance* of the product.

Several studies have been conducted in an effort to clarify how customers' expectations and preconceptions of performance affect the subsequent level of customer satisfaction or dissatisfaction with actual performance. In the jargon of the 'confirmation/disconfirmation paradigm', we can say that:

- *confirmation* results when the two performances match but
- *disconfirmation* results when the two performances do not match; this can be of two types:
  o *positive disconfirmation* when the perceived performance exceeds expectations and
  o *negative disconfirmation* when the perceived performance falls below expectations.

Because service experiences are inherently *personal* experiences, this confirmation or disconfirmation leads to an emotional reaction – referred to as 'arousal'. That is, if a product or service appears to be performing above or below expectations, the customer experiences an emotional reaction of significance (a sense of growing pleasure or a sense of growing concern).

Understanding expectations

As we have seen, the *perceived quality* of a given service is the outcome of an evaluation process during which consumers compare their prior expectations of the service with what they have actually received. That is, having received the service, they put the *perceived* service against the *expected* service.

The term 'expectations', as used in the literature on consumer satisfaction, differs from the term as used in the literature on service quality. In the consumer satisfaction literature, expectations are viewed as predictions made by the customer about what is likely to happen during an impending transaction. In contrast, in the service quality literature, expectations are viewed as what the customer desires, or wants, or thinks should happen. The crucial difference is between what consumers expect a service provider *will* offer and what they think the provider *should* offer. This subject will be discussed in more detail below (see 'the gaps principle' below).

This difference (between an expectation of what is *likely* to happen as opposed to what *should* happen) raises the question of what factors influence expectations – that is, the identification of variables that *contribute to* customer expectations. These include previous experiences of the service or a similar service, word-of-mouth advice from other consumers, and conclusions drawn from various cues surrounding the service – including tangible cues such as furniture, fittings, and equipment associated with the service.

Aim to exceed expectations

Organizations can achieve a strong reputation for quality service only when they consistently meet or exceed customer service expectations. As we have seen, service quality is a measure of how well the services (as received) match expectations (as preconceived). And, as outlined above, these expectations might be expressed in terms of what is *likely* to happen or in terms of what *should* happen. Firms that satisfy what is *likely* to happen will do well. Firms that satisfy what *should* happen will do even better. Truly successful firms are those that consistently exceed these customer expectations.

However, it should be noted that the goal of exceeding expectations has been debated in the service literature. For example, exceeding expectations implies that organizations have continued to do more in order to deliver excellent service and delight their customers. Scholars argue that exceeding expectations is not always necessary, can be very costly, and in some cases is unsustainable as it might increase customers' expectations of subsequent service.

The importance of quality

Product differentiation and competitive advantage

Conventional theory recognizes two generic strategic alternatives for developing a sustainable competitive advantage. The first is *product differentiation*, and the second is *overall cost leadership*. Quality control is a crucial element of the first of these. Although product differentiation can take many forms, superior quality is the most common basis of differentiation. If customers see a clear-cut quality advantage, they usually favor that product, without trying to weigh all other factors. Quality rules – but with a caveat! Quality comes with many conditions and variables – what is quality to one person may not be to another. And quality to one market segment may not be to a different segment.

Customer satisfaction and loyalty

In addition to the above economic outcomes of effective service quality management, businesses can also achieve a range of qualitative aspirations by consistently delivering a quality service to their customers, including satisfaction, repeat purchase, loyalty, word-of-mouth behaviors, and so forth. These concepts will be discussed throughout the book; however, we offer an overview here to emphasize the importance of pursuing service quality for business success.

Some confusion often exists between the concepts of satisfaction and quality, yet they are distinct terms and thus it is important for managers to understand the similarities and differences. Satisfaction can be defined as the degree of fulfillment provided by the consumption of a product, service, or experience; while quality, on the other hand, is less about 'consumption' and more about 'observations' or 'attitudes'. Customers generally develop satisfaction with a company as a result of frequent and consistent positive experiences, whereas perceptions of quality are developed on a transactional basis or through the service encounter.

Research has shown that there is not a direct correlation between the two. In other words, a customer may perceive the service to be of high quality but may not necessarily be satisfied with the firm. Service quality is only one driver of overall satisfaction and quality does not always guarantee satisfaction. Nevertheless, there is strong evidence to suggest that the right service provided at the right level of quality for the customer leads to higher levels of satisfaction, which in turn leads to customer loyalty.

Thus, another positive outcome for businesses that deliver service quality is customer loyalty. This term has been defined in various ways, but in general it reflects the degree to which customers repeatedly transact with the firm as well as their level of attachment or affection toward a company. Loyalty is said to be either attitudinal (a person feels or says they are loyal to a firm) or behavioral (when this attitude of loyalty is converted into repeat patronage and even word-of-mouth advertising). Although both are important, managers ultimately aspire for behavioral loyalty – the actions of customers to continue to repurchase and share their positive experiences with others. The business concept of customer lifetime value (CLV) is important here, which describes how a firm seeks to maximize profitability over the lifetime of a customer.

Linking satisfaction and loyalty

It is worth noting here that there is no linear relationship between satisfaction and loyalty. As there are many factors that influence satisfaction (quality being one of them), there are also many factors that influence loyalty. Thus, while satisfaction is a necessary step in the formation of loyalty, it does not guarantee the result. Research shows that loyal customers can still defect to the competition, thus organizations must strive for extremely high levels of satisfaction (rather than merely satisfaction) to achieve customer loyalty. Research shows how the relationship between satisfaction and loyalty can change depending on circumstances (see Figure 4.1). Note that in markets with little competition, customers can be very dissatisfied, but still remain loyal (as they have few choices to switch to the competition). However, in highly competitive markets, even moderate levels of satisfaction do not equate with commensurate levels of loyalty.

Knowing and understanding the drivers of customer satisfaction and loyalty is critical. In other words, managers must realize that achieving

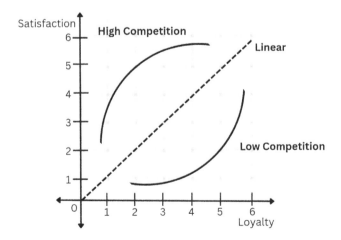

Figure 4.1 The nonlinear relationship between satisfaction and loyalty *(Adapted from Jones and Sasser (1995))*

satisfaction is not a 'one size fits all' situation, therefore customers' specific needs and context of service should be taken into consideration.

Customer delight

Another positive outcome of service quality is customer delight, which has been described as a profoundly positive emotional state generally resulting from having one's expectations exceeded to a surprisingly large degree. However, this is a contentious strategy because at some point it becomes unsustainable to exceed the expectations of a customer who regularly patronizes a business. Studies also suggest that in many service settings, such as phone-based and self-service interactions, loyalty is driven not by how dazzling the service experience might be, but rather by how well the company can deliver on the very basic service promise. Therefore, delighting customers does not by itself build loyalty; rather, reducing the required effort of the customer and solving problems quickly does.

Burner India: Excelling through Service Quality

By Dr. Mayank Bhatia and Dr. Samik Shome,
Institute of Management, Nirma University

Burner India, established in 2001 with manufacturing facilities in Gujarat, India, specializes in industrial oil, gas, and dual fuel burners, along with power packs and blowers. The company caters primarily to business-to-business (B2B) clients in industries such as cement, printing, dairy, food processing, and ceramic. In addition, it also supplies burners for road construction, tea gardens, and powder coating units. Burner India believes in building long-term, trusting relationships with clients by providing customer-centric service, which helps them to build a competitive advantage.

The uniqueness of Burner India is based on the service that they provide; in other words, they compete primarily on service rather than on product. The firm aims to be known as one that delivers high-quality service to its clients by focusing on the following areas:
- Customer-centricity and lifetime value
  - Providing a high-quality service that also includes after-sales service such as installation, technical information, and training to operate the burner, plus guaranteed problem rectification within 48 hours (irrespective of any non-working days or holidays).
- Timeliness and responsiveness
  - Catering to companies that require service on an immediate basis, which the majority of Burner India's competitors cannot

provide. These clients are mostly micro and small enterprises, and any type of disruption to the burners (which are considered the heart of their operations) leads to a break in their production process. Thus, they are never in a position to wait for service to be delivered at a later time.
- Differentiated service culture
  - A dedicated team of 40 service executives (accounting for 37% of the total number of employees), who work all year round to provide service to their clients with a turnaround time of 48 hours for resolving a problem.
- Quality management accreditation
  - Burner India has taken an ISO 9001:2015 certification, with the aim of achieving high-quality standards to ensure that the company meets customer and other stakeholder needs within statutory and regulatory requirements related to a product or service.
- Fulfilling service promises
  - A commitment to fulfilling their service promises and resolving any problems their clients encounter over the operation of burners, whether it is installed in India or abroad. Depending on the urgency of the issue, the service executives are sent to the client's plant location, even via air travel in order to maintain their 48-hour turnaround time. For global locations, Burner India has partnered with various technical service providers to resolve any problems and deliver the after-sales service requirements within the stipulated time.
- Service innovation
  - Adopting state-of-the-art technology so that customers have access to technicians round the clock via video call. Burner India has shown service innovation in their operations throughout the COVID-19 pandemic (while the travel of technical service personnel has been restricted) by employing technology to provide virtual support to their clients. All technical service executives were trained to use online meeting platforms like Zoom, so that whenever clients faced any problem with their installed burner, these executives resolved the problem through video calls by providing instruction to the technical operator of the burner in the client's plant.

The competitors of Burner India who operate with a similar client structure lack this kind of service commitment. Burner India's customers trust in the quality of service provided, which makes them loyal to the organization and provides a competitive advantage.

> It is not the profitability that makes Burner India well-known (the company is enjoying almost 30% business growth year-on-year), but rather the superior service they provide. This has earned them loyalty from customers and to receive their positive word-of-mouth. Because of the excellent quality, fast turnaround times, and fair pricing, the company has made its presence very strong across the industry.

Service quality approaches

A variety of approaches

So, how do customers assess service quality? What parameters matter in their assessment? How can service quality be analyzed in conceptual terms?

There have been various models proposed by researchers in the field, which reflect both similarities and differences in ideas and arrangements of factors. The variety of conceptions in the service literature demonstrates the difficulty in developing a single acceptable model which adequately describes all aspects of service quality. After all, it is not easy to find a single model which takes into account every aspect of something as complex as how human beings make a subjective assessment of a personal experience.

The Nordic approach

The Nordic-based service researchers often took a slightly different approach to service management than their American-based contemporaries. For example, Grönroos (1982a) developed a model of service quality that suggests service quality is a combination of *technical* quality and *functional* quality (see Figure 4.2). In discussing *technical* quality, he suggested that although services are basically intangible, and although production and consumption are virtually simultaneous, the material content in the buyer–seller interaction is still important in the customer's assessment of perceived service quality. Examples of this technical quality include:

- food in a restaurant;
- computerized systems in a bank;
- machines used in a car-repair service center;
- an employee's technical ability in serving a firm's customers (e.g., know-how, technical knowledge, and experience); and so on.

In short, *technical quality* relates to *what* the customer receives (for example, in a dental service, the cleaning of teeth, or in a car repair, and the oil changed).

76 Understanding service quality

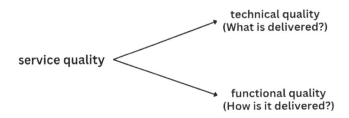

Figure 4.2 Technical quality and functional quality in service quality *(author's presentation)*

Functional quality represents the way in which the technical quality is delivered, based on the fact that services are subjective experiences of the customer, and because these experiences are produced through close interaction with the employees of the service firm, the technical quality dimension alone cannot account for customers' perception of the total quality they have received. Customers will be influenced by *the way in which the technical quality is transferred to them*. Examples of this functional quality include:

- the behavior of a restaurant waiter;
- the friendliness and perceived competence of the dentist;
- the attitude of a car-repair service provider; and so on.

In short, *functional quality* relates to *how* the customer receives a service.

In a competitive market, technical quality is the required essential to survive. However, it is the functional quality that clearly distinguishes one service provider from the other. Similarly, Pine and Gilmore (1998) would also agree, as they see the *how* (i.e., the experience) as being of greater importance than the *what*. Pine and Gilmore argue that the world has entered a fourth economy – the experience economy – where *experiences* have emerged as the key competitive battleground for both B2C and B2B companies.

In addition to the idea that service quality involves both technical quality and functional quality, Grönroos (1982b) incorporated the concept of 'corporate image', since this determines the way in which consumers perceive the firm. The most important part of a firm, as seen and perceived by its customers, is its service. Combining this with his idea of technical and functional quality, Grönroos argued that corporate image is derived mainly from a combination of a firm's technical quality and its functional quality. He went on to suggest that corporate image often influences customer expectations, and helps to reinforce the organization's advertising, marketing, and public relations activities.

An example of the power of corporate image is that of Apple products. Many customers all around the world buy Apple products simply because they have strong brand recognition and are known for reliable, easy-to-use,

Understanding service quality 77

and attractive technology items such as phones, computers, tablets, and smartwatches. In a case of such strong and positive brand recognition, customer perceptions of service quality can often be significantly influenced not by the item or the service itself, but rather, or partly, by the image of the firm. *Service organizations that can create a strong brand image can significantly increase value and quality perceptions.*

The 'Gaps' principle

Predominant in the service quality literature is an approach to measuring quality based on the difference – or 'gap' – between customer *expectations* of a service and their perception of the *actual service* delivered. In other words, customers assess service quality by comparing the service they *receive* (perceptions of 'what I get') with the service they *desire* (expectations of 'what I want'), as illustrated by Figure 4.3. This principle forms the foundation for many service quality models or measures, including SERVQUAL that is further described below.

This gap is actually made up of several other gaps – all of which are potential breaks in the links of the relationship. In developing this idea of four intermediate gaps (and a resulting overall fifth gap, being the total of the other gaps), the researchers looked beyond a single transaction and developed a model of service quality (called 'the Gaps model') representing customer judgments across multiple encounters involving service design, communication, management, and delivery.

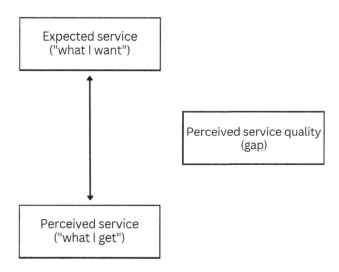

Figure 4.3 Perceived service quality gap *(author's presentation)*

The Gaps model

Research has identified four intermediate gaps which, taken together, lead to the overall gap between expected quality and the perceived quality of service received (Zeithaml 1988).

Gap 1 is the difference between consumer expectations and management perceptions of consumer expectations, also known as a 'listening gap'. According to Parasuraman (1985), management might not always understand what features connote high quality to consumers, what attributes a service must have in order to meet consumer needs, and what levels of performance of these particular features are necessary to deliver high-quality service. Furthermore, the gap between what consumers *expect* and what managers *think* they expect might be considerably larger in service industries than is the case in goods manufacturing.

Gap 2 is the difference between management perceptions of consumer expectations and the means by which these expectations might be met, often referred to as the 'service design and standards gap'. Even if knowledge of customer expectations *does* exist, the means to deliver services that match or exceed customer expectations might not exist. Managers frequently cite various constraints to explain the fact that services have not been designed effectively to meet customer needs, such as difficulties with resources and/or markets. Many managers go further than this and believe that it is actually *impossible* to meet customer needs and thus cannot establish specifications to meet those needs. In these cases, the gap between customer expectations and the means by which these expectations might be met can be attributed to the absence of meaningful management commitment to service quality. Therefore, a variety of factors – resource constraints, market conditions, and/or management indifference – can result in a discrepancy between management's perception of consumer expectations and the actual specifications established for a service.

Gap 3 is the difference between the specifications for the service and the actual delivery of the service. It can be referred to as the 'service-performance gap' – that is, the extent to which service providers do not perform at the level expected by management. The service-performance gap occurs when employees are unable or unwilling to perform the service at the desired level.

Gap 4 is the difference between service delivery and external communications – or the 'communication gap'. Media advertising and other communications by a firm can affect consumer expectations. Such media advertising might contain exaggerated promises or might not contain certain vital information about aspects of the service delivery. This can create discrepancies between external communications and actual service delivery.

Gap 5 is the overall difference between expected service and perceived service. It is made up of the sum total of the preceding four gaps and is thus determined by the nature of the gaps associated with the overall design, marketing, and delivery of services.

In comparing expectations and final perceptions across this overall gap, Berry (1990) suggested that:

- if expectations are met, service quality is perceived to be satisfactory; if expectations are not met, service quality is perceived to be less than satisfactory; and if expectations are exceeded, service quality is perceived to be more than satisfactory;
- quality evaluations derive from both the service process and the service outcome; the manner in which the service is performed (politeness, willingness to help, trustworthiness, and so on) can be a crucial component of the service from the consumer's point of view; and
- service quality is judged against (i) expectations of regular service and (ii) expectations of exceptional services; the first refers to the quality level at which the regular service is delivered (such as a bank teller's typical handling of a transaction), and the second refers to exceptions or problems (such as a monthly credit card statement being incorrect, and how the service provider responds).

SERVQUAL

The most widely researched and adopted measure of service quality was developed by Parasuraman (1988), who developed a tool called 'SERVQUAL' for evaluating a customer assessment of service quality. SERVQUAL consists of survey questions about a number of service quality attributes or dimensions and has been used successfully across many sectors of the service industry.

The authors identified five service dimensions as factors that are considered highly by customers when assessing the quality of service (see Figure 3.4). These dimensions include:

- *reliability* – ability to perform the desired service dependably, accurately, and consistently;
- *tangibles* – physical facilities, equipment, and appearance of personnel;
- *responsiveness* – willingness to provide prompt service and help customers;
- *assurance* – knowledge, competence, ability to convey trust, confidence, and credibility; and
- *empathy* – provision of caring, individualized attention (Figure 4.4).

For each of the above dimensions, SERVQUAL measures the gap between:

- the service *expectations* of the consumer and
- his or her *perceptions* of the service received.

80   Understanding service quality

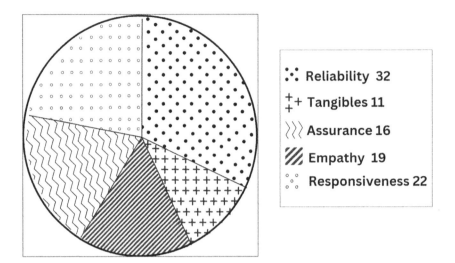

Figure 4.4 Relative importance of service dimensions in meeting expectations *(author's presentation)*

The SERVQUAL questionnaire consists of 22 questions across all five dimensions. These questions are asked twice – before and after the customer had the experience. The difference between these two measurements is then assessed and used as an indication of service quality. In the SERVQUAL model, quality is defined as a weighted average of the quality determinants. The weights used in the model are effectively defined by the consumer, according to the relative importance of each quality attribute.

There are some criticisms of the general applicability of the SERVQUAL model. Some customers have difficulty differentiating among many of the scale items, and it is sometimes impractical to ask customers about their expectations before consumption and then again immediately after consumption. Despite these misgivings, this instrument is a concise multiple-item scale with good reliability, and it has been widely accepted as a valid instrument in the measurement of service quality.

Zone of tolerance

In subsequent work, Parasuraman (1991) further examined variances and nuances of customer expectations and argued that the five dimensions could be further broken down into *process dimensions*, being responsiveness, empathy,

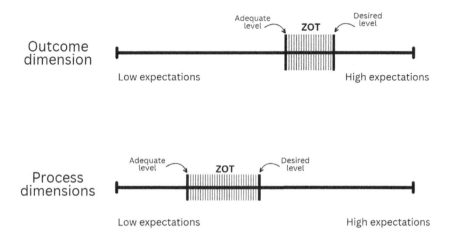

Figure 4.5 ZOT's for outcome and process dimensions (*Adapted from the concept proposed by Parasuraman, Berry, and Zeithaml (1991)*)

assurance, and tangibles, and one *outcome dimension* being reliability. The authors conceptualized a 'zone of tolerance' (ZOT) for customer expectations (see Figure 4.5) for process and outcome dimensions. They concluded that even though reliability is the most important element in meeting expectations, it is also the most difficult service quality dimension in which to *exceed* expectations (because customers expect reliability and have minimal tolerance for this expectation not being met). On the other hand, the process dimensions (especially responsiveness, empathy, and assurances) are the key to *exceeding* expectations. This is because with the process dimensions, the opportunity is present to surprise customers with uncommon swiftness, grace, courtesy, competence, commitment, or understanding, and go beyond what is expected.

Service quality in the digital age

The early conceptualizations of service quality occurred in the 1970s and 1980s – before the advent of the Internet and the explosion of online retailing. Some of the original researchers involved in the development of service quality measures have turned their attention to how customers would evaluate service in an online platform. 'E' service quality was therefore broadly defined to encompass all phases of a customer's interactions with a website – including the extent to which website facilities create efficient and effective shopping, purchasing, and delivery. Through another complex research process a measure of 'E' service quality was developed by Parasuraman and his colleagues (2005), called 'E-S-QUAL' (for electronic service quality). The items proposed to measure online service quality are composed of two parts: 'Core' and 'Recovery'.

The 'Core' elements include:

1. *efficiency* – refers to the ability of the customers to get to the website, find their desired product and information associated with it, and check out with minimal effort;
2. *fulfillment* – incorporates accuracy of service promises, having products in stock, and delivering the products in the promised time;
3. *reliability* – associated with the technical functioning of the site, particularly the extent to which it is available and functioning properly; and
4. *privacy* – includes assurance that shopping behavior data is not shared and that the website is safe.

These researchers found that three additional dimensions are important when online customers run into problems. These were conceptualized as 'recovery' and include:

1. *information* – once customers have a problem, having mechanisms for handling returns and providing online guarantees;
2. *compensation* – the dimension that involves receiving money back, and return shipping and handling; and
3. *contact points* – the need for customers to be able to speak to a live customer service agent online or through the phone, requiring seamless multiple-channel capabilities on the part of online retailers.

There have been many other developments in the sphere of measuring service and now experiential quality. We are in a period of very dramatic and rapid rates of change linked to technology and globalization. Moving from quality, to service quality, to online service, and now to experience quality, has meant endless research studies, books, and ideas about how to capture the many nuances of these subjective ideals. Rather than overviewing these in detail, instead, we offer a number of references for your further reading; however, we emphasize that the principles above provide a grounded and timeless foundation for understanding managing and marketing in the service and experience economy.

Summary of chapter

To remain competitive, businesses must be able to offer quality service to increasingly demanding customers. Failure to maintain consistent quality standards jeopardizes a firm's reputation and its ultimate profitability. Quality has thus become an essential yardstick to predict business performance.

Although the importance of product quality has long been recognized in the manufacturing industry – in which various quality management concepts and strategies have been developed and implemented over the years – the service sector has historically been less aware of the importance of these matters. However, the current economic importance of the service sector highlights the need for management to gain an understanding of quality strategies that are specifically appropriate for service firms.

In today's economy, service is crucial to customer satisfaction and business success in every industry. For a service firm, the ability to provide quality service is, in fact, the most effective means of differentiating itself from competitors. But the distinctive nature of service (IHIP) means that the quality of service is different from that of manufactured goods. Service quality is also more difficult to define, measure, and control since a firm's service quality is significantly affected by the subjective judgment of its customers.

Indeed, service quality is the most important determinant of customer satisfaction. It is therefore imperative that managers in both a B2C and B2B context understand the factors that influence a customer's perceptions, expectations, and satisfaction with services – and design their strategies accordingly.

This chapter has offered an overall understanding of quality concepts in general, as well as specific information pertaining to quality management and measurement in a service context. It should thus provide assistance to managers, as service providers, to focus their efforts and resources effectively on improving their firms' market position through quality services and customer satisfaction.

Review questions

1. Analyze the importance of quality in terms of costs and benefits.
2. Briefly describe the concept of 'total quality management' (TQM) and its core principles.
3. What is your understanding of service quality? How is service quality different from product quality?
4. Briefly describe the service quality concepts and theories presented in this chapter.
5. Choose any service quality model as described in this chapter and analyze and apply the model in the context of a hospitality operation.
6. Briefly describe the techniques for measuring service quality as presented in this chapter and describe some of the changes needed due to technology and the rise of the experience economy.

Suggested readings

Bank, J. (2001). *The essence of total quality management*. New York, NY: Prentice Hall.

Berry, L. L., Zeithaml, V. A., & Parasuraman, A. (1990). Five imperatives for improving service quality. *Sloan Management Review*, Summer, 31(4), 29–38.

Brown, W. S., Gummesson, E., Edvardson, B., & Gustavson, B. (1991). *Service quality: Multidisciplinary and multinational perspectives*. New York, NY: Lexington Books.

Bustamante, J. C., & Rubio, N. (2017). Measuring customer experience in physical retail environments. *Journal of Service Management*, 28(5), 884–913.

Crosby, L. A. (1991). Expanding the role of CSM in total quality. *International Journal of Service Industry Management*, 2(2), 5–19.

Grönroos, C. (1991). The marketing strategy continuum: Towards a marketing concept for the 1990s. *Management Decision*, 29(1), 7–13.

Kandampully, J., Mok, C., & Sparks, B. (2001). *Service quality management in hospitality, tourism and leisure*. New York, NY: Haworth Hospitality Press.

Kimes, S. E. (2001). How product quality drives profitability: The experience at Holiday Inn. *Cornell Hotel and Restaurant Administration Quarterly*, June, 42(3), 25–28.

Klaus, P., & Maklan, S. (2012). EXQ: A multiple-item scale for assessing service experience. *Journal of Service Management*, 23(1), 5–33.

Kuppelwieser, V. G., & Klaus, P. (2021). Measuring customer experience quality: The EXQ scale revisited. *Journal of Business Research*, 126, 624–633.

Lewis, B. R., & Mitchell, V. W. (1990). Defining and measuring the quality of customer service. *Marketing Intelligence and Planning*, 8(6), 11–17.

McColl-Kennedy, J. R., Zaki, M., Lemon, K. N., Urmetzer, F., & Neely, A. (2019). Gaining customer experience insights that matter. *Journal of Service Research*, 22(1), 8–26.

Parasuraman, A., Berry, L. L., & Zeithaml, V. A. (1991). Understanding customer expectations of service. *Sloan Management Review*, Spring, 32(3), 39–48.

References

Berry, L. L., Zeithaml, V. A., & Parasuraman, A. (1990). Five imperatives for improving service quality. *Sloan Management Review*, Summer, 29–38.

Grönroos, C. (1982a). A service quality model and its managerial implications. Working paper presented at the Workshop of Research into the Management of Service Business, January.

Grönroos, C. (1982b). Seven key areas of research: According to the Nordic school of service marketing, emerging perspectives on services marketing. In L. L. Berry, G. L. Shostack, & G. D. Upah (Eds.), *Emerging perspectives on services marketing* (pp. 108–110). Chicago: American Marketing Association.

Jones, T. O., & Sasser, Jr., W. E. (1995). Why satisfied customers defect. *Harvard Business Review*, November–December, 88–99.

Marchese, T. (1991). TQM reaches the academy. *American Association for Higher Education*, 44, 3–9.

Parasuraman, A., Berry, L. L., & Zeithaml, V. A. (1991). Understanding customer expectations of service. *Sloan Management Review*, 32(3), 39–48.

Parasuraman, A., Zeithaml, V. A., & Berry, L. L. (1985). A conceptual model of service quality and its implications for future research. *Journal of Marketing*, *49*(4), 41–50.

Parasuraman, A., Zeithaml, V. A., & Berry, L. L. (1988). SERVQUAL: A multi-item scale for measuring consumer perception of service quality. *Journal of Retailing*, *64*(1), 12–40.

Parasuraman, A., Zeithaml, V. A., & Malhotra, A. (2005). E-S-QUAL: A multiple-item scale for assessing electronic service quality. *Journal of Service Research*, *7*(3), 213–233.

Pine, J., & Gilmore, J. (1998). Welcome to the experience economy. *Harvard Business Review*, July–August, 97–106.

Chapter 5

Customer centricity in practice

Study objectives

Having completed this chapter, readers should be able to:

- Understand the categories of customers from a managerial perspective;
- Define the concept of 'customer centricity' and understand how organizations (whether B2C or B2B) can become customer centered;
- Appreciate the importance of listening to customers to identify their needs and expectations, and be familiar with the major techniques of gathering such information; and
- Understand the cross-functional relationships among service employees and the importance of internal marketing for successful external marketing.

The framework of this chapter

This chapter is set out as follows:

- Introduction
- Customers of a service organization
  o Categories of customers
- Customer centricity
  o Defining the concept
  o From product centricity to customer centricity
- The path to customer centricity
  o Characteristics of customer-centric organizations
- Engaging external customers
  o The importance of listening to external customers
  o Methods for listening to external customers
    - In-depth interviews with individual customers
    - Focus-group interviews
    - Market surveys
    - In-house customer satisfaction surveys

DOI: 10.4324/9781003470373-6

- Net promoter score
- Critical-incident technique
- Complaint analysis
- Mystery shoppers
- Customer-to-customer communication
  o Responding to customer feedback
- Engaging internal customers
  o The importance of listening to internal customers
    - Employees as 'listening posts'
    - Inseparability makes employees important
    - Interdependency makes employees important
  o Encouraging employee feedback
  o Employees as customer 'advocates'
  o Creating brand communities
- Summary of chapter
- Review questions
- Suggested readings
- References

Introduction

To remain competitive in the twenty-first century, businesses must be customer centered. In other words, they must view the customer as the starting point and continually strive to understand and satisfy their customers' needs and expectations. Meeting or exceeding these needs and expectations of customers is the essence of service quality. Having explored the concepts of quality, satisfaction, and loyalty in Chapter 4, we now move on to the present chapter to explore the concepts of *customers* and *customer centricity* in greater detail.

From a managerial perspective, the term 'customers' encompasses more than those from whom an organization earns revenue. This chapter explores the idea that a service firm really has *multiple* groups of customers in two broad categories – 'external customers' and 'internal customers'.

The very nature of service emphasizes the role of human beings in producing service products and delivering service experiences to other human beings. To offer quality service to *external* customers (those who ultimately pay for the final service offering), service firms must first realize the importance of the *internal* customers (the staff who render the various services that make up the final service offering to the external customer). It might seem strange to describe employees as 'internal customers', but these people actually give and receive services from one another as part of an internal chain of collaborative co-creation of products and services preceding the final delivery of promised service to the external customer. This concept is explored in greater detail later in this chapter and further elaborated on in Chapters 7 and 8.

To fulfill customers' expectations and enhance their perceptions of *service quality*, service firms must continuously collect customer information and measure customer satisfaction as a basis on which to assess performance. This chapter presents various methods of acquiring and using customer information, and explores the role of service employees in gathering and providing management with customer feedback.

This chapter therefore examines two very important themes – internal and external customers, and the importance of customer feedback and continual communication. In so doing, this chapter focuses on the ultimate measures of service quality – customer satisfaction, loyalty, and referrals – and outlines how firms can become more customer-oriented.

Customers of a service organization

Categories of customers

Firstly, it is important to understand the term 'customer' and which stakeholders are encompassed by the various definitions. It is useful to consider that customers can be categorized into five broad groups:

- *internal customers* – employees and leaders of a firm, as well as suppliers and intermediaries who assist the firm in servicing its external customers;
- *current external customers* – a firm's current end-users or consumers;
- *competitor's customers* – those whom the firm would like to attract and make its own;
- *ex-customers* – those who have chosen to no longer engage with a firm and now use a competing firm's products and services; and
- *potential future customers* – consumers who are likely to engage with the firm in the future.

While each of the above categories is vital for a full understanding of customers, this chapter focuses predominantly on *external customers*. It should be noted too that the concepts covered here can be applied by managers operating in both B2C (business-to-customer) and B2B (business-to-business) contexts. Firms that excel in customer experience adopt the position that everyone has a customer. Take Disney for instance – widely accepted as a world leader in delivering exceptional experiences. Within the ecosystem of their organization, there are 'frontline' employees who directly engage with *external customers*, as well as 'backstage' employees who serve *internal customers* by playing vital roles in the costuming, maintenance, and marketing departments, to name a few. Thus, everyone who works at Disney *has* a customer and is simultaneously viewed *as* a customer. This holistic perspective of an organization's network is a critical component of customer centricity.

Customer centricity

Defining the concept

Customer centricity, or customer orientation, is defined as a total organizational approach that focuses on the needs, wants, and resources of customers as the starting point of all organizational activities. This is not a new idea! As early as 1954, Peter Drucker emphasized the importance of customers when he said that it is a customer who ultimately defines what a business is, what it produces, and whether it will prosper, and to satisfy a customer is the mission and purpose of every business.

Drucker accurately foreshadowed a radical shift in gravity, highlighting that the increasing speed and availability of information meant that for all organizations the center of power would be the customer. This represented a fundamental shift in power away from suppliers and manufacturers. Levitt (1981) also mirrored these predictions when he proposed that firms should not focus on making and selling products, but rather on fulfilling customer needs.

As we have learned in Chapter 1, a firm's competitive advantage is primarily achieved by focusing on the service components of its offerings, rather than the product components. In other words, it is service excellence that often determines customer satisfaction and loyalty, and that provides a point of differentiation. Competing firms may provide a similar type of service; however, customers will be compelled to return to those that offer a customized experience and demonstrate a commitment to their customers. Indeed, customer perceptions of a firm's service quality, and its perceived value, offer firms the most sustainable basis of differentiation and their most powerful competitive weapon.

Managers therefore need to focus on meeting customers' expectations and enhancing their perceptions of service quality. Research studies have repeatedly confirmed the strategic advantage of adopting a customer orientation if firms wish to improve market share and profits. As firms have shifted their focus from production to service, managers have realized that their primary responsibility is to satisfy the customer. Accordingly, this customer-centric focus has emerged as a prerequisite for gaining market dominance.

From product centricity to customer centricity

Placing the customer at the center of a firm's focus may sound simple; however, shifting away from the traditional firm focus and product focus requires a reappraisal of every element of a firm's operations and a reorientation of its culture. In most cases, a product focus tends to have originated from the firm and transactions-centric focus. On the other hand, a customer-centric

Table 5.1 Product-centric versus customer-centric approaches

	Product-centric Approach	Customer-centric Approach
Core business philosophy	Focus on selling products	Focus on fulfilling customer needs and value co-creation
Business orientation	Managing transactions	Developing relationships
Organizational structure	Product departments and sales teams focused on increasing market share	Customer relationship managers focused on increasing the value of each customer ('share of wallet')
Organizational focus	Internal orientation toward products and efficiency	External focus toward customer relationships and loyalty
Performance metrics	Profit by product and department	Customer loyalty, customer satisfaction, and social media advocacy
Selling approach	'How many customers will buy our product?'	'How many products will each of our customers buy?'

focus will guide the firm to the concepts of superior service and customer experience. This then allows the firm to focus primarily on service to provide higher value for the customer, which will ultimately bring benefit to the firm. Table 5.1 outlines the key differences between a product-centric approach in comparison to a customer-centric approach.

While these approaches represent two ends of a spectrum, the reality is that most firms will adopt elements of both depending on their competition and customers. Despite the concept of customer centricity being a feature of management discourse for decades, firms still struggle to fully align with a customer-centric approach (the common challenges firms experience will be discussed later in this chapter). However, research evidence continually shows that most managers believe their firm *should* be more customer centered, and that there is likely a correlation between a firm's success and its degree of customer centricity. One firm that has achieved such a transformation in approaches is PayTm Gold, as outlined in the example below.

PayTm Gold: Transforming Product to Service

By Dr. Mithilesh Pandey, Department of Marketing & Strategy, ICFAI Business School (IBS), Hyderabad

Globally, India is the second largest consumer of gold after China. In Indian culture, both women and men wear gold jewelry as a symbol of prosperity and social status. Gold is also an attractive investment option, due to its high liquidity. However, possessing gold in its physical form carries certain disadvantages, such as risk of theft, damage, and cheating by manufacturers. Hence, PayTm identified an opportunity to address consumers' aspirations of investing in gold and reducing the risks associated with purchasing physical gold.

The company designed a technological solution called 'PayTm Gold', which allows customers to buy, store, and sell 24k gold (999.9 purity) without any physical transaction. In other words, it is a form of 'virtual gold' or 'digital gold'. This scheme eliminates the risk associated with purchasing physical gold, while giving customers a convenient way to invest via a mobile app.

The service process is simple; customers register for a PayTm account and can then purchase or sell gold at the prevailing market rate in either rupees or grams. The gold price given on the PayTm Gold platform is in alignment with the London Bullion Market Association (LBMA), and customers are able to invest in as little as Rs 1 or 0.001 grams. PayTm Gold also offers the option of converting digital gold into physical gold in the form of coins that can be delivered to a customer's address of choice. If a customer opts for digital gold, the company will store it for free for a period of 5 years from the date of purchase, after which time certain charges will be applicable. This flexible approach makes investing in gold easy and accessible for a large consumer market.

As the most widely used mobile wallet in India, PayTm was a recognized name prior to launching PayTm Gold. Hence, the brand already carried a level of consumer trust and market value. The company enhanced trust in PayTm Gold by adding certain safety and support features, including:

- offering 24k gold with 999.9 purity from MMTC-PAMP (India's most trusted and advanced precious metal refining and minting company);
- insuring and keeping gold in the vaults of MMTC-PAMP;
- setting transparent gold prices by linking with the London Bullion market; and
- providing 24x7 customer support.

Furthermore, PayTm Gold is highly valued by consumers due to the following service features:

- convenience of buying, selling, and storing gold through a mobile app;
- flexibility in buying options (starting from as low as Rs 1 or 0.001grams);

- delivery of the physical gold to the customer's doorstep if desired;
- the option of a systematic plan to invest in gold at regular intervals; and
- provision of gifting the gold through the PayTm Gold platform.

Overall, PayTm Gold has improved consumers' investment experience with gold and transformed what was traditionally a physical product transaction into a seamless service process. The company has successfully used service to clearly differentiate itself from other gold 'products' in the market. PayTm Gold offers superior value and has built a high level of trust and loyalty among its customers by seamlessly delivering on the basic service promise, addressing inherent risks, and catering to its customers' desires.

The path to customer centricity

If customer centricity is so important, then why don't all organizations adopt this approach?

Despite the growing understanding that such a strategy can help to establish a competitive advantage, firms typically struggle to fully align themselves to the customer-centric paradigm. The following table outlines the fundamental issues and challenges that firms typically face, along with proposed changes and strategies that managers can implement to steer them on the path to customer centricity.

Perhaps the most important ingredient for achieving customer centricity that underpins all of the following strategies is unwavering leadership commitment. To become a 'gold star' customer-centered organization requires strength from all leaders at all levels – from the CEO to the frontline supervisors. A strategy needs to be in place that makes it abundantly clear that customers are core to all functions of the organization, and this needs to be reflected through all leadership messages. The company's vision, mission, values, policies, procedures – EVERYTHING – must be aligned and signal a customer-centered focus. Table 5.2

It is important to note that not every organization will require each of these strategies in the same amounts. In other words, the specific path taken to achieve customer centricity will depend on each firm's unique circumstances. Making the change will require time, patience, commitment, and strong leadership – but it will be worth it!

Table 5.2 Potential challenges and proposed strategies for customer centricity

Potential challenges	Proposed solutions
Organizational culture	Culture change
<ul><li>The organization's values, norms, symbols, and beliefs can often be deeply embedded</li><li>Many firms have been operating as product-centered for a long time</li><li>Culture is a barrier because of how difficult it is to change!</li></ul>	<ul><li>Leaders can create a customer-centric culture through their actions and discussions, which employees take as cues to what's important</li><li>For example, managers can ensure all team discussions regarding costs and revenues have a parallel discussion about customer outcomes</li></ul>
Organizational structure	Systems realignment
<ul><li>Product-centric companies are typically organized around functional silos and defined by product categories</li><li>Yet in customer-centric organizations all functional activities must be integrated and aligned to deliver customer value</li><li>It is often difficult to change the deeply rooted incentives, motivations, and priorities distinct to each organizational function</li></ul>	<ul><li>Instead of structuring organizations by function or product category, managers can adopt a more integrated or 'horizontal' organizational structure that ensures all departments are interacting harmoniously</li><li>For example, managers should ensure that information is readily shared across the organization and that KPIs are aligned with customer measures</li></ul>
Organizational processes	Integrated HRM functions
<ul><li>Typically, the collection of tasks and activities within a business are not customer centered</li><li>It can be difficult to change these habits to place the customer at the heart of the exchange process</li><li>Organizations can also struggle with breaking down their customers into distinctive groups with different needs and expectations, which is important for value co-creation</li></ul>	<ul><li>Customer-centered organizations integrate all HRM functions across the organization</li><li>For example, HRM managers need to recruit, select, and retain the right people who have customer centricity under their skin, which can be achieved by aligning job ads, interview questions, and performance reviews around the customer</li></ul>
Use of metrics	Revised metrics
<ul><li>It is very common for organizations to get stuck on 'cost cutting' and focusing on short-term profits</li><li>Creating a system of metrics to measure customer centricity is hard work and requires transforming years of accounting terminologies</li></ul>	<ul><li>Managers must ensure that the way they measure performance aligns with customer-related metrics such as customer satisfaction, customer loyalty, and customer advocacy on social media</li><li>Remember, what gets measured gets done!</li></ul>

Characteristics of customer-centric organizations

To illustrate the power of customer centricity, the authors of this book have examined the practices of some of the world's most beloved service organizations – those which have become part of 'Service Excellence Folklore'. A common feature of these companies is their *obsession* with the customer experience across *every* level of the firm – both internally and externally. To demonstrate, we include a case study about Nordstrom in the box below. Stories of how the company had exceeded customers' needs and expectations would circulate, becoming part of their organizational folklore and fuelling their customer obsession.

- Research has identified a number of other common characteristics of highly customer-centered organizations. Specifically, a customer-centric firm:
- collects important and detailed information from customers;
- uses that information to build trust and deeper relationships with customers;
- actively engages customers in developing new ideas;
- emphasizes *value for customers* rather than focusing on the product or service itself; and
- ensures that everyone in the organization is aware of the critical importance of customers.

Nordstrom's Customer Obsession

Adopted from Solnet and Kandampully (2008)

Terms such as 'Nordy Stories' and 'Nordstronmisms' emanate from this customer-oriented company. Examples of Nordstrom's practices include the presence of 'personal shoppers' in their stores, for those customers who prefer to take a guided personal shopping experience. Customer comfort is ensured by the strategic placement of chairs and couches throughout the store. The aisles are wide enough to accommodate parents and children walking side-by-side (passing other shoppers). There are signs in meeting rooms, espousing sayings such as, 'we built our business one customer at a time' and 'is the customer having an exceptional experience?' Stories about employees' extraordinary efforts to assist customers pervade not only the employee orientation programs at Nordstrom, but also the press. However, Nordstrom often prefers to downplay its legendary customer stories, preferring rather to let the stories be told by the recipients of the experience.

Nordstrom is renowned (through storytelling and word-of-mouth) for its exceptionally liberal returns policy – offering an unconditional

> guarantee and a no-questions-asked policy on returns. There are numerous stories circulating in the press about this policy. One often cited example is a story about a disoriented customer who tried to return a set of tire chains to Nordstrom, even though Nordstrom does not sell tire chains (some stories suggest it was tires – it depends on which myth you hear!). The employee, following the company's focus on customer satisfaction, accepted the chains and gave the customer the refund! Nordstrom's philosophy is that its policy is aimed at the 98 percent of customers who are honest. Nordstrom not only 'accepts' returns, they actually encourage them. For example, all mail orders through Nordstrom contain a filled-in exchange/return packing slip just in case! Nordstrom employees are consistently reminded about the company's commitment to customers by the note on the bottom of their paychecks (or stubs) which reads, 'from Bruce Nordstrom, on behalf of the customer'.

To put the first of these points into practice, the next section looks at how organizations can collect important customer information through a variety of customer-perception research methods. Indeed, a feature of great service organizations is the way they have created a genuine 'customer listening' organizational culture (see Chapter 8 for further discussion on culture).

Engaging external customers

The importance of listening to external customers

The most important component of any business endeavor is the customer. Organizations conduct various forms of research to obtain information about the needs, expectations, and perceptions of their present and prospective customers. These expectations and perceptions are constantly changing, as is the nature of the service offered by competing organizations. It is therefore important that research into these matters is administered on a continuous basis – so that any changes can be picked up quickly and acted upon as appropriate.

Research might establish answers to the following sorts of questions:

- Why did a customer buy (or not buy) a particular product or service?
- What were the customer's expectations about the product or service before purchase and consumption?
- Is the customer satisfied or not with the product or service?
- How do customers experience the different components of a given service?
- Will the customer return?
- What are the trends in customer preferences over time?

- What are the current trends among particular customer segments?
- Would the customer recommend the product or service to someone else?

Although some researchers have offered a spirited critique of this approach, Reichheld (2003) argues that this final question in the list above, regarding a customer's willingness to recommend the firm to someone else, is the most accurate gauge of customer loyalty. The act of recommending a product or service demonstrates that a customer is so faithful that they're willing to place their own reputation on the line in support of the firm, which makes them the most effective firm marketers!

The way in which the information is utilized is of the utmost importance. It is the responsibility of management to collect, analyze, and interpret information accurately, and to communicate the findings to employees. Such information – gathered from the customers and fed back to the employees – is a powerful tool in effecting changes in both the 'controllable' aspects of services (service systems, methods, and processes) and the 'uncontrollable' aspects of services (the quality of the service encounter as perceived by the customer).

It is also important to select carefully the people from whom the information is to be collected. They should constitute a reasonably representative sample of the customer population being studied. Ideally, the sample should include people who have never bought the service, as well as those who have. It is also helpful to collect information from people who prefer the services of a competitor – because disgruntled customers can provide information that is as valuable as that from happy customers.

Methods for listening to external customers

Customer-perception research usually employs a combination of qualitative and quantitative methods, to enable managers to gain a better understanding of the organization from the perspective of their customers. *Quantitative research* involves the collection of statistical data on various *measurable aspects* of customer behavior, whereas *qualitative research* involves identifying the *attitudes* of current (and potential) customers, as well as those of the wider community. This might involve eliciting information from journalists, intermediaries, and even competitors.

The objective of customer-perception research is the identification of the characteristics of the service product that are most critical and valuable to the customer, and thus to isolate characteristics that can form the basis for successful differentiation of the organization's service product from others in a competitive market.

In the past, the most commonly used methods for learning about customers' perceptions were:

- in-depth interviews with individual customers;
- focus-group interviews with selected groups of customers;
- in-house customer satisfaction surveys;
- statistical market surveys of representative customer populations;
- critical-incident technique (complaint analysis); and
- employee opinion/attitude surveys.

Today, there is a number of commonly used methods that enable companies to get a more regular 'pulse' on customers' moods, trends, and interests, including:

- Net Promoter Score (NPS);
- mystery shoppers (customer experience survey); and
- customer-to-customer communication/social media.

However, it should be noted that online community-based feedback presents many challenges in terms of accuracy of information.

Each of these techniques for assessing customers' perceptions will be discussed in more detail below; but first, some general observations.

Managers should also strive to select the most appropriate methods depending on their circumstances, rather than attempting to employ all the methods listed above. Ultimately, the purpose of utilizing a combination of qualitative and quantitative research techniques is to learn more about the firm's customers.

In-depth interviews with individual customers

In an in-depth interview, the interviewer asks numerous questions about all aspects of the service product. This might involve half-an-hour or more (perhaps extending to several hours) with a single customer. Because of the time and expense involved, this type of interview is the least frequently used particularly for those firms that have many customers. However, in some contexts it proves to be effective because it provides the most pertinent and current information. The aim of the interviewer is to uncover the key attributes of the service that customers deem to be important and desirable, and the attitudes of customers toward these attributes.

In-depth interviewers 'actively listen' – to detect 'cues' that reveal aspects of the experience about which customers seem to feel strongly. The effectiveness of the interview lies in discovering more about customers' feelings, needs, and expectations regarding particular aspects of the service, and knowing which aspects to explore in greater detail. The interviewer needs skill in knowing which 'cues' to follow.

Following a series of interviews, the interviewer will frequently detect that a certain pattern of response is developing. At this point, nothing new seems to be forthcoming, and the interviewer can assume that it is reasonably safe to stop interviewing and compile the results. An analysis usually identifies recurring themes in the customers' statements regarding aspects of the service and its delivery. From this, the researcher might be able to draw up a list of attributes that defines the total service experience, as perceived by this customer.

Focus-group interviews

Customer focus groups can provide a continuous source of information on customer expectations. The purpose of focus-group interviews is similar to that of individual interviews, but the discussion techniques are somewhat different.

Groups of customers, usually frequent users, are regularly brought together to allow a study of their opinions about the present quality of service or to gain their views on some of the changes the firm is planning to undertake. The interviewer (or a facilitator) tries to involve everyone in the group and attempts to draw out as many various opinions as possible. If one person states a strong opinion and there appears to be a general consensus, the interviewer probes to ascertain whether there are opposing views that are not being stated.

These groups can be usefully employed to monitor the introduction of a new or revised service. While for established and ongoing services, the use of continuous groups can be a means of anticipating problems. Discussion in the group might reveal emerging issues of importance that can be addressed before they become real problems.

The validity of this research is dependent on how accurately the views of the group represent those of consumers as a whole. Careful selection should therefore be undertaken to ensure that the group possesses the same characteristics as the population of customers being analyzed – in terms of social, economic, and demographic factors, and in terms of frequency of use of the service. Having chosen such a group, the accuracy of focus-group information is then dependent on the skill of the researcher in ensuring that all views are heard, and in ensuring that an apparent consensus is a true consensus – representative of the group as a whole, and therefore likely to be representative of consumers as a whole.

Market surveys

Statistical questionnaire surveys are often used if customer-perception information is required from a relatively large number of people. Individual interviews and focus-group interviews (as described above) might not involve a large enough sample to make statistically valid judgments about the customer base. However, in-depth interviews and focus-group interviews can be useful prior to developing market surveys, since such interviews can serve a crucial role in determining the questions to be asked. In other words, the interview process involving a small number of people provides the basis of a research model for questionnaires aimed at a bigger population.

A research model involves the selection of desired demographic groups to be surveyed, and a list of key topics about which information is desired – opinions or preferences about the key attributes of the service being offered. This information can be processed statistically to develop a profile of the service preferences of the customers and their attitudes toward the organization and competing organizations. All of this information can be expressed as a demographic breakdown of preferences in terms of age, gender, educational level, and income level.

Today, market surveys are typically conducted electronically using online platforms such as SurveyMonkey, Survey Gizmo, and Qualtrics, to name a few. These tools offer a simple and easily accessible way to disseminate questionnaires for little effort and investment. However, despite the user-friendly format of these online tools, managers need to tailor their approach and not rely on 'off-the-shelf' templates. Careful consideration should be given to the way to ask questions, how to measure certain variables of interest, and the types of analysis which will provide the most relevant, accurate, and insightful information.

In-house customer satisfaction surveys

The use of customer satisfaction surveys has become increasingly common in service industries, with many organizations now realizing the importance of accessing direct feedback from their guests or consumers. Such surveys usually ask customers to relate positive and negative features of the service experience, as well as suggestions for improving the service.

The surveys are usually distributed via hard-copy cards, or electronically via text message or email. Some companies also use their point-of-sale system to include a link or QR code on a customer's bill, directing them to an online survey about their experience. In some cases, firms may even choose to offer a small gift to encourage customers to participate in the survey. While these techniques are currently the most common, mechanisms and channels for deploying such surveys are constantly changing; thus, readers are encouraged to conduct their own research into the latest online customer feedback options.

Net promoter score

With the ever-increasing demands on customers to give feedback, it is becoming increasingly difficult to ask customers to fill in satisfaction surveys. There is growing evidence of customer feedback 'fatigue' where customers become impatient when asked to complete even a short questionnaire. This fatigue has led researchers to develop more concise measures of satisfaction and loyalty. One such measure, also widely adopted by practitioners, the Net Promoter Score (NPS), asks only a single question about how likely the person would be to recommend the product or service using a 10-point scale.

Fred Reichheld (2003) developed this idea and labeled it the 'ultimate question'. It allows a firm to identify the percentage of 'Detractors' (0–6 – unhappy customers who can potentially damage the brand and business), 'Passives' (7–8 – unenthusiastic customers who are vulnerable to competitive offerings and not fully committed to the business), and 'Promoters' (9–10 – enthusiastic customers who become ambassadors for the brand, keep coming back, and fuelling the growth of the business). NPS is calculated as the difference between promoters and detractors – the higher the number the better! In use, the NPS can range from a low of -100 (if every customer is a Detractor) to a high of 100 (if every customer is a Promoter). This metric is suggested to be a powerful and accurate way to measure customer satisfaction and predict business growth.

While easy to implement, NPS has its shortcomings. The metric itself does not offer much insight into potential areas of improvement. To overcome this limitation, many companies ask a follow-up open-ended question that is designed to elicit qualitative comments from those who haven't chosen a '9' or a '10'. There is growing consensus that the most effective approach to adopting the NPS is to capture both the numerical rating in addition to written comments that customers are asked to explain their response. Recent studies (McColl-Kennedy et al., 2019) have shown that the most important insights firms can gather exist in the written comments, *even from those who score 9 or 10*. If NPS is used, managers should be aware of its limitations and the simple fact that the original claims of NPS – its links to loyalty – have been disproved over time in many academic studies. Nonetheless, it is a very common measure and can be used to identify opportunities to improve customer experience.

Critical-incident technique

Incident-based measurement, or critical-incident technique (CIT), is based on the principle that long-term total customer satisfaction can be achieved only by identifying a list of all the problems that customers experience when using a service. Management needs to know what worries customers. A related phenomenon is observed in many surveys – when it is often the case that the 'additional comments' made by customers at the end of the survey prove to be the most valuable of all the information elicited from surveys.

The fundamental idea of all incident-oriented measurement thus hinges on efforts to express the quality experiences of customers as precisely as possible through evaluation of *their own accounts* of these experiences. CIT focuses on the active and systematic investigation of customer experiences of critical incidents. In general terms, for an incident to be defined as 'critical', it must deviate significantly from what is expected – either positively or negatively – and it must be possible to describe it in detail.

The aim of this method is therefore to compile and evaluate 'critical incidents' in a systematic and planned manner. CIT can assist management to identify problems in service delivery, and can also help management to redesign the service delivery system. The important point is that any such redesigned system is firmly based on the most important quality attributes *as perceived in practice by the customers* – not as perceived in theory by the management.

Complaint analysis

Research has provided convincing evidence that significant rewards are available to organizations that handle complaints creatively and appropriately. Appropriate management of complaints goes beyond merely 'handling' dissatisfied customers. Rather, it involves the active *encouragement* of complaints, followed by identifying problem areas and taking corrective actions so that similar errors will not happen again.

The idea of actively encouraging complaints might seem strange. However, the idea is firmly based on some well-established guides driven by years of research, for example:

- the average business never hears from 96% of its unhappy customers; for every complaint received, the average company has actually had 26 customers with problems, six of which were 'serious' problems;
- complainers are more likely than non-complainers to do business again with the company that upset them, even if the problem is not satisfactorily resolved;
- of the customers who register a complaint, 54–70% will do business with the organization again if their complaint is resolved; this percentage goes up to a staggering 95% if the customer feels that the complaint was resolved quickly;
- the average customer who has had a problem with a firm tells 9–10 people about it; of people who have a problem with an organization, 13% recount the incident to more than 20 people; and
- customers who have complained to an organization and had their complaints satisfactorily resolved tell an average of five people about the treatment they received.

Complaints can become part of a larger process of staying in touch with customers. In particular, complaints can provide important information about the failures or breakdowns in the *overall service system*, and not just about isolated incidents. If compiled, analyzed, and fed back to employees who are empowered to correct the problems, complaints can become an inexpensive and continuous source of adjustment for the overall service process. Ultimately an active policy of responding to complaints quickly and effectively is essential if the objective – good service first time, every time – is to be achieved.

Mystery shoppers

Mystery shopping is a means of auditing the standard of service offered. In this case, the main focus is to assess the capacity of service personnel to offer service at the established standards. Regular checks on the levels of service performance are essential for any service organization if it is to maintain a consistent quality of service. Indeed, eliminating or reducing variability is one of the major tasks of service managers. The function of mystery shopper surveys is to monitor the extent to which specified quality and experience standards are actually being met.

When correctly implemented, mystery shopping can provide service managers with detailed information about what is being routinely experienced by customers at the front line of the business. To be effective, mystery-shopping surveys must be:

- independent;
- objective; and
- consistent.

The researcher must have a comprehensive knowledge of the industry, job tasks, and procedures – combined with good observation techniques. This can entail the ability to differentiate quite subtle nuances – for example, there is a difference between an initial greeting of a guest (which is crucial and must be done in a way which makes the guest feel special) and a passing acknowledgment later on (which is of lesser significance, and can be more casual and less 'intense'). Such differences can be subjective; thus, mystery shopper data is *qualitative* and must be conducted by people who know what they are doing. Even so, the qualitative subjective data must be validated by a carefully designed and tested measurement process (and mystery shoppers must be trained and clearly understand their role, focus, and priorities for their evaluation).

Done well, a mystery shopper program puts pressure on the organization to design and clarify the exact expectations for service – a template of the 'perfect customer experience'. This questionnaire then serves the dual purpose of being an assessment tool and a training tool, making it clear to all employees what the company aspires to give its customers.

Customer-to-customer communication

As noted in the section in Chapter 1 regarding online platforms in the sharing economy, the growth of the Internet, mobiles, and smart technologies has allowed consumers to interact directly. Online platforms, such as blogs, social networking sites, and video sharing sites, have fuelled the spread of 'user-generated' content through which consumers can communicate with each other en masse. While this has presented new opportunities for managers to gather 'live' feedback from their customers, it has also meant that firms have lost some control over the messaging surrounding their brand.

One of the earliest examples of these user-generated interactive forums is TripAdvisor.com, an online platform that allows customers to rate and review their experiences at hospitality and tourism businesses. Today, reading reviews online has become a habit for most consumers and an important part of their path to purchase. According to TripAdvisor's 2017/18, Trip Barometer report revealed that '86% of travelers will not book accommodation without reading reviews first' (TripAdvisor, 2018, p.6). Thus, this type of customer-to-customer (C2C) communication represents a new form of 'word-of-mouth' referral and has a significant influence on purchasing decisions.

This has implications for firms wishing to obtain 'real' feedback from customers and respond to comments. While we caution anyone who believes that user-generated conversations represent statistically and methodologically valid customer research, most firms today monitor this 'traffic' and learn about trends and general perceptions about customer experiences in their business. There is a vast array of challenges to consider as well, mainly about the truthfulness of the reviews, and the degree to which consumers and competitors can sabotage these communications or start a thread of negativity that can spread and in many ways distort the messaging. Nonetheless, service firms today must:

- be aware of these communications;
- engage in conversations where it would be beneficial to respond to concerns or fallacies; and
- decide to what degree they will allocate resources to this.

Such easy access to customer communication has also led to changes in the fundamental relationships of firms with their customers. For instance, many businesses today actively encourage and incentivize customers to 'like' their social media pages. In this new era of customer relationship management, it is thus becoming increasingly important for firms to have an online presence and to engage in conversations with their customers in this domain.

Similarly, it is important for firms to monitor their online reputations and respond to customers' comments in an authentic and timely way.

It is also important to be aware that different methods of communication are more effective for different age groups. For instance, while the 'Millennials' and 'Generation Z' demographics may prefer online platforms, there is still a large group of 'Baby Boomers' who are not comfortable using digital technology and thus may prefer to communicate via more traditional channels. The key point is for managers to clearly define which customer groups they want to engage with and tailor the methods for gathering information according to their preferences.

Responding to customer feedback

Regardless of the method used, it is vitally important to have a mechanism whereby any urgent customer feedback is considered and acted upon by management immediately. However, this is often far from reality in the vast majority of organizations. If such surveys are to be beneficial to management, customers, and employees, planning and management of the feedback system is essential. Questionnaires should have a definite purpose, and the survey should deal with a limited number of issues at any one time. Moreover, a definite time period should be designated for the gathering of information, and for subsequent action on any identified issue.

Once the data is collected, it needs to be interpreted. One of the challenges which firms often face is an overabundance of data, and the management concern about how to store and appropriately interpret the data. The sheer amount of information now collected also provides major challenges in how to respond to important concerns in a timely way.

Engaging internal customers

The importance of listening to internal customers

The customers of first concern to a firm should be its internal customers – its own service personnel. Management's primary task is to 'sell' its service concept to the firm's employees, before attempting to sell it to external customers. And the most important of these employees in this context are those who actually deliver the service to the external customers. Management thus needs to develop trust and strong relationships with its own internal customers – a philosophy of 'internal marketing'.

The concept of internal marketing is relevant to virtually all organizations. It is particularly important, however, for labor-intensive service organizations. The concept of the internal customer should be viewed as a managerial philosophy that has strategic and tactical implications throughout the company and its various business functions. In any service organization, employees are both receivers and providers of some services. Hence, service offered and received by internal customers inside the organization invariably affects the service offered by the firm to its external customers.

Employees as 'listening posts'

In a service business, *everyone* is responsible for managing service, and front-line customer-contact employees represent one of the most valuable means for gathering information about customers. By eliciting information about customers, these employees are ideally placed to help senior management know their customers better. They are, in effect, 'listening posts' (Heskett, 1997). And a service firm probably has more such 'listening posts' than management commonly believes – virtually every employee can function as a valuable 'data-collection center' and on-the-spot 'market researcher'.

Inseparability makes employees important

As previously noted on several occasions, one of the distinctive features of service is 'inseparability' – that is, services are produced and consumed simultaneously, and services therefore differ from physical goods in that there are no channels of distribution to isolate the producer from the consumer. Service personnel meet and communicate personally with the customer each time a service is rendered. Service personnel are thus the direct 'face' (or 'marketer') of the organization, and they are the most important link in a service organization's communication with its customers.

Interdependency makes employees important

Because a single isolated service is of limited use to the customer in the absence of various supporting services, customer demands on most service organizations are 'cross-functional' in nature. Services are *interdependent* and cannot exist or function independently. It is therefore essential that the various departments and personnel work collaboratively to offer service commensurate with the customer's requirements.

It can be argued that all personnel in a service organization receive or offer service from other members of the organization. In this sense, everyone in a service firm *is* a customer and *has* customers. For example, a surgeon receives a service from the care and nursing staff (the provision of various information about the patient's health reports and many other pre- and post-operational information) and subsequently the doctor provides a service to the patient (the surgery or other types of medical intervention). Essentially, this is the idea expressed by the concept of the 'internal customer' – it indicates the interdependency of every function within the service organization.

The success of every service organization is dependent on collaboration between the internal customers (the employees) of every department. No service firm can give its external customers the service they want and expect without the active participation of all of its employees. Unless employees receive good service from their fellow employees with whom they interact, they will be unable to serve their customers well. Quality internal service and satisfied internal customers are essential if an organization is to establish an effective customer-oriented service culture.

Encouraging employee feedback

In the words of Deming (1982), effective two-way communication can 'drive out fear'. Such communication is one of the critical factors in the success of any service organization. But the emphasis must be on effective *two-way* communication. Unless management makes itself easily accessible and approachable, upward communication will not take place. Top management must emphasize a company philosophy in which the focus is on the customer and must demonstrate its support of those employees who actively live this out by really serving customers.

Management must recognize the importance of feedback from employees, and actively encourage it. If information regarding customers' expectations and perceptions, as obtained by customer-contact employees, is passed onto top management, management's understanding of their customers *must* be enhanced. Indeed, in most companies, management's understanding of their customers largely depends on such communication as received from customer-contact personnel. However, large organizations often have an organizational structure consisting of many levels and usually communicate through fixed and formal systems. Such formal communication systems can prevent the full benefit of feedback information, which might otherwise be more readily available from employees in less-formal arrangements.

Managers must encourage and support employees in their service endeavors, and senior managers must make themselves available to receive feedback. They must be active in personally seeking feedback from employees and transparent in their willingness to act upon it. A good example is a restaurant group in Australia, where an entrepreneurial owner of four very successful restaurants in Noosa (a beach resort town) makes a very concerted effort at an 'open door' policy that he lives and breathes everyday. His promise is that any staff member (of hundreds) who has an idea, innovation, or feedback can come to talk to him directly and privately – and he will always make every effort to implement their ideas, even at the risk of failing. This creates an atmosphere of trust and responsibility where everyone feels that they have the power and authority to think and help the business, and have direct access to the owner in a nonthreatening way. What a great approach that has seen dozens of employee ideas implemented over the years!

Employees as customer 'advocates'

Employees should be encouraged to become 'advocates' for the customer. Indeed, many employees have a natural tendency to do so. In many service-interface situations, employees take customers 'under their wings' to ensure that their needs and wants are met and that their problems are solved. By doing so, a door is opened to much important information about the buyer of the service. If employees begin to function as customer advocates, a new sense of responsibility for knowing those customers 'inside–out' will develop.

A customer advocate goes beyond providing a service or product to the customer. In many service situations, a personal relationship with the customer becomes established (as is evident in the case of many professional services, such as educational services, medical services, and so on – see also the example of Indian Coffee House in the box below). As customers become known on a more intimate basis, their trust grows and their willingness to express their concerns, wishes, and preferences increases.

Indeed, relationships can develop such that frontline employees sometimes prove to be more loyal to their customers than to management. This is consistent with the Japanese management approach, whereby employees are constantly informed that their loyalty *should* be with the customers because, ultimately, the customers are paying their wages. This sort of strong commitment to customer orientation is to be encouraged. It can ensure a service firm's survival, in even the most turbulent market conditions.

Customer Centricity at Indian Coffee House

By Dr. Vibha Arora, Department of Marketing,
ICFAI Business School (IBS) Gurugram and Dr. Ravi Chatterjee,
IMT Business School, Dubai

At its core, Indian Coffee House (ICH) is guided by the belief that 'satisfaction of the customers is our destination'. ICH, with a century-old history and more than 400 outlets, is not just a restaurant but a place that holds significant importance in the lives of many individuals. The company is run by 13 cooperative societies and its staff are the co-owners. ICH is a meeting place for its customers, with each venue being promoted as a place to socialize and share interests. As a cooperative, there is no single owner; rather, ICH's owners are the coffee-serving waiters who grow as the business grows. This egalitarian business model and strong focus on employee empowerment has sustained the company over time and ICH now stands as a unique brand in the market.

ICH truly embodies the concept of customer centricity, and the importance of 'internal customers' in delivering on the service promise is deeply understood. Indeed, employee empowerment was being practiced at their workplace long before the concept of empowerment became a topic in management books! At ICH, each waiter is both a part owner of the firm and serves the customers as a host. All staff are encouraged to adopt a 'no hurry attitude', hence they are fully empowered to find their own unique way to establish a relationship and provide customers with a friendly experience.

The positive customer experience created at ICH has resulted in a high level of loyalty, with dedicated customers visiting on a regular basis for coffee or tea. Customers have also established a strong connection with the brand as the moments spent by them at ICH during their school or college days carry a level of nostalgia. This is enhanced by the décor and ambience of most of its branches, which remains the same and thus helps its customers to relive their experiences with the brand. There is no extravagant component associated with ICH; their 'unique selling proposition' is simple – to deliver quality coffee and food, alongside genuine and authentic service. The friendship shared between the servers and customers of ICH is a unique connection that keeps them coming back, and it is this personalized service that creates a customer experience that is hard for competitors to replicate.

Creating brand communities

Employees can and should become directly involved in the process of collecting customer feedback for the following reasons:

- to create an opportunity to extend appreciation to customers for their business; and
- to establish communication back to customers, to reassure them that they are being listened to.

It might be desirable to implement service quality 'circles' as a deliberate formal mechanism for gathering customer feedback. Many service settings provide the opportunity for joint problem-solving activity, involving both the customer and the contact person. Through such active communication, employees who provide services can identify the customer's needs and find a configuration of the service that best satisfies those needs. This encourages employees to participate actively in problem-solving and decision-making.

This improves morale in the workplace and fosters a positive customer-oriented culture.

Regular feedback communication systems ensure a continuous flow of information from employees to management, and back to the employees. This communication system should have formal and informal channels to capture the full spectrum of available customer knowledge, and thus to provide maximum benefit in tailoring effective quality of service.

More recently, with the introduction of interactive digital media, many consumption communities have come into existence. The most effective brand communities are all based on a combination of social media and other technology-based mechanisms to connect customers around the passion for a brand, along with connecting employees around how to physically and virtually engage in these communities. Harley Davidson is famous for creating a community-based phenomenon known as the 'brotherhood of riders', united by the passion for riding Harley Davidson motorcycles. These groups hold events around the world to meet and share their enthusiasm for the brand, and the company sends employees to assist with these events to connect customers to firms. Research has shown that it is the social connection formed between customers that creates the brand loyalty and brand community, rather than the products themselves (Fournier & Lee, 2009). It has been reported that supporting and managing brand communities effectively can assist service firms to increase brand advocacy, improve customer loyalty, and increase positive word-of-mouth.

Summary of chapter

In today's competitive marketplace, businesses must adopt a customer-oriented managerial approach to attract and retain their customers. As discussed in previous chapters, the distinctive nature of service forces organizations to place even more emphasis on *customers* in the design, development, and delivery of their service offerings. It is thus imperative that the firms understand customer expectations and perceptions, as well as the factors that influence their evaluation and satisfaction with the service.

Managers must be up to date with new market trends in customer needs, perceptions, and expectations. And service providers who are able to anticipate customer needs and desires before they become apparent in the marketplace will be advantaged in gaining a competitive position. To gather, analyze, and act on market information effectively is thus of paramount importance to service providers who wish to stay ahead.

This chapter has emphasized the importance of understanding the needs and desires of service customers from different perspectives – those of the customer, management, and employees. In addition, this chapter has discussed some of the most effective methods of customer research. These methods, which can be used independently or in conjunction, can assist managers in understanding the behavior and characteristics of their customers, and in improving their managerial effectiveness and business performance.

Review questions

1. Briefly explain why customer centricity is so important for service organizations, and why it can be so difficult to do.
2. How do organizations traditionally use 'metrics' and why are these approaches barriers to true customer centricity?
3. What are the different types of 'customers'? Provide examples of each.
4. Briefly describe the techniques for gathering customer information, as presented in this chapter.
5. What are the pitfalls of the Net Promoter Score system of measuring customer loyalty?

Suggested readings

Baehre, S., O'Dwyer, M., O'Malley, L., & Lee, N. (2022). The use of Net Promoter Score (NPS) to predict sales growth: Insights from an empirical investigation. *Journal of the Academy of Marketing Science*, 50(1), 67–84.

Bitner, M. J. (1990). Evaluating service encounters: The effect of physical surroundings and employee responses. *Journal of Marketing*, 54(2), 69–82.

Crosby, L. A. (1991). Expanding the role of CSM in total quality. *International Journal of Service Industry Management*, 2(2), 5–19.

Lewis, B. R., & Mitchell, V. W. (1990). Defining and measuring the quality of customer service. *Marketing Intelligence and Planning*, 8(6), 11–17.

Parasuraman, A., Berry, L. L., & Zeithaml, V. A. (1991). Understanding customer expectations of service. *Sloan Management Review*, 31(3), 39–48.

Prokesch, S. E. (1995). Competing on customer service: An interview with British Airways' Sir Colin Marshall. *Harvard Business Review*, 73(6), 100–118.

Reichheld, F. F. (1996). Learning from customer defections. *Harvard Business Review*, 74(2), 56–69.

References

Demining, W. E. (1982). *Quality, productivity, and competitive position*. Cambridge, MA: Massachusetts Institute of Technology Center for Advanced Engineering Study.

Drucker, P. F. (1954). *The practice of management*. New York, NY: HarperCollins.

Fournier, S., & Lee, L. (2009). Getting brand communities right. *Harvard Business Review*, April. Retrieved from https://hbr.org/2009/04/getting-brand-communities-right

Heskett, J. L., Sasser, W. E., & Schlesinger, L. A. (1997). *The service profit chain: How leading companies link profit and growth to loyalty, satisfaction and value*. New York, NY: Free Press.

Levitt, T. (1981). Marketing intangible products and product intangibles. *Harvard Business Review*, 59(3), 94–102.
McColl-Kennedy, J. R., Zaki, M., Lemon, K. N., Urmetzer, F., & Neely, A. (2019). Gaining customer experience insights that matter. *Journal of Service Research*, 22(1), 8–26.
Reichheld, F. F. (2003). The one number you need to grow. *Harvard Business Review*, December, 46–54.
Solnet, D., & Kandampully, J. (2008). How some service firms have become part of "service excellence" folklore: An exploratory study. Managing Service Quality *an International Journal*, 18(2), 179–193.
TripAdvisor. (2018). *TripBarometer 2017/18: Global report.* Retrieved from https://www.tripadvisor.co.za/TripAdvisorInsights/wp-content/uploads/2018/10/TripBarometer-2017-2018.pdf

Chapter 6

Translating service vision to action

Study objectives

Having completed this chapter, readers should be able to:

- appreciate the importance of a service vision and service strategy to an organization's long-term success;
- understand the importance of a well-designed service system;
- understand some of the most practical techniques for managing quality service operations; and
- be aware of the role of service employees in impacting customer experience.

The framework of this chapter

This chapter is set out as follows:

- Introduction
- Service vision
  - Like an architect's drawing
  - A point of differentiation
  - Ensuring widespread adoption
  - Customer-centered vision
- Service strategy
  - A distinctive formula
  - Marketing implications
  - Changing needs require changing strategies
- Service process
  - The actual delivery of a service
  - Quality at every stage
- Service system
  - Coordinating processes for consistency
- Aligning service vision, strategy, process, and system
- Service design

DOI: 10.4324/9781003470373-7

- o Key elements of service design
- The employee–customer 'interface' or 'touchpoint'
  - o What are 'moments-of-truth'?
  - o The 'cascade' in moments-of-truth (or the customer journey)
  - o At the 'coalface' or the 'frontline'
  - o Not to be left to chance
- Optimizing the customer experience
  - o Customer journey mapping
- Summary of chapter
- Review questions
- Suggested readings
- References

Introduction

Having discussed the needs of customers in Chapter 5, we now proceed in the present chapter to discuss how a service firm might organize its internal (organizational, process, operational, human resource, and the like) arrangements to ensure that these needs are met.

Successful service organizations pursue visions of service excellence that clearly indicate to customers and employees the service direction of the firm and its position in the marketplace. This *service vision* provides the foundation upon which the firm designs its service offerings such that they are always consistent with the overall image which the organization has attempted to create in the minds of customers.

A key feature of successful service organizations is that every aspect of the business reinforces who they are and what they are good at. A service manager's role is thus to ensure perfect alignment between the big picture and the small daily actions that contribute to achieving this vision. Thus, both clarity of purpose and outstanding execution are critical.

When it comes to execution, remember too that it is the firm's employees who are of paramount importance; these 'frontliners' are primarily responsible for building relationships with customers and creating positive experiences. The frequent employee–customer interactions are instances where strategy is translated into action, or in other words, where 'the rubber hits the road'. This connection between *broad service vision to the actual delivery* is the focus of this chapter and critical to fully understanding service management.

The nature of service experiences makes the service delivery process especially important. It is imperative that firms design service systems that effectively organize the firm's processes to produce the desired outcome. To this end, various techniques, such as blueprinting and customer journey mapping, have been developed to visualize interrelationships of service processes, to identify common pitfalls, and to enable firms to channel their efforts efficiently to achieve maximum benefits.

This chapter addresses the above issues from a managerial perspective to provide readers with a broader awareness of a more *strategic* level of service management, along with an understanding of the more important *techniques* in service operations management. Remember that for service marketing to happen successfully, the organization must not operate in silos. Instead, all of the management processes must operate in harmony. Hence the importance for service marketers to work closely with the whole team.

Service vision, service strategy, service process, and service system

This chapter talks about (i) service vision, (ii) service strategy, (iii) service process, and (iv) service system. These terms are obviously interrelated, but they do have distinct meanings and applications.

A *service vision* is an overall vision of a firm's service orientation and position – a sense of self-awareness (perhaps even a sense of 'self-destiny') which explains to staff and customers what the organization stands for and what it aims to offer.

A *service strategy* is a distinctive formula for delivering the above service vision – a unique plan of action which guides an organization and effectively defines the practical meaning of the word 'service' for that firm.

A *service process* is the actual delivery of the service – a series of acts or performances which make up the very essence of a service. Not *what* is done, but *how* it is done – in other words, a step-by-step outline of how the service is delivered. Process requires the implementation of various tools, techniques, and people.

A *service system* consists of management systems, departments, delivery systems of products or information, organizational structures, and technologies.

Service vision

Like an architect's drawing

The service vision represents all that a service organization stands for – the image of the organization as the customers see it. From a theoretical point of view, it is this concept which explains to both employees and customers what the organization's purpose is and what it aims to offer. An analogy is an architect's drawing of a building – indicating how a building will look when its construction is complete. In designing a building, an architect's task is to visualize the final product and then to fulfill that vision with a detailed plan that indicates all the components to be put together to bring the plan to fruition. In the same way that a good design from an architect is necessary for a builder to deliver the final desired construction, the service vision is necessary as a statement of the final service benefits that an organization proposes to deliver. The service vision is the expression of the planned service offer, including the delivery systems and procedures required to achieve this objective.

A point of differentiation

All outstanding service companies have a compelling service vision of their own position of leadership in the marketplace. This sense of self-awareness (perhaps even a sense of 'self-destiny') provides outstanding firms with a direction that differentiates them from other companies. In a sense, firms with such a vision of superior service do not have to compete – because they always stand apart from other firms. Their vision represents quality, superiority, and value to the customer, and this service vision nurtures, motivates, and binds every member of the organization in pursuit of a common goal. For example, the message Federal Express (FedEx) communicates to the market is its well-known slogan 'When it absolutely, positively, has to be there overnight'. This compelling vision provides a clear message of the standard expected from every employee to work toward meeting this promised standard. Customers, suppliers, and employees all know that FedEx stands for fast delivery!

As they work toward this compelling vision of superior service, successful service organizations are able to meticulously orchestrate every employee, every individual process, and every system into a unified focus on service. In turn, this uncompromising vision of superior service stimulates the energy of its employees, attention of customers, provides value to those customers, and gains the loyalty of those customers.

Of note, the service vision statement should not be confused with a mission statement. The terms are often used interchangeably, but mission statements are present-based statements designed to convey a sense of why the company exists to both internal and external stakeholders. Vision statements are future-based and are meant to inspire and give direction to the employees of the company, as its primary purpose.

Ensuring widespread adoption

Given the intangible nature of service outcomes, it is imperative that all service personnel – from 'the boardroom to the shop floor' – know and understand the service vision. The service vision must be nurtured, promoted, and 'sold' to everyone in the organization until it becomes ingrained in the firm's fabric and collective thinking. The vision should communicate what the organization is, what it does, and what it believes in.

The service vision of an organization should provide employees with clear information as to:

- the service offerings of the organization and
- the specific needs and wants of the customer that the organization is promising to fulfill.

That is, every person in the organization needs to have a clear vision of *what* the firm is trying to do for its customers, and *why* it is trying to do these things. Once these basic goals are established, the service vision moves on to the more practical questions of establishing unique strategies, identifying effective processes, and designing a structure that is capable of producing desired outcomes every time.

Customer-centered vision

Service vision is an umbrella concept covering the whole service offering of a firm. However, in discussing the *firm* in detail, it is easy to lose sight of the fact that the whole purpose of the service vision is to serve the *customer* – not the firm. Thus, in talking about how a firm proposes to operate, the service vision should never lose sight of the fact that the *customer* is the focus and purpose of the whole concept.

The service vision should therefore guide the core service that the firm proposes to offer to the customer, the facilitating and supporting services it proposes to offer to the customer, how the basic package is to be made accessible to the customer, how customer interactions are to be developed, and how customers are to participate in the process. In other words, the service vision is not ultimately defined in terms of products or services. Rather, it is defined in terms of *the results produced for customers and how this is assessed by them.*

Hilton Hotels provides a good example of this alignment in action. Their company vision (which is in essence their service vision) is to 'fill the earth with the light and warmth of hospitality by delivering exceptional experiences – every hotel, every guest, every time'. But words are meaningless without energy, policy, and commitment across the whole company and its hundreds of worldwide hotels. To bring this vision to life, Hilton has a stated mission 'to be the most hospitable company in the world – by creating heartfelt experiences for Guests, meaningful opportunities for Team Members, high value for owners, and a positive impact in Communities'. And then they have a set of values that align with the letters HILTON: hospitality, integrity, leadership, teamwork, ownership, and now. This vision, mission, and set of values guide all managerial activities at Hilton. These elements inform who is hired, how people are rewarded, how incentives are offered, and how they measure success. Done well, service organizations like Hilton convey clear language, a shared understanding, and an unwavering commitment from all levels of management. The next section introduces the way a service organization can strategize to achieve this outcome (see below an example of this full system in action including an audit process).

Service strategy

A distinctive formula

If a service vision is an overall concept of a firm's service orientation and position, a *service strategy* can be defined as a distinctive formula for delivering that service vision. Strategy represents an integrated set of plans for building and maintaining a sustainable competitive advantage. In its original sense, strategy is derived from the Greek word, *stratēgia,* a military term used to describe a General's plan for arraying and maneuvering forces with the goal of defeating an enemy army. In business, a strategy is a framework for businesses to pursue superior performance. This occurs on two levels: 'Whereas a firm or corporate level strategy considers the broad direction of a firm – growth, stability, or retrenchment – a competitive or business strategy outlines how a business unit competes within its industry' (Parnell, 2010, p. 305).

By developing specific strategies, rather than vague 'wishes', management has an opportunity to reassess and reorganize its options in its attempts to establish and maintain an effective competitive position. A service strategy is thus an organizing principle that allows everyone in a service organization to focus their efforts within the overall plan of action. An overall strategy can be made up of smaller strategies related to specific benefits or promises that are valuable to customers.

A service-oriented strategy that permeates effectively through the entire organization underpins the service culture from the inside and thereby strengthens the image of the organization as perceived from the outside. It clearly communicates to every member of the organization what the business is all about, including its key operational priorities and the things that they should all try to accomplish. If comprehensively explained to all employees, it establishes itself as the firm's corporate strategy, and as the personal strategy of every individual employee.

Marketing implications

A service strategy ultimately promotes the development and maintenance of an organization's market position. If the service strategy has been effectively communicated to all staff members, the basis of the firm's marketing strategy should already be apparent to all. Thus, marketers should already have a definite strategy on which to base their creative efforts and their marketing campaigns.

The service strategy therefore not only determines the conception and delivery of the service offering but also uses a unique mechanism to set its service at a different position in the market. For example, Southwest Airlines in the United States was one of the pioneers in the airline industry to offer its customers the opportunity to purchase flight tickets online, which accounted for nearly 85 percent of its ticket sales (a dramatic increase at the time). Although this approach is used by all airlines now, it was highly innovative when they started to do this and it created a significant marketing edge – convenience, transparency, and speed. Southwest's website was among the first to have customers make reservations and check-in, thereby creating a direct relationship with their customers. Supported by technology, Southwest's customers are able to review the options available and make a choice based on their needs and affordability. Southwest's e-tickets, online check-in, self-service kiosks, and open seating strategy benefits both customers and employees, as it frees up the time spent by employees. This provides employees with additional time to interact and assist customers with valuable friendly support, while also providing enormous convenience and efficiency to customers.

Changing needs require changing strategies

Service organizations have an ongoing need to make themselves aware of important changes in customer needs, preferences, and buying motivations. Customer-focused strategies must therefore continuously anticipate changes in such needs and motivations, and must adjust accordingly.

Ideally, readjustment of the service strategy should take place before the trend in the marketplace has become apparent. Systematic market research and other methods of feedback information concerning current and changing customer behavior can provide appropriate information (see Chapter 4).

The following example of Nahari highlights how a unique service business emerged through an awareness of the needs of customers (tourists) as well as the needs of the local community (who ultimately become internal customers/employees). Their distinctive formula proved so successful that the concept has been replicated and new modes of delivery explored, thus enhancing value creation.

Nahari: Meeting Needs through a Transformative Service Initiative

By Ardhendu Shekhar Singh, Symbiosis International (Deemed University), Sanjai K Parahoo, Hamdan Bin Mohammed Smart

University, and Madhavi Ayyagari, Managing Partner, Mindsbourg Consulting, Dubai, UAE

BAIF Development Research Foundation is an Indian not-for-profit organization founded in 1967. Its mission is to uplift the disadvantaged rural population by creating gainful self-employment while nurturing good human values. One of its most successful initiatives is Nahari, a culinary enterprise that is based on an innovative and sustainable business model in the Dang district of Gujarat, Western India. Dang is home to a predominantly tribal population and the inhabitants are largely subsistence farmers who sell any extra produce that might remain. Unfortunately, this provides a very meager income and many inhabitants feel compelled to migrate to nearby cities for their livelihood.

To remedy this situation, BAIF conducted a study on the theme of eco health and its potential for tourism. Blessed with scenic beauty and proximity to a hill station in the Western Ghats, Dang attracts a large number of tourists. Under the leadership of BAIF, in 2006, two enterprising groups collaborated to launch a restaurant named 'Nahari', which means 'breakfast' in the local language. They offered ethnic cuisine using locally grown ingredients like finger millet, lentils, traditional chillies, wild tubers, seasonal vegetables, and other forest foods. The interior decor and ambience was designed to reflect the tribal culture. Soon Nahari became a popular attraction for tourists and city dwellers alike looking for a unique sensory experience, by offering a source of healthy, nutritious, and tasty food in a native setting.

In terms of operations, Nahari is fully managed and run by the local women, organized in teams, with each one working for ten days a month. This arrangement is pragmatic, enabling the women to combine their work for Nahari with their own household chores.

The success of this venture inspired more women's groups to adopt the Nahari model. Under the tutelage of BAIF, ten more outlets were launched and Nahari grew into a chain of restaurants run by tribal groups. The reach was further extended through 'Nahari on Wheels', a mobile restaurant as well as catering company for special occasions. The positive impacts of the project include the creation of livelihoods, local cluster development, and empowerment of tribal women. There is also immense potential for replicating this concept across villages to extend the benefits to a wider group of stakeholders. The Nahari initiative has created shared value by effectively embedding a sound business rationale in a social enterprise structure. This project demonstrates how creative homegrown solutions based on celebrating cultural traditions and local cuisine can provide sustainable livelihoods for disadvantaged groups.

Service process

The actual delivery of a service

Having described the service vision (the overall service philosophy of a firm), and the service strategy (the distinctive formula for delivering that service vision), we now turn to the actual delivery itself – the *service process*. Service is an act or performance that is often carried out in a series of steps, which together makes up a service process. As previously noted, service has certain features that distinguish it from physical goods (see Chapter 2). These include the fact that service is produced and consumed almost simultaneously, and that customers participate with the service organization in the process of production and consumption.

Production and consumption of service, and consumer involvement in these, all occur at about the same time. Simultaneously, the quality of service is judged by the consumer. The design of a service process – the mapping out of how a service is to be rendered – is thus of vital importance in maintaining the quality of service. Process is so important that many scholars describe process as being the very *essence* of a service.

Quality at every stage

Given the importance of process, quality must be built into *every component* of a service delivery system if total quality is to be achieved (see Chapter 3 for more on service quality). In order for managers to understand a service process properly and identify areas for quality improvement, it is important to analyze and assess:

- what has to be done;
- how it has to be done (and by whom); and
- how the customer responds to it.

Such an analysis will help managers to identify the unique combination of steps and activities that make up the overall process. And as we know from Chapter 4, improved quality of service comes from *improving the process*.

Ultimately, the design and coordination of the service process lead to the creation of a complex *system* that produces the overall service experience.

Service system

Coordinating processes for consistency

The *service system* is a collection of delivery systems (e.g., management systems, organizational departments and structures, and technologies) that help to coordinate the service processes. It is important that all processes are aligned and follow a regular pattern to ensure a consistent customer experience and delivery of the firm's service vision or promise.

In appreciating the significance of service quality, it is important to recognize that most services are experienced by customers as a *process* and as an *outcome*. Both are significant in the assessment of quality. For example, consider a customer who takes their car to be repaired. If a service provider has put systems in place that shorten the customers' wait time (the *process*), while also ensuring that the car is properly repaired (the *outcome*), then the customer's perception of quality is likely to be high. However, if the customer is kept waiting for an unreasonable length of time (in an uncomfortable waiting area) and misses an important appointment because they are stuck at the repair center, their perception of quality is likely to be low despite the car being properly repaired in the end.

According to this view, the output of any service 'takes form' during the whole transaction and is simultaneously being judged by the customer during that transaction. By coordinating the process carefully (and the quality of that process), the output quality can also be controlled. Thus, service quality can be achieved through management taking responsibility for the processes involved in the delivery of service. Service managers need to analyze each of the processes in the overall service offering and should ensure that they are coordinated and effective as an integrated system.

Aligning service vision, strategy, process, and system

The preceding sections have introduced us to the foundational elements of service vision, strategy, and process. Each of these is important to understand as distinct concepts, yet their value to an organization lies in service managers' ability to bring them together in a clearly communicated package that serves to strengthen the firm's internal culture and external image.

To reach alignment, it is important that managers conduct an audit that ensures organizational policies and procedures support overarching goals. Such an audit results in consistency of communication, which means managers are sending a clear message to employees about the practices and actions that are expected and that have value to the organization. Ultimately, misalignment causes confusion, while alignment can lead to organizational success when employees understand the message. Such alignment includes links to external messaging but also to HR processes to ensure that all recruited employees match the firm's vision and understand the business before even starting to work there.

This work on alignment emphasizes the importance of service organizations being clear about who they are and what they aspire to do. Having mechanisms in place – including feedback and measurement – can ensure that this occurs from start to finish.

The case study below illustrates the links between a vision and how this is brought to life in a healthcare context. This chapter then proceeds to examine some of the principles and techniques that can be used to perfect the way service vision, strategy, and process create a service system.

Narayana Health: Transformative Leadership in Health Care Service

By Kameshwar Rao V.S. Modekurti, Finance and Accounting, ICFAI Business School (IBS), Hyderabad, India

'India will be the first country in the world to disassociate affluence from health care'

'My dream is to cure the world's poor for less than a dollar a day'

– Dr. Devi Shetty, Chairman, Narayana Health

Narayana Health (NH), formerly known as Narayana Hrudayalaya (meaning 'an abode of God's Compassionate Heart' in Sanskrit), is a multispecialty chain of 20 hospitals, six heart care centers, and 19 primary health care centers (as of August, 2020). Founded in 2001 by Padma Bhushan Dr. Devi Prasad Shetty, NH is now the second largest hospital system in India offering affordable health care. When NH was founded, critical care was only accessible to the affluent; health insurance covered only 10% of the population of India, and around 5% of the patients who needed critical cardiac surgeries could afford them. Dr. Shetty wanted to provide affordable health care solutions to the masses and lead by example to demonstrate that 'low cost and high quality are not mutually exclusive' and that 'being philanthropic is not necessarily unprofitable'.

Dr. Shetty started NH with 225 beds and offered only cardiac care, yet he envisioned it becoming a world-class center of excellence in the practice and research of treatment for various life-threatening diseases. By 2020, NH's operations had expanded to 5,900 beds across Asia, Africa, and the Middle East, offering services related to over 30 critical ailments, and being staffed by 16,500 employees and 3,500 doctors. Dr. Shetty's commitment to offering affordable health care has not wavered, demonstrated by his team undertaking open heart surgeries at an average cost of around $2,500 (compared to around $100,000 in the United States, with equally comparable quality).

Dr. Shetty's visionary leadership has shaped an innovative service delivery system at NH. Telemedicine technologies and mobile cardiac diagnostic labs are used to connect specialty surgical care in major cities with coronary care centers located in villages. Preliminary screenings are undertaken in these villages by trained personnel and general practitioners, who receive expert advice via teleconference facilities, and patients are only moved to the city centers in case of emergency or surgical necessity. NH's telemedicine network is offered for free and has become the largest across India. This service is supported by several key strategic partners, including the Indian Space Research Organization who provide Internet through satellite connectivity, NGOs like Rotary International and the Lions Club which provide logistic and outreach support, and the Karnataka government who sponsor some of the coronary care centers. Effectively, the best cardiac care is now being offered in villages with the collaborative involvement of multiple agencies, which is attributable to Dr. Shetty's transformative business model.

Other key elements of NH's successful service delivery system include a focus on task specialization and talent development. NH allocates all tasks that constitute the complete cardiac care service to respective specialist personnel, who deliver a near-zero defect service. This level of professional specialization and proficiency is translated into a higher capacity to serve, with NH surgeons performing around 550 procedures per year, which is about eight times the average of other Indian competitors. To nurture a skilled talent pool, Dr. Shetty has coordinated with the university system in India to offer the first Diploma in Cardiology, which has created an entirely new employment profile in the cardiac care services sector, complimented by NH's fellowship programs in various intensive procedures.

Dr. Shetty's unique approach is also evident in NH's service process. For instance, the technique of performing complicated cardiac surgeries on a beating heart is a differentiating procedural innovation that has eliminated the need for a heart–lung machine and also reduced postoperative complications. Furthermore, in collaboration with Stanford University, NH has created learning modules for training friends and family members of patients to undertake all the non-intrusive monitoring of non-ICU patients in the post-operative phase (who are supervised by a minimum number of nursing and ward personnel). By engaging these stakeholders as co-creators in the service process, this strategy has improved recovery rates, reduced post-surgical complications and emergency visits, and reduced costs in the post-operative phase.

Dr. Shetty's transformative leadership in health care service also extends beyond NH. Another of his business model innovations that offers affordable health care to the masses is a micro health insurance scheme called 'Yeshasvini'. For a payment of US$1.20 per year (in 2002), the beneficiaries have access to both surgical and nonsurgical treatments of up to US$2,000 at around 150 non-NH hospitals in the entire state of Karnataka. The Karnataka government has since adopted Yeshasvini, sponsored 50% of the premium, and extended it to other social groups. Dr. Shetty also designed 'Udaan', a program that identifies, mentors, and financially supports aspiring medical professionals from rural and underserved sections of society to help them pass the medical entrance examinations.

Through NH, Dr. Shetty has transformed the lives of his patients (customers) and their family members. He has created significant improvements in their well-being, nurtured service practitioners, designed customized services, innovatively trained service providers, strategically developed solid service partnerships, and has worked in alignment with social networks. The health care offered at NH minimizes consumers' suffering long beyond the service encounter and impacts many more facets of human life than just health. Dr. Shetty's clarity of vision and sincere commitment to alleviating the suffering of the weak and poor resonates through his statement: 'while the world perceives us as a low-cost Indian health care service provider; what we are engaged in is a passionate journey to establish ourselves as the lowest-cost, high-quality healthcare service provider of the world'.

Service design

Adjusting the strategy, changing the personnel, and improving the general 'know-how' of those involved will not improve the final result if the overall service system is defective. We often wonder why so many of the service systems that we encounter in our daily lives are so ineffective in meeting customer needs. Rather than being deliberately designed, some systems just evolve by chance. But if an organizational system is allowed to evolve on its own, it is certain to evolve in the direction of the self-convenience of the people inside the organization, rather than for the benefit of the people whom they are supposed to be serving.

Allowing a service system to evolve is insufficient. It is imperative that service delivery is *systematically designed* if the organization is to offer reliable, superior service. The goal of systematic design is to eradicate or minimize any policies or processes that stand between the service and the customer.

The basis of a well-planned and executed service system in any line of business is:

- keep the service itself simple and uncomplicated;
- make the service truly customer-centric; and
- add value for the customer.

But how does a service organization design such a system?

Key elements of service design

The term *service design* refers to making a service system 'tangible' in the form of drawings, flowcharts, specifications, computer programs, instructions, and so on. There is a wide variety of forms in which the design can be visually presented, such as service blueprints and customer journey maps, which will be discussed later in this chapter. This sort of tangible representation clarifies what the service includes and how the service is to be performed. In essence, it is an operationalized version of the service vision.

Frei (2008) proposed four key elements that should be considered when designing a service, although each context will dictate the actual actions. But these four elements offer a flavor of the fundamentals and are useful in designing a service:

- the *offering* (i.e., what experience are you offering to customers?);
- the *funding mechanism* (i.e., how will the service be paid for?);
- the *employee management system* (i.e., how will employees be enabled and motivated to achieve service excellence?); and
- the *customer management system* (i.e., how will the customer engage with the firm?).

Again, there is no one-size-fits-all approach and the decisions made in one element should be supported by the decisions made across the other three elements. Ultimately, what is most important for managers to remember is that *service design should not be left to chance!*

Designing a service system is a logical, step-by-step process. But this does not mean that it is a static process in which a step is taken and assumed to be firmly established for all time. Rather, designing a service system is an interactive process, in which the customer plays a crucial role. As previously noted, in all service situations the customer actively participates in the production of the service. Flexibility is required to receive customer feedback and promote an effective interactive environment during service design. For employees too, designs cannot be inflexible and prescriptive. There must be a balance between programmed behavior and personal initiative.

While service design is a complex process, which can employ a number of tools such as customer journey maps that offer a holistic overview of the customer experience (from the viewpoint of the customer), it is each and every touchpoint between the company and customer that matters the most. Each touchpoint is an opportunity for the company to either deliver on their vision and fulfill the promise, or not! These touchpoints are formed through the interaction that occurs between the customer and the organization and are known as 'service encounters'. While these interactions are often hard to fully predict and foresee, it is important to understand how they contribute to the overall customer experience. A more detailed discussion about managing those 'encounters' or 'touchpoints', and the many challenges inherent in striving for high quality and consistency, is covered in Chapter 7.

The employee–customer 'interface' or 'touchpoint'

Part of the role of service managers and marketers in creating a seamless service system is the way the firm delivers excellence across the multitude of interactions between its employees and its customers. This interaction is known as the 'service encounter' or the 'employee-customer interface'. A *service encounter* can be defined as the dyadic interaction between a customer and service provider or, more broadly, as a period of time during which a consumer directly interacts with a service (and therefore the firm). This somewhat broader definition encompasses *all* aspects of the service firm with which the consumer interacts – including its personnel, its physical facilities, its technologies, and other tangible and intangible elements. This wider definition alerts managers to think laterally about the nature of all service interactions or touchpoints and their implications for marketing.

Ultimately, the most important issue in managing service encounters is the firm's interaction with their customers at the critical times of service delivery – the so-called 'moments-of-truth'. While earlier sections in this chapter have focused on what happens 'in the boardroom' (i.e., the planning of vision, strategies, processes, and systems), in a sense, all of this is preliminary to the *real issue* – the management of the 'critical encounters' or 'moments-of-truth' when the customers personally experience the service. In many ways, this is the *end point of all management strategie*s for service industries. This is what it is all about! This phenomenon is a critical consideration for service managers in taking into account the complexity of linking and aligning the service vision to the customer experience.

What are 'moments-of-truth'?

Moments-of-truth are critical individual interactions that have the potential to determine a customer's attitude toward the overall service offering. These are numerous episodes that illustrate, to the customer, the *true value* of the organization – at least as the customer perceives it. Such moments-of-truth can 'make or break' a service experience. There can be no doubt as to the importance of these personal experiences. *They are the single biggest determinant in customer perceptions of service quality.*

> **'Moments-of-truth' in Japan**
>
> The best way to illustrate the nature of 'moments-of-truth' is to give an example. Albrecht and Zemke (1985) narrated an incident which happened to one of their friends who was travelling alone in Japan on vacation. At a train station in Japan he inquired in his limited Japanese which train he should take to go from Sapporo, where he was at the moment, to Tokyo. The man behind the counter wrote out all the information for him – times, train numbers, and track numbers. He even took the trouble to write it in both English and Japanese, in case our friend should lose his way and later need to show the note to some other Japanese person. This was a moment-of-truth, one of many that happened that day. At that instant our friend had an opportunity to form an impression of the train company, or at least of that one employee. He came away thinking, 'that was a nice experience, there's somebody who really takes the trouble to help people'. But the story goes even a bit further. Whilst waiting in the waiting area a few minutes later, he saw the information man come bustling through the crowded waiting hall looking for him. Locating him at last, the man gestured for the return of the paper. He wrote something on it, gave it back, bowed quickly, and hurried back to his post. He had figured out a faster, more convenient sequence of trains, and came back to correct the note! Such moments-of-truth can 'make or break' a service experience.

The 'cascade' in moments-of-truth (or the customer journey)

Each of us has personal memories of moments-of-truth in our own experiences. As customers, we have experienced awful moments when it seemed that people or systems (or both) went out of their way to be difficult or unhelpful. And we have also had shining moments – when we felt appreciated, cared for, and genuinely valued. As customers, as receivers of the service, each of us experiences the moment-of-truth as an intensely personal matter.

It is often the service interactions that occur in the first and final stages of an overall service experience that are particularly critical. A failure at an early point in the relationship results in a greater risk of dissatisfaction at each ensuing stage because we tend to take things personally, and interpret each successive failure as further evidence of the personal 'insult' that we have initially received. Conversely, a cascade of goodwill can occur. If the first interactions are positive and affirming we tend to look positively on each ensuing interaction, anticipating goodwill and looking for satisfaction.

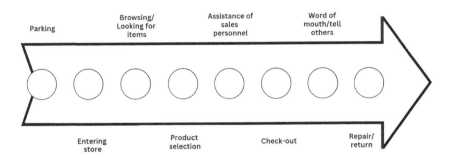

Figure 6.1 Moments-of-truth 'cascade' in a basic retail setting *(authors' representation)*

This phenomenon, both positive and negative, is known as the 'cascade' in moments-of-truth. Similarly, the final memory of a service experience is more easily retained by the customer. If positive, memorable, and impactful, it has positive implications, and if negative, it is likely to poorly impact the customer's memory of that experience. Figure 6.1 offers a basic example of how moments-of-truth cascade for a visit in a retail store context. Service managers must first understand which of these areas are most likely to be problematic and which ones are viewed as more important by customers (remember heterogeneity, which tells us that not every customer is the same!).

This 'cascade' (or as we explain later, the 'customer journey') has real and practical implications. For example, the Disney Corporation estimates that each of its amusement park customers experiences about 74 service interactions during each visit. This is a significant number, and the cascade phenomenon becomes very important when it is realized that a negative experience in any one of these 74 experiences, especially early ones, increases the risk of the next interaction being negatively interpreted. In turn, this substantially increases the risk of a negative evaluation of the overall service experience. Conversely, each positive experience reinforces the likelihood of the next encounter being viewed positively, and of the overall experience being perceived as enjoyable.

Jan Carlzon and Scandinavian Airlines

As an example of the importance of moments-of-truth, consider the case of Scandinavian Airlines (SAS). This is an old but still very relevant story about how the moments-of-truth concept was first conceptualized and executed by SAS. This event helped to turn the entire company from near bankruptcy to profitability and represents a perfect case in excellence in service management.

Jan Carlzon, former president of SAS, used the phrase moments-of-truth to rally the employees of his airline at a time when the organization was in dire economic straits. Carlzon convinced his staff members that every contact between a customer and employee of the airlines constituted a moment-of-truth, and that these moments-of-truth had a cascading effect. In these brief encounters, Carlzon argued, the customer made up his or her mind about the overall quality of service offered by SAS.

Carlzon communicated to his employees that we do not fly planes, but *fly people*. Therefore, the focus should be on serving the travel needs of the public. Carlzon estimated that the company created 50 million moments-of-truth per year, based on 10 million customers, each of whom engaged with five employees for 15 seconds each. SAS managers' task is thus to manage these moments-of-truth to convince customers of their trustworthiness and service superiority. In other words, SAS has about 50 million moments-of-truth to deliver on the service promise and create relationships with their customers. Therefore, the concept of moments-of-truth is critical to help manage customers' interactions with the firm.

The matter of cascading moments-of-truth is addressed more comprehensively through the customer experience and customer journey mapping literature, which are discussed further below.

At the 'coalface' or the 'frontline'

In assessing the importance of service encounters, it must be recognized that the service provider who is the 'face' of the organization is typically the very last link in the chain of service production. This customer-contact person, even in a world of growing self-service technology, is arguably the most important – bearing enormous responsibility for conveying the 'personality' of the organization – yet is quite often the least-valued member of the service firm in terms of status and pay. In the eyes of the customer, at the point of service encounter, these contact employees *epitomize* the company.

In a very real sense, service quality is *created* by employees but *judged* and *defined* by customers. The fact that customer-contact employees are often underpaid and under-trained can result in low levels of motivation, job dissatisfaction, high turnover, and, ultimately, in dissatisfied customers and unsuccessful marketing.

Effective management and marketing of the service encounter involve an empathic understanding of the motivation and behavior of such employees – behavior that can make the difference between a highly satisfactory service encounter and an unsatisfactory one. In other words, effective management and marketing is synonymous with a real appreciation of the importance of the people at the 'coalface', and a firm's commitment to their training, recognition, and welfare (read more on this in Chapter 8).

Not to be left to chance

The challenge of managing service interactions is thus vital for the successful marketing of any service organization. But, although it is generally recognized that the consistent quality of encounters is vital to the success of service operations, many organizations leave much of the process to chance.

The critical moments-of-truth vary depending upon the nature of the business, the nature of the product, and the nature of the service provided to the customer. But one thing is common in all cases – the critical moments-of-truth, if left unmanaged, invariably lead to loss of customer confidence. And once a firm loses the confidence of its customers, loss of loyalty and loss of repeat business follow soon after. The ability to customize delivery, to diagnose needs, and to respond to these needs at each moment-of-truth thus makes the competitive difference for service firms.

Every service interface can be broken down into its critical moments-of-truth. To manage service effectively, it is imperative to identify, analyze, and manage these individual episodes of interpersonal interaction to ensure positive experiences, desirable customer reactions, and effective marketing of the entire service organization. There are various tools and techniques that service managers can utilize to better understand the service encounter, customer experiences, and enhance performance quality at every stage. Two of the most popular – customer journey mapping and service blueprinting – will be discussed in the sections that follow.

Optimizing the customer experience

Building on the evolution from a product management mindset through to a service orientation, and more recently the move to the overall customer experience (CX), has also brought the development of tools, mechanisms, and processes that are vital to managing and marketing service.

For example, the concept of service 'blueprinting' was developed in the 1980s and used for many years as a way to visually illustrate all of the moments-of-truth in a service process. A *service blueprint* is essentially a detailed planning and diagnostic document that depicts the service events and processes as a flowchart – or a 'map' of intersecting paths. A blueprint represents, in diagrammatic form, the various processes that constitute the entire service system, and the interrelationship among these individual processes. The service blueprint is a versatile and practical instrument that allows management and employees to visualize, organize, and manipulate the entire service system, and facilitates service improvement and innovations.

Service blueprints support service managers with:

- a bird's eye view of the total moments-of-truth from all perspectives;
- depicting all the processes and activities involved in the production and delivery of the service;
- providing insights into what/how the service is being offered;
- a detailed planning and diagnostic document;
- identifying services that are valuable to customers;
- identifying possible fail points or 'hotspots'; and
- offering the opportunity to plan the 'tangibilization' of intangible services.

Blueprints are generally *organizationally centered*, by taking an organizational point of view on the customer experience. More recently, the terminology and perspective developed through blueprinting has transformed into what is known as customer journey mapping. These maps, in turn, take a *customer perspective* and are being used extensively by many organizations to better manage the complexity of the customer journey.

Customer journey mapping

The service encounter involves multiple 'touchpoints' or moments-of-truth between the customer and the organization – either in-person or digitally – each of which presents opportunities to spark delight ('joy points') or frustration ('pain points') for customers. These cumulative touchpoints make up the 'customer journey'.

Customer journey mapping allows service managers to look closely at the path customers take, the personnel they interact with, and the enablers and obstacles along the customer journey. By identifying the joy points and pain points (or 'hotspots'), service managers can identify opportunities to implement changes in the service system to enhance the overall customer experience.

These customer journey maps can take several forms – either linear or circular. In creating a customer journey map, service managers need to:

- identify all of the touchpoints and
- consider whether each touchpoint sparked joy or pain from the customer's perspective.

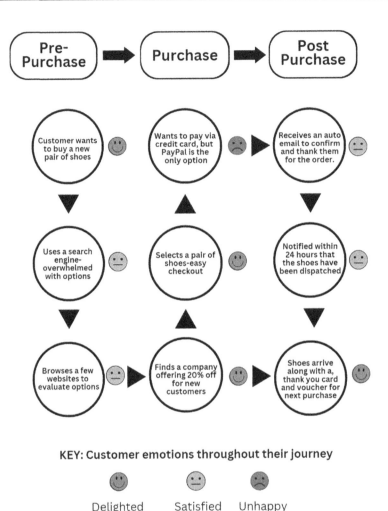

Figure 6.2 Example of a customer journey map (*authors' representation*)

This visual representation can easily highlight where potential problems lie, if any patterns are occurring, and which touchpoints need to be addressed as a priority by the organization. There is no universal template for drawing a customer journey map; however, there are some principles that lead to more effective maps. These principles include showing the stages or phases of the journey (e.g., pre-purchase, consumption/purchase, and post-consumption/purchase), and highlighting the places where there are possible 'fail points' and also where there are opportunities to exceed customer expectations.

Figure 6.2 offers a simple example of a customer journey map, in this case an online shopping experience. This particular map breaks down the customer experience into stages and highlights the level of (dis)satisfaction with each of them, thus identifying possible 'pain' and 'joy' points. Other possible elements to consider in mapping journeys include divergences in customer journeys depending on the customer segment/persona, if and how emotions and senses can be used to trigger satisfaction, and the nature of each touchpoint (human vs. digital).

Ultimately, customer journey maps help service managers to take a holistic view of the customer experience and see which elements of the service encounter work well and which need improvement from the customer's perspective.

Summary of chapter

Successful service organizations understand the complexities of delivering consistently outstanding customer experiences. This chapter has outlined the links between a service vision, strategy, process, and design, and culminates with introducing the customer journey and journey mapping. Critical to this chapter is understanding the many interconnected parts in getting this right – requiring the whole firm to be aligned and in-sync about the company (service) vision, so that all efforts from all areas of the business can have a singular purpose.

Emphasized in this chapter is the role that service employees play in bringing the vision to life through the many moments-of-truth that customers face with service organizations. Indeed, the best firms in the world place great importance on managing these moments and creating positive memories for customers to share with others.

This chapter addresses the above issues from a managerial perspective to provide readers with a broader awareness of a more *strategic* level of service management, along with an understanding of the more important *techniques* in service operations management. Remember that for service marketing to happen successfully, the organization must not operate in silos. Instead, all of the management processes must operate in harmony. Hence the importance for service marketers to work closely with the whole organization

Review questions

1. Why must a service organization have a clear and compelling service vision?
2. What is the relationship between service vision and service strategy? Give an example of how strategy can bring a vision to life.
3. What are 'touchpoints' and why are frontline employees a vital element in ensuring positive touchpoints? Relate your answer to the moments-of-truth concept.

4. Discuss the link between 'cascading' moments-of-truth with the evolution of customer journey maps.
5. Describe how customer journey maps can be of particular benefit to managers and marketers striving to enhance the overall customer experience.

Suggested readings

Crotts, J., Dickson, D., & Ford, R. C. (2005). Aligning organizational processes with mission: The case of service excellence. *Academy of Management Executive*, *19*(3), 54–68.

Larivière, B., Bowen, D., Andreassen, T. W., Kunz, W., Sirianni, N. J., Voss, C., ... De Keyser, A. (2017). "Service encounter 2.0": An investigation into the roles of technology, employees and customers. *Journal of Business Research*, *79*, 238–246.

Rawson, A., Duncan, E., & Jones, C. (2013). The truth about customer experience. *Harvard Business Review*, *91*(9), 90–98.

Rosenbaum, M. S., Otálora, M. L., & Ramírez, G. C. (2017). How to create a realistic customer journey map. *Business Horizons*, *60*(1), 143–150.

References

Albrecht, K., & Zemke, R. (1985). *Service America: Doing business in the new economy*. Homewood, IL: Dow Jones Irwin.

Frei, F. X. (2008). Four things a service business must get right. *Harvard Business Review*, April, 70–80.

Hilton Management Services. (2022). *Your Hotel, our brand & management team*. Retrieved from https://managementservices.hilton.com/en/who-we-are/

Parnell, J. A. (2010). Strategic clarity, business strategy and performance. *Journal of Strategy and Management*, *3*(4), 304–324.

Chapter 7

Managing customer experience and service failures

Study objectives

Having completed this chapter, readers should be able to:

- understand the importance of the service encounter triad;
- identify important obstacles and strategies in managing the service encounter;
- be mindful of the inevitability of service failure, and how service recovery is a critical element for service managers; and
- understand the principles and benefits of service guarantees and how they can be implemented for a competitive advantage.

The framework of this chapter

This chapter is set out as follows:

- Introduction
- A reminder about customer experience
  - o Pre-consumption
  - o Consumption
  - o Post-consumption
- Harmony between organizations, employees, and customers
  - o The service encounter triad
  - o The employee–customer interface
    - Identifying the challenges
    - Strategies to overcome the challenges
  - o The important role of frontline employees
  - o Building long-term relationships
    - Innovation and customer engagement
    - A holistic view
- When things go wrong: Service failure
  - o Categorizing service failures

DOI: 10.4324/9781003470373-8

- o Identifying service failures
  - o Service recovery
    - Why recovery is important
    - Service recovery strategies
    - The benefits of service recovery
    - Implementing service recovery strategies
- Strategies to support the delivery of customer experience
  - o Service guarantees
    - Implementing service guarantees
    - The benefits of service guarantees
    - A commitment to service excellence
- Summary of chapter
- Review questions
- Suggested readings
- References

Introduction

In recent years, more and more firms across all industries have begun to see the importance of making 'customer experience' (CX) a top priority. Practitioners have also begun appraising the management of customer experience as one of the most promising management approaches for meeting market challenges and developing a competitive advantage. A system of marketing strategies and technologies that focus on customer engagement, satisfaction, and managing customer experience has become a top priority for many of the world's top companies.

This system asks firms to think and act more holistically than ever before and to create an integrated approach that considers the full end-to-end customer journey including the way a person learns of a firm, considers a purchase, and engages with the firm after purchase. This may sound logical and straightforward but ensuring that each and every interaction between the firm and customer is positive necessitates a series of harmonious actions and relationships between customers, employees, and firms. Again, while this sounds sensible we know that there are usually challenges and friction between these parties – so this chapter assesses these challenges and proposes possible remedies and strategies to overcome any lack of harmony. This chapter first focuses on frontline service employees, all of whom can be labeled 'part-time marketers', and how customers serve as co-producers/co-creators of service experiences.

Further, to maintain their position in today's competitive marketplace, leading organizations must continuously improve their service offerings and the full end-to-end customer journey, and communicate the superiority of these offerings. However, because service is intangible, quality is difficult to quantify. And with nothing tangible to assure them of promised quality, service customers understandably perceive a risk in purchasing. The reality is that regardless of how well prepared a firm is to manage the customer experience, or how well-trained the employees are, problems, challenges, and even service 'failures' are inevitable. And the best companies in the world have distinct strategies and processes in place to address failures – or perceived failures.

The high level of human involvement in both the production and consumption of service means that mistakes, or service failures, are unavoidable. For these reasons, service companies attempt to establish effective *service recovery strategies* to back up the system in the event of failures occurring. This chapter will address some of the fundamentals of a good service recovery strategy.

This chapter also explores another approach taken by many service organizations to mitigate service failures (or failing to meet expectations) – offering *service guarantees*, which are an explicit communication of their commitment to service, and an assurance to the customer that if the service promise is not kept, some kind of compensation will be offered.

This chapter proposes a systematic approach to gaining a sustainable competitive advantage by continually improving the customer experience through a combination of strategies – service *recovery* and service *guarantees* – to form a system that facilitates superior service quality, while simultaneously reducing customer perceptions of risk and the chances of service duplication by competitors. The next chapter goes further by examining the internal structures and strategies that are required to facilitate service excellence.

A reminder about customer experience

Exceptional, consistent, and ever-improving customer experience has been identified as one of the most important success factors in all industries. Researchers and managers agree that offering positive customer experiences – in both offline and online contexts – can provide economic value for firms. In this competitive market, customer satisfaction and quality needs have been supplemented with the need for superior experiences. Therefore, service firms must enhance customer experience at every moment-of-truth. It is only through positive experiences that firms will have the opportunity to engage customers to become their brand ambassadors.

In today's connected society, many firms have realized that customers are their best advocates (which is reciprocal to the role of employees as customers' advocates, discussed in Chapter 5) and are far more effective than any other form of marketing. Moreover, customer-induced product and service innovations not only create customer engagement but, more importantly, also provide a powerful resource for the firm (see Chapter 10). Leading service firms thus ensure that they create and manage positive customer experiences throughout the entire service process, namely, pre-, during, and post-consumption stages. These stages are instrumental in forming the basis for how service firms can more holistically understand the customer experience, visually depicted in customer journey mapping (see Chapter 6).

A customer's experience with a firm's service often begins before they visit either physically or online. Similarly, customer experience in most cases extends far beyond the context of service delivery. In fact, service firms seek ways by which they can maintain lasting relationships with the customer and gain their continued engagement. Successfully providing positive customer experiences through the entire chain of interactions requires both internal and external collaboration and coordination.

There are three principal stages or parts to the customer journey: pre-consumption, consumption, and post-consumption (see Figure 7.1). Each of them, and associated challenges, are unpacked below. While technology-led innovations may assist in rendering the journey more efficient and smoother, it is, however, the human elements (i.e., people) involved in the co-creation and delivery of service that often contribute substantially to the overall customer experience since frontline employees have the advantage of engaging with customers to build trust and relationships. There is a recognized need for a unified approach to harmonize the blend of technology and human factors to create a unique advantage in service firms.

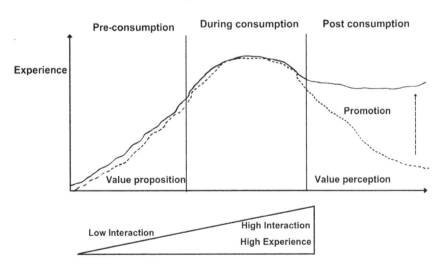

Figure 7.1 Three stages of service consumption along the value and experience continuum (authors' representation)

Pre-consumption

Most traditional approaches to marketing and advertising are ineffective in service contexts, since intangibility makes it difficult for customers to assess the benefit of a service before consumption. Customers depend heavily on word-of-mouth information from others who have already experienced the service (most often now received through electronic means such as social media and online ratings). Apart from such word-of-mouth, customers also seek cues to gain an indication of the likely quality of the service outcome (such as the cleanliness of a restaurant). Because services cannot be pre-tested before consumption, marketing of service is thus more effective if directed toward the consumption and post-consumption phases of service delivery.

Consumption

During the consumption stage, the firm is able to showcase its competency to provide superior service through its employees. It is through personalized service that employees create the all-important relationship with customers. Thus, in most service contexts, the most important task of marketing happens during the consumption stage when relationships are created and maintained by employees. This also implies that marketing is most effective during the consumption stage to convince the customers of the firm's service quality. Positive customer experience is far more reliable and impactful than a fancy website or glossy marketing brochure!

It is thus imperative that the firm convince the customer of its superiority through exceptional service and by providing customers with a memorable positive experience – the all-important moments-of-truth (see Chapter 6). If this opportunity is missed, very rarely will customers give the firm a second chance. All marketing efforts will prove worthless if the firm has not utilized the opportunity to impress customers during the consumption stage.

Post-consumption

Once a firm has delivered a superior customer experience, the emphasis is on engaging customers to contribute to the brand through positive word-of-mouth. Promotion thus plays a different role in service marketing. In this context, promotion serves to extend the memory of the positive experience they received and to entice them to take up the role of brand ambassadors.

Customers communicate experiences to others in many different ways, for example, word-of-mouth, testimonials, blogging, and social media. Generally, consumers regard the opinions of *other users* as more important and reliable sources of information. Word-of-mouth, however, is not something that happens following every service delivery. Service managers have to plan and create circumstances that provide customers with a unique story to tell their friends. In today's digital world, both positive and negative word-of-mouth can have a considerable impact via the Internet and social media, given these platforms' broad reach.

Technology-mediated connectedness between customers has given rise to a new form of customer voice, primarily directed at other customers. User-generated content and shared experiences communicated through online channels, such as blogs, virtual communities, and social networks, have gained substantial popularity, leading to customers' increasing reliance on other customers' information. Therefore, firms actively seek to encourage their customers to serve as ambassadors and positively influence other consumers' purchase decisions and loyalty.

Managing customer experience also requires a focus on monitoring and measuring. For example, Uber effectively uses a two-way experience monitoring system – taking reviews from customers to drivers and from drivers to customers. Uber then creates an average rating for each driver based on customers' feedback. If a driver's rating slips below a certain average, the driver is prompted to improve their service. If the driver's average does not improve within a certain period, the driver is let go from Uber. This online system helps prevent poor service while protecting the experience of their customers. On the reverse side, drivers can let Uber know about problematic customers, which in turn helps their drivers to feel safe. This example shows how Uber utilizes customer reviews in a positive way and manages the experience they offer to their customers consistently.

Ultimately, managing the three phases of the customer journey requires effort from the entire firm and also necessitates a balanced and harmonious relationship between the firm, its employees, and its customers.

Harmony between organizations, employees, and customers

The service encounter triad

In nearly all interactions between a customer and an organization, there are at least three main parties involved – the customer, the service employee, and the service organization – known as the 'service encounter triad' (see Figure 7.2). Each party is critical to the overall outcome of the service encounter. In a perfect scenario, there is a collaborative, harmonious relationship between each of the three parties – engaged employees, fully supported by their organization, serving customers who are loyal and satisfied. But such harmony is rare!

Great service organizations realize the importance of this harmony and employ various strategies to limit potential tensions between the firm, its employees, and its customers. For example, Singapore Airlines (SIA) is renowned as a preferred employer, which suggests that employees aspire

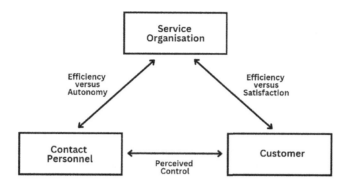

Figure 7.2 The service encounter triad (*authors' representation*)

to work for the company. SIA clearly focuses on its people to ensure that they are empowered and supported, and in return SIA employees make every effort to successfully deliver superior service. SIA's employees can also help mitigate tensions, for example, when the organization reduced legroom and in turn decreased comfort for customers to keep prices down. Such a scenario could create a perceived tension between the organization and the customer, which can be mitigated by exceptional service interactions by employees.

The service encounter triad highlights the importance of collaboration and harmony between the three main parties involved in customers' interactions with a firm. However, service managers also need to remember the importance of collaboration and harmony between the three main functions involved in creating superior service experiences – including operations, human resources, and marketing. Operations primarily links the firm's employees with its customers, human resources links the employees with the firm, while marketing is considered to be the primary function linking the firm to its customers. Just as exemplar service organizations have realized the value of collaboration with all stakeholders both within and outside the firm, they also break down barriers between the traditional functions of operations, human resources, and marketing to create a seamless service experience for its customers.

Service management is thus about focusing all the energies of the organization – including all the various functions and individuals of which the organization is composed – on developing *harmony, collaboration, and positive relationships*. In focusing the energy of the organization in this way, service management can be likened to a laser. A laser, in itself, is a weak source of energy. It takes a few kilowatts of energy and converts this into a coherent stream of light. It is the collective convergence of energy that provides a laser with the strength to outperform other (apparently stronger) sources of energy. In the same way, service firms have to converge the energies of the

142 Customer experience and service failures

organization to the specific goal of creating positive customer experiences. If a company has a customer focus of this sort, it possesses a powerful laser-like ability to dominate the market.

The employee–customer interface

As introduced in Chapter 6, the service encounter can be defined as that period of time or moment(s) when a firm and customer interact – also referred to as the 'employee–customer interface' or 'touchpoints'. Such contact is not necessarily limited to interactions between people, as technology is becoming an increasingly vital and ubiquitous component of service interactions.

The concept of the employee–customer interface is critical to understand for effectively operating and managing service organizations. The majority of accepted measures of service quality and satisfaction (see Chapter 4) give significant consideration to these 'encounters' or 'touchpoints'. This is even more important given how value is created – that is, in service and experiences, value is co-created during production by all parties – and that negative inputs from any of the parties can have serious impacts on customers' perceptions and experiences. The following section offers a range of challenges and practical solutions to managing these critical interactions.

Identifying the challenges

Planning and managing the service encounter is far easier said than done! Yet the great service organizations seem to get these moments-of-truth right, more often than not. There are many challenges facing service managers with respect to managing the employee–customer interface, which are outlined in Table 7.1.

Strategies to overcome the challenges

Great service organizations employ many strategies and actions to proactively combat the challenges above. Like a professional athlete who spends hours in the gym preparing their body for their sport, great service organizations work hard 'behind the scenes' to create a culture grounded on a service vision, which facilitates excellent and consistent employee–customer interactions.

The list below, although not exhaustive, offers a glimpse into some of the ways that great service organizations overcome the aforementioned service encounter challenges. Above all, remember that consistent, high-quality service does not happen by accident. Great service organizations continually use a culture of excellence, training, and continuous improvement to underpin

Table 7.1 Common challenges with managing the employee–customer interface

Challenge	Description
Employee stress	A state of emotional, mental, and physical exhaustion that service workers can feel, caused by job 'burnout' or excessive/prolonged stress. Workers can begin to exhibit indifferent and distant attitudes toward work and a lack of satisfaction. In addition, role conflict or ambiguity, where the specific responsibilities for a worker are unclear, or role 'creep' where a person's job subtly changes over time, can increase the stress and strain on a worker.
Emotions and moods ('emotional labor')	The emotional exertion that a service employee must provide over and over again each day by acting or showing emotions (e.g., sincerity, empathy, friendliness) that the worker may not genuinely feel. This can be difficult and cause stress for service employees, since the emotion they must display may be counter to their actual mood.
Customer variability	As we know, heterogeneity – from both a customer and employee perspective – is a common feature of service organizations. This variability creates challenges for service employees in determining exactly what each customer wants and how to best cater to their needs and expectations.
Other customers	The behavior of some customers can impact the service experience for others and hence affect their perception of service quality (e.g., loud children in a cinema could mean others miss hearing parts of the movie). These customers may not be intentionally disruptive; however, since their actions may be impacting other customers' experiences, this is a challenge that service managers need to be aware of.
Customer and employee deviance	When a customer or employee is intentionally disruptive, or tries to negatively impact the service encounter, it is known as 'deviance' or 'sabotage'. Similarly, the term 'jay customer' has been used to define those customers who deliberately act in a thoughtless, harmful, or abusive manner, often intentionally disregarding common sense etiquette and consideration for others.
Balancing service quality and financial performance	As important as service excellence is, there are competing dynamics in any organization where there are financial expectations. Many service firms have to strike a balance between service quality and profit. It is not uncommon for financial pressures to put a strain on resources and impact service.

their competitive advantage (discussed further in Chapter 8). It never just happens! (Table 7.2).

There are many other organizational practices for overcoming service encounter challenges, including creating an organizational culture and climate that are strategically focused on service (see Chapter 8) and service blueprinting (see Chapter 6).

Table 7.2 Strategies for managers to overcome challenges in the service encounter

Strategy	Description
Understand service	Top-performing organizations understand and practice service management principles. They know that the first step in creating a loyal customer is to understand that service is central to customer perceptions and satisfaction, and that the best 'product' in and of itself does not lead to long-term customer loyalty.
Smiling and impression management	Impression management is the process whereby a firm strategically works on creating a positive impression by having staff who are both competent and likable. Great service organizations spend time and resources facilitating authentic smiles among their employees, understanding the positive effect this can have on customers, since emotional 'contagion' suggests that strong emotions felt and displayed by one person easily rub off on others.
Human resource management (HRM) practices	Great service organizations find a way to attract and retain high-performing, service-oriented employees. This does not happen by accident! The types of activities involved in HRM include staffing planning, innovative recruitment techniques, strong 'employer brand' presence in the marketplace, clever interview approaches, effective reference checking, and an ongoing commitment to 'human' resources.
Optimism	Optimism can be defined as a tendency to expect the best possible outcome or dwell on the most hopeful aspects of a situation. Optimists generally deal with stress in a more positive way. Great service organizations consider personality in their recruitment process, as well as nurturing optimism in the workforce (e.g., through individualized support, modeling behavior, reward and recognition, and cognitive training).
Listening skills	To set the stage for high-quality customer service, managers must develop a strong service culture and what Brownell (2008) calls a 'listening environment'. In order to serve customers well, employees must know and understand their needs and expectations. Thus, great service organizations teach listening skills – focused on listening to customers *and* listening to each other.
Service 'scripting'	Many service firms systemize the employee–customer interaction with scripts. Scripts are used to help ensure a more consistent process. A service script creates a guide for frontline employees – including a predetermined set of words, phrases, gestures, and other expectations – to be used during each step of a service process.

The important role of frontline employees

In almost all circumstances, customers wish to develop relationships with their service providers. These relationships are important – whether interaction with the firm is frequent or intermittent. For example, a customer might visit a local retail outlet once a week, a hairdressing salon once a month, a dental clinic every six months, and a tax agent once a year. Whatever the frequency of visits, customers will choose to go back to the service provider with whom they have formed a good relationship.

In almost all cases, employees' interactions have a profound effect on customers' perception of the quality of the service experience. Every employee within a service organization thus plays an important marketing and relationship-building function, in addition to carrying out the operational requirements of their position. When interacting with customers, service personnel are simultaneously producing and marketing the firm's service. Employees are thus *'part-time marketers'* using their people skills to create a lasting, positive impression on the customer, which can lead to a long-term relationship with the firm. Since the service 'factory' is at the point of interaction between the employees and the customer, it is imperative that frontline employees receive appropriate encouragement, incentives, and training to help them market their own service effectively to customers, whether in person, via telephone, or online (discussed further in Chapter 8). Therefore, in service organizations, the marketing, operations, and people skills of employees are integral to their role.

We would like to emphasize a very important point about the growth of technology across service touchpoints. While many elements of the employee–customer interaction may now be either supplemented or replaced by technology, in most cases people still have a critical, if not changing, role in service delivery. Of course, there are firms like Amazon where a customer will rarely have an interaction with an employee. Even so, employees play a role in designing the service.

For the great majority of service organizations, employees are still critical. Bowen (2016) proposed four new roles where service employees' tasks are increasingly impacted by growing technology integration (known as the 'service encounter 2.0'). These roles are 'Innovators', 'Differentiators', 'Enablers', and/or 'Coordinators'. For instance, service employees may be 'Innovators' because machines are still generally unable to do many tasks innately human (e.g., creative writing, reading, and responding to and displaying emotions). Indeed, research shows that people in service frontline roles that require them to be innovative results in employees producing a significantly greater volume of innovation and performing at a higher level.

Building long-term relationships

The primary focus of service firms should go beyond merely attracting customers to proactively cultivating their loyalty and their patronage for the long term. Such loyalty is not easily obtained and is usually the result of ongoing relationship-building with its customers. Thus, relationship management plays a vital function in securing and retaining the trust and loyalty of people inside and outside the organization. Customer loyalty has been widely accepted as central to firms' success. Furthermore, managers and marketers have realized that the firm can benefit considerably more if loyal customers exhibit attachment and commitment to engage with the company in a proactive way (such as engaging in brand communities and writing reviews).

Customer engagement and their positive word-of-mouth are of greater value to a firm than passive loyalty of the customer. As mentioned above, evidence indicates that customers' word-of-mouth recommendations are one of the most important influences on other customers for their purchase decision, as they are seen as a more trustworthy source of information. Customer's positive word-of-mouth is arguably the most important outcome of a customer–firm relationship and is also widely considered an important form of loyalty.

Engaging customers and co-creating value

Given the competitive nature of business today, service innovation is an important ingredient to sustain leadership in the market, not only to attract customers but more importantly to provide them with a unique experience. Technology has changed customers, industries, and societies considerably (discussed further in Chapter 9). These changes have compelled firms to adopt innovative approaches to engage with customers and to build long-term relationships.

Many customers today take up an active role not only as *co-producers* of value but also as the more important function of *co-ownership* of the brand and its potential success. For example, online communities allow customers to help other customers solve problems for many products and services. It is often easier, faster, and more authentic to first ask questions to an online community rather than through normal organizational service touchpoints, which can be of great value to the organization (or harm if the narrative is negative!). The strategic focus here, beyond mere customer loyalty, is to achieve active engagement of customers as co-owners and co-creators of value as they disseminate marketing messages among their networks.

Engaging customers in the process of innovation on an ongoing basis has numerous advantages for companies. For example, Starbucks invested and built its own online co-innovation community platform, *MyStarbucksIdea.com*, in order to engage its customers and to participate actively in the community. Starbucks enticed the tech-savvy community members with various incentives to share, vote, discuss, and see the ideas in themed categories. As a result, over 196,000 ideas were generated on *MyStarbucksIdea.com*, and over 1,000 ideas were put in action for the improvement of Starbucks' products and services, while at the same time enhancing customer experience and involvement. Other widely cited online co-innovation communities include *Heineken Ideas Brewery, Lego Cuusoo, Dell Ideastorm, Best Buy IdeaX*, and *McDonald's Mein Burger*, to name a few. Through the effective use of online innovation communities, these firms were able to successfully engage their customers to co-create and co-innovate products and services (see Chapter 10 for more on fostering innovation).

A holistic view

For service businesses, *all* relationships matter. The growth and prosperity of a service organization is dependent on the harmonious growth of relationships among all of their partners, including customers, employees, suppliers, and shareholders. While the primary relationships are with its customers and employees, these are affected by the strength of its secondary relationships with its suppliers and shareholders. Thus, a firm needs to go beyond its 'core relationships' to encompass a more 'holistic' view of relationships in which *all* stakeholders are involved.

Relationship and experience marketing thus involves all stakeholders in the success of the firm. If proactive strategies are developed to nurture relationships and manage experiences on an ongoing basis among all stakeholders, the value of the firm's service offered in the marketplace will inevitably increase. This is particularly true of firms operating within industries in which service differentiation is difficult to achieve – such as hospitality and tourism, professional services, high-tech industries, the healthcare industry, and so on. The whole organization must be committed to enhancing the relationships and experiences of all stakeholders. The example below of Crimson Cup Coffee & Tea demonstrates how a service organization has focused on establishing strong relationships with all stakeholders, and as a result has achieved a unique advantage that is hard for competitors to replicate.

An Integrated Relationship and Supply Chain: Crimson Cup Coffee & Tea

By Vishakha Kumari, The Ohio State University, USA

Crimson Cup Coffee & Tea has found an innovative way to develop a *relationship chain* to support and strengthen its *supply chain*, which has given the company a unique advantage in the highly competitive coffee market. Founded in 1991, Crimson Cup Coffee & Tea is a wholesale coffee business based in Ohio, USA. The Founder and CEO, Greg Ubert, has built a culture of sharing and giving back into the fabric of his company. The values of trust, relationship, and sustainability are at the heart of everything the company does, while Crimson Cup's employees, coffee roasting team, coffee shop owners, and coffee growers in different parts of the globe all believe in and uphold this unique value proposition. Crimson Cup's success has been recognized through the multiple accolades won, including the Golden Bean North America Award, Smart 50 Innovation Award, and Good Food Awards in 2017 and 2020, to name a few! What makes this wholesale coffee business unique lies in many factors, yet the one that competitors may find hardest to replicate is the strength of the relationship chain that Greg has built that underpins Crimson Cup's supply chain.

Crimson Cup emphasizes the importance of an *integrated* and relationship-focused supply chain model, where all parties understand the importance of these relationships and trust in each other to uphold sustainability as a unifying shared goal. The three crucial links in the company's relationship and supply chain include:

- the farmers (who provide the raw materials in the form of coffee beans);
- the coffee roasting team (who hand-roast the beans in small batches); and
- the individual coffee shop owners (who brew the best-tasting coffee for the final customers).

In this integrated chain, the links do not work in silos; instead, they are in continuous interaction to build trust and understanding of the needs of others. For instance, Crimson Cup farmers visit the roasting facilities and individual coffee houses to see and experience the outcome of their crop. Similarly, the coffee shop owners and the coffee roasting teams visit the farmers to understand their needs to better support their well-being. Accordingly, Crimson Cup has been able to build trusting relationships across the supply chain, founded on a sense of common purpose and shared goals in both the upstream and downstream flow of the business.

Crimson Cup has developed several innovative initiatives to support the first link in its supply chain – the farmers. For instance, in 2011, the company launched the Friend2Farmer program, which has helped farmers and cooperatives to connect and collaborate, thus eliminating the need for any 'middlemen' and providing farmers with better economic stability. Crimson Cup has also invested in multiple quality labs across the United States and key coffee-growing regions such as Uganda, Guatemala, and Colombia, which provide farmers with a clear understanding of the value of their coffee beans as they pass through different stages of the supply chain. Furthermore, the sourcing team travels more than 86,000 miles each year to meet with the farmers and provide useful information and techniques that have helped farmers to grow higher quality coffee, achieve higher productivity, and ultimately gain higher prices.

Crimson Cup also maintains strong relationships with the other two key partners in their integrated supply chain – the coffee roasting teams and the independent coffee shop owners. For instance, Greg Ubert invests his personal time in coaching coffee shop owners and offers them step-by-step guidance to manage a profitable business. This unique leadership style of Crimson Cup's Founder and CEO stems from his core belief that trusting relationships with the entire supply chain is imperative for organizational success.

Ultimately, Crimson Cup's unique approach to relationship and supply chain management is underpinned by the core values of sustainability and giving back. The organization's driving philosophies of L.Y.F.E. (Leave You Feeling Energized) and L.O.V.E. (Leave Others Very Energized) also keep its partners motivated and connected. Crimson Cup's commitment to supporting its supply chain stakeholders and fostering economic stability for all has created a ripple effect that has positively impacted the communities in which they work.

When things go wrong: Service failure

For service organizations where so much of the offering is intangible and delivered by and to people, breakdowns, or service 'failures', are inevitable. The service might not fail in the eye of the provider, but if it does not meet the customer's expectations then it has failed from their point of view. And since service organizations must be customer-centric (see Chapter 5), customer *perception* is a service firm's *reality*! Remember too that it only takes *one service failure* in *one step* of a service process to make a customer dissatisfied (see Chapter 6 on the service encounter)! Excellent service organizations want to hear about service failures through easy and ongoing communication with customers. Great service organizations also ensure that there are clear pathways for customers to provide feedback – good and bad – with every piece of feedback being an opportunity to learn and improve (see Chapter 5).

Categorizing service failures

Service failures can be perceived differently by the various stakeholders involved and can occur for many different reasons. However, from a customer's perspective, what caused the failure might not matter! It is important for service managers to be clear about the types of failure so that appropriate responses can be implemented. Failure can occur in relation to the service *process* (something went wrong with the way a service was delivered) or in relation to the service *outcome* (a customer was simply not satisfied overall). Research has identified four types and causes of service failures, including:

- *The service itself.* In this case, the 'core' (or 'technical') offering was perceived by the customer to be incorrect. For example, a hairdresser cut a person's hair in a style that wasn't to their liking.
- *The service provider.* This type of service failure is primarily caused by the way in which the service was delivered ('functional' quality). For example, in the case above of the hairdresser, the stylist may have had a negative attitude toward the customer or was too rough when washing their hair. There is much evidence to suggest that it is an uncaring or rude attitude of a service employee that causes the majority of dissatisfaction with a service.
- *Things outside the control of the service provider.* In some cases, service failure can occur outside of the direct control of the service firm. For example, a hairdresser's service could be impacted by a power or water outage in the area.
- *The customer(s).* Also outside of the direct control of the service provider are the actions of customers themselves. Earlier in this chapter, we introduced some of the challenges firms face in managing the service encounter, one being deviant or difficult customers. The simple fact is that customers themselves can be complicit in causing a service failure. For example, coming excessively late for an appointment only to find that the hairdresser has given away the time slot to someone else can cause a customer to feel dissatisfied and therefore result in a service failure. Additionally, customers in the establishment, for instance, who are loud, can lead to service failure from the perspective of other customers whose experience is impacted as a result.

Identifying service failures

Despite everyone's best efforts, service failure is inevitable. In a perfect world, customers would feel compelled to proactively communicate with the service firm about instances of failure and dissatisfaction. However, the challenge for service managers is that the majority of people (some research suggests 90%) never complain! Although most of the research on service failure has been on service *recovery*, linked to those people who *do* complain, there is some research which examines that very important group of customers who do not complain. One notable research project (Voorhees et al., 2006) labeled this group of dissatisfied customers who do not complain as 'The Silent Masses'.

These researchers attribute the lack of complaining to a multitude of reasons, broken into six major themes:

- *time and effort* (i.e., not worth the time or didn't have time to complain);
- *service provider's responsiveness* (i.e., nobody to complain to or didn't think anyone would take any corrective action);
- *personality factors* (i.e., customer assertiveness, mood, or empathy toward service workers);
- *organization-initiated recovery* (i.e., before the customer could complain, the firm proactively dealt with the service failure);
- *miscellaneous* (i.e., did not realize failure until too late, customer loyal regardless, failure is rare, etc.); and
- *alternative action* (i.e,. customer simply switched service providers rather than saying anything).

Service managers benefit from first understanding that unhappy customers or those who have experienced a service failure do not necessarily complain, and second from proactively putting measures into place which address the themes presented above. The reason is that service failures can have various damaging consequences, including a decline in customer confidence, customer defections, and negative word-of-mouth. It is thus important that service failures are recognized and result in a satisfactory recovery for the customer.

Service recovery

It has been reported that many firms never hear from the majority of their unhappy customers. This means most unhappy customers never complain but also never return to the service provider. In turn, customers who have complained to an organization and had their complaints satisfactorily resolved tell many people about the treatment they received. Therefore, *service recovery* is a very important strategy for all service firms to invest their time and energy into.

Service recovery is a proactive strategy to continually assess situations or points in the service system that are prone to failures, using blueprinting and establishing a procedure that employees can undertake to recover from the failed service to the satisfaction of the customer. Therefore, service recovery is the set of actions a company takes to re-establish customer satisfaction and loyalty after a service failure, to ensure that failure incidents encourage learning and process improvements, and to train and reward employees for this purpose. Great service organizations respond not only to those problems that might be their fault but also provide service recovery strategies linked to events that may not have been their fault!

Why recovery is important

Although it might sometimes seem that there is an unlimited pool of potential customers for any given service firm, the primary goal of an organization must be to focus on maintaining the loyalty of its existing customer base. This is because customer recruitment is always more costly than customer retention. Indeed, it has been argued that it costs five times as much to attract a new customer as it does to retain an existing one. In addition, the time spent searching for new customers can mean that present customers are treated less well, with a resultant loss of customer satisfaction and brand reputation.

Various researchers have indicated that the loyalty, retention, and repurchase intentions of existing customers are inextricably linked to customer satisfaction. The main reason for customers leaving familiar service providers and seeking new ones has been repeatedly shown to be failure in the core service of the firm. And dissatisfied customers not only defect but also trigger a chain of negative word-of-mouth comments. Except in a few rare instances, complete customer satisfaction is the key to generating customer loyalty and securing long-term financial viability of the firm.

This long-term perspective has produced a strong emphasis on orienting service strategy toward fulfilling service promise, increasing customer loyalty, and reducing customer dissatisfaction. Thus, it is imperative for service managers to have recovery strategies that can be implemented when failures inevitably occur.

Service recovery strategies

As noted above, the human element in service is so prominent in both production and consumption that mistakes are unavoidable. Given the inevitability of error, the way in which a service organization responds to mistakes becomes a crucial factor in customer retention. Once a service failure has occurred, managers can adopt a range of service recovery strategies such as:

- apology;
- correction;
- empathy;
- compensation;
- follow-up;
- acknowledgment;
- explanation;
- exceptional treatment; and
- managerial intervention.

Service managers need to know which strategy is the appropriate one for any circumstance. The list above generally follows a sequence, in that an apology and correction would be used in the first instance and in almost any service failure situation. Research suggests that service firms could enhance their competitive position by simply understanding that customers generally are not looking for anything unreasonable, but rather a simple acknowledgment of a mistake and some small effort to make a correction (depending on severity).

Most customers understand that service failures do occur despite a firm's commitment to offer superior service. Customers are, in fact, generally forgiving in these instances, yet they can become unhappy if the service organization is unwilling to accept responsibility for the mishap. More importantly, they are especially unhappy if the service provider is unable (or, worse, unwilling) to take immediate action to fix the situation. Indeed, Kelley (1993) claimed that regardless of the type of failure experienced, customers will remain loyal to a service firm *provided that an effective recovery is executed*.

From a customer perspective, recovering failed service demonstrates fulfillment of the firm's promise and thereby confirms a firm's commitment to superior service. The example below of how Zomato handles service failures highlights how firms can embed recovery strategies into their service design to successfully maintain customer loyalty.

Recovery with a Smile: How Zomato Effectively Handles Service Failure

By Dr Malini Majumdar, Army Institute of Management, Kolkata, India

The food delivery unicorn Zomato has revolutionized Indians' dining experience. This restaurant aggregator app offers a range of benefits to consumers, including timely meal delivery to homes or offices, exclusive discounts, and live tracking features. Zomato's spirit is reflected in its tagline: '*Never have a bad meal*', while the company's success is evident in its rapid scale (serving in more than 10,000 cities across 24 different countries) and profitability (in the first quarter of FY 2020, Zomato recorded a record 225% increase in revenue). Some of their main services for both restaurants and customers include POS systems, restaurant search and discovery, table reservations and management, and online ordering.

The basis of Zomato's service is the ability to connect food sellers and consumers through a discovery algorithm that is unparalleled in India. The company manages a fleet of delivery personnel who serve over 65 million people every month; thus, their service delivery process involves frequent interpersonal interaction and hence a high degree of heterogeneity. Naturally, service failures occur. For instance, while the

Zomato app shows an expected time of food delivery based on an algorithm that takes into account several factors (such as preparation time, time of the day, changing traffic conditions, and distance to the customer's location), customers do not always get their orders in the stipulated time period. Other service failures can involve issues with packaging, billing, incorrect orders, rude behavior, and the quality of food.

The company recognizes the need to implement a smooth and effective recovery system; thus, to ensure a timely response when failures occur Zomato utilizes an online customer service platform. Furthermore, as part of its failure recovery mechanism, the company has trained its workforce to treat consumer complaints with empathy and professional efficiency. Every unsatisfied customer wants to be heard, have their issue resolved quickly, and be acknowledged by the service provider. Accordingly, Zomato has embedded the following in its service design:

- a live tracking feature on the app that allows full transparency at every step of the order process;
- multichannel communication options to reach Zomato's customer care department (including via social media, a chat functionality in the account section of the app, or through the website);
- effective and personalized communication, with an engaging tone of voice and a response that shows care and concern to consumers (for instance, customer service representatives manage queries from their own social media handles to make their responses more personal and conversational in nature);
- conducting a detailed 'root cause analysis' for every service failure, which allows Zomato to provide constructive feedback to its partner restaurants; and
- keeping a record of complaints and problems to use for training staff members and refining the service delivery process to reduce errors (for instance, delivery partners are trained on using technology, behavioral skills, personality development, guidelines for safe riding, and skill development through customized simulation and case studies).

The professional approach toward Online Reputation Management (ORM) practiced by Zomato is clearly identifiable in how it handles service failure and recovery. For instance, after a failure has occurred, a phased ORM practice is employed to dilute any online negativity with more neutral or positive publicity. The company's responsiveness, resolution time, and volume of appreciation visible on social media help

> to build its reputation as a trustworthy service provider. Furthermore, the empathy shown by their customer service representatives helps to establish a positive connection with their customers. This approach has enabled Zomato to stand apart from its competitors and become one of the two largest food delivery platforms in India.

The benefits of service recovery

As noted above, firms are able to regain the trust and satisfaction of customers following a failure provided that a service recovery strategy is successfully executed. Indeed, effective service recovery leads to enhanced perceptions of the firm's competence and a favorable image in terms of perceived quality and value.

There is also a peculiar irony evident in the service literature known as 'the service recovery paradox'. This concept has been defined as a situation in which customer satisfaction can *exceed* pre-failure satisfaction. The lesson for service managers is that in service recovery situations, a customer who experiences a gracious and efficient handling of a complaint can become a company's best customer and advocate. Nevertheless, we are not advocating failure for the purpose of achieving the service recovery paradox!

Furthermore, a firm can gain additional benefit for itself if it makes use of the information gained from the experience to prevent future failures. Every service failure and recovery experience should trigger a learning process across the whole organization – to prevent a recurrence of the mistake. This concept of 'learning from failure' is crucial if an organization is to improve its people, its systems, and its procedures. Modern service firms, taking advantage of technology, use databases to record, categorize, and disseminate information to the entire organization to help everyone learn from their mistakes.

Implementing service recovery strategies

The effective implementation of service recovery requires a range of complementary strategies, including a *service guarantee* to ensure an immediate response to failure, and *employee empowerment* (see Chapter 8) to ensure successful corrective action to recover from that failure. The literature on service recovery and service guarantees stresses that recovery is most effective if a firm's response is focused on each customer's individual needs, and if employees have highly developed interpersonal skills that enable them to react flexibly to each situation.

Service recovery, service guarantees, and employee empowerment are complementary strategies that reinforce one another in practice and engender a spirit of mutual trust between management and frontliners – everyone is committed to the same goal of delivering quality service. The integration of these three complementary strategies within an organization results in an effective service culture that is not easily emulated by competitors and thus constitutes a unique competitive advantage. We now turn to a consideration of how firms can successfully implement service guarantees.

Strategies to support the delivery of customer experience

Creating competitive advantage requires service organizations to have outstanding customer-centric practices built into the fabric of the business. Furthermore, as we know, it is imperative to manage a customer's entire experience with the firm through numerous touchpoints. Customer perceptions of each of these touchpoints (or moments-of-truth) play a major role in gaining customer satisfaction and in influencing future purchase decisions. Each of these encounters presents an opportunity for a firm to prove its superior quality of service or, alternatively, to lose its customers' trust and loyalty.

Before examining service guarantees in more detail, it is important to stress that this strategy should be seen as part of a *cohesive system*. Strategies such as innovative and service-focused people-management practices, creating a workplace culture where frontline staff are empowered to make decisions (see Chapter 8), and a proactive service recovery process (as discussed above) are inherently complementary. A successfully coordinated system of strategies will permeate the whole organizational culture, and thus making it difficult for other organizations to emulate and leading to a sustainable competitive advantage.

Service guarantees

Every business encounter involves risk. And in every business encounter, one stakeholder always assumes more of the risk than the other. When customers purchase a service, they usually take a relatively higher risk than when they purchase a physical object because the intangible nature means they cannot examine or pre-test the outcome. In effect, the customer makes a purchase based on the trust and expectation of receiving a good result.

To encourage prospective customers to avail themselves of its service, an organization should therefore seek ways to reduce the perceived risk. In practice, this means offering the customer a guarantee of service. A *service guarantee* can be defined as: 'an explicit promise made by the service provider to (a) deliver a certain level of service to satisfy the customer and (b) remunerate the customer if the service is not sufficiently delivered' (Hogreve & Gremler, 2009, p. 324).

A guaranteed service transaction will be seen by the prospective customer as an added bonus – something that enhances the value of the offer by increasing the likelihood that they will receive what they wish to receive. However, the reality is that no one can ever guarantee that mistakes will never be made. The best that can be done is a promise to make every effort to eliminate foreseeable and controllable error, together with an undertaking to make good any mistake that does occur – and to do so promptly.

Service guarantees should strive to be as 'unconditional' as possible, with a view to assuring the customer of service reliability. In essence, a service guarantee is a vow that service delivery will meet company promises; and if it does not, that the company will promptly compensate the customer.

Implementing service guarantees

It is not enough to offer a service guarantee as a public relations exercise – cynically designed to attract attention and prospective customers – with no commitment to the concept of a real guarantee. An effective guarantee must be carefully designed and effectively organized as part of an overall focus on sustaining a service-oriented culture.

Such a service-oriented guarantee should be:

- *unconditional* – because when excuses are given, the customer feels cheated;
- *easy to understand and communicate* – specific and clear to both customers and employees;
- *meaningful to the customer* – promising something of real value if service is not delivered properly;
- *believable/credible* – promising something that could legitimately be delivered upon;
- *easy to invoke* – an unpleasant situation should not be exacerbated by a service guarantee that is difficult to deliver; and
- *easy to fulfill* – when a customer invokes a guarantee, the service provider should pay out immediately.

Incorporating these sorts of features into a service guarantee ensures that it is real and effective. A guarantee reinforces a company's service promise to its customers and makes that promise 'tangible'. Once established, service guarantees should constitute a permanent part of an organization's operating philosophy, and be supported by an advertising campaign to reinforce the fact.

Furthermore, when implementing a service guarantee strategy, the use of a reward system can be very useful. Such a reward system, by which customers are rewarded for their comments, and by which employees are rewarded for solving problems, encourages feedback and compels the organization to respond to that feedback.

The benefits of service guarantees

So why should an organization go to the trouble of guaranteeing its service offering? The above section has outlined what a service guarantee should look like in theory, but do such service guarantees really deliver value in practice?

Indeed, service guarantees have benefits beyond the obvious – assuring reliability and thereby encouraging doubtful customers – and these wider advantages permeate through the whole organization.

In summary, service guarantees have the following benefits:

- assuring reliability and positively influencing sales;
- encouraging customer feedback and facilitating immediate corrective action;
- improving operational efficiency and service delivery systems (i.e., it 'lifts the game' of the entire organization);
- identifying 'fail points' in the service system;
- increasing customer satisfaction, trust, and loyalty;
- improving employee performance through training/education programs;
- developing a general service-oriented culture in the business; and
- maintaining competitiveness in the marketplace.

Taking these points together, a service guarantee sets a standard that cannot be compromised. This strategy effectively coordinates every system in the organization to become focused on better serving the customer. It can thus be considered to function as an internal 'auto-alignment' system.

A service guarantee does deliver value by fulfilling both an effective marketing function and an effective operational function. That is, it simultaneously enhances an organization's (internal and external) marketing effectiveness and its operating competency. Therefore, it is apparent that a service guarantee is an effective and valuable management tool, which all service organizations should embrace because:

- it forces an organization to focus on the customer's definition of good service, rather than relying on management's assumptions of what constitutes such service;
- it sets clear performance standards;
- it generates reliable data on poor performance (through records of complaints and payouts);
- it forces an organization to examine its entire service delivery system for possible failure points;
- it builds customer loyalty and enhances positive word-of-mouth recommendations; and
- it encourages employees to show initiative and commitment to the firm and its customers.

A commitment to service excellence

Above all, customers appreciate such guarantees for the commitment to service which they represent. A service guarantee is essentially a way of demonstrating an organization's *trust in its customers* – in the full knowledge that some customers will attempt to take unfair advantage of the offer. Such trust makes customers feel valued. It communicates one half of a partnership reaching out to the other – thus facilitating a long-term partnership.

Take Costco for example – a US company that has been ranked as one of the top businesses in the retail industry, which can be attributed to their belief that every aspect of the organization should focus on customer satisfaction and service excellence. To combat any possible service failures, Costco offers a very generous 'Risk-Free 100% Satisfaction Guarantee'. Costco's focus is to offer its customers a positive service experience, so they guarantee customers' satisfaction on every product they sell with a full refund without question. Costco also offers a guarantee on their membership, which means they refund customers' membership fee in full at any time if they are dissatisfied. In order to achieve this, Costco proactively empowers and relies on employees to closely monitor customer experience. The organization's service guarantee strategy is thus one part of a cohesive system, which includes a focus on workplace culture and a commitment to supporting their employees through above average-wages and benefits. With this approach, Costco has been able to build a sense of trust between their employees and customers alike – and they know that customers' trust and loyalty are built up over many years, thus offering a service guarantee will pay back many times over.

Ultimately, service guarantees create a customer-driven standard for service which defines the service promise of an organization to its internal and external customers simultaneously. That is, service guarantees not only set criteria by which customers can evaluate the quality of service they receive but also establish the standard to which an organization needs to train its workers, so as to ensure that the staff are capable of delivering such quality service. The effect of this is that service guarantees create a commitment to the delivery of excellent service, and reciprocal trust on both sides, resulting in an impressive customer (and employee) retention rate.

Summary of chapter

To achieve and maintain a competitive edge, it is imperative that a service firm systematically identifies and manages the factors that influence the customer experience across the full customer journey at all interactions between a firm and its customers. The service encounter 'triad' was introduced as a way to understand the importance of a balance of power between the firm, a customer, and the employee – and some of the many challenges firms face in ensuring that service encounters are maximized for mutual benefit. We highlighted changes to service roles with the growth of technology, more often altering the role of employees but rarely fully replacing them.

Regardless of how well a service firm performs, failures are inevitable – and the best firms plan for failures and proactively address situations when customers are disappointed. Service recovery, a systematic process undertaken by an organization in an effort to return aggrieved customers to a state of satisfaction after a service has failed to live up to expectations, is a vital element for service firms. Great service organizations respond not only to those problems that might be their fault but also provide service recovery strategies linked to events that may not have been their fault, knowing that customers who feel that a firm worked hard to overcome a perceived failure can become exceptionally loyal.

Service guarantees serve as a unique selling point that aims to promote the firm's customer orientation with real commitment. Such a service guarantee not only targets external customers but also employees – who become acutely aware of the firm's service philosophy and service vision. The service guarantee thus establishes and communicates the firm's image and market position to its customers, employees, and competitors. Ultimately, it will be reflected in customer satisfaction and loyalty.

Review questions

1. Why is it important that service managers and marketers view the firm, customers, and employees as equal, harmonious partners in the customer experience?
2. Although technology is making strides in reducing some labor in service organizations, explain why frontline employees remain critical to customer experience success.
3. What are Bowen's 'four new roles' for service employees, and in what context might each be adopted?
4. Why is a proactive service recovery strategy (and not just reacting to complaints) so important?
5. Is it worth the risk to offer a service guarantee? Why or why not?

Suggested readings

Dhebar, A. (2013). Toward a compelling customer touch point architecture. *Business Horizons*, 56(2), 199–205.

Groth, M., & Grandey, A. (2012). From bad to worse: Negative exchange spirals in employee–customer service interactions. *Organizational Psychology Review*, 2(3), 208–233.

Hart, C. W., Heskett, J. L., & Sasser, Jr. W. E. (1990). The profitable art of service recovery. *Harvard Business Review*, 68(4), 148–156.

Kandampully, J., & Butler, L. (2001). Service guarantees: A strategic mechanism to minimize customers' perceived risk in service organisations. *Quality: Managing Service an International Journal*, 11(2), 112–121.

Van Vaerenbergh, Y., & Orsingher, C. (2016). Service recovery: An integrative framework and research agenda. *Academy of Management Perspectives*, 30(3), 328–346.

Van Vaerenbergh, Y., Varga, D., De Keyser, A., & Orsingher, C. (2019). The service recovery journey: Conceptualization, integration, and directions for future research. *Journal of Service Research*, 22(2), 103–119.

Wu, C. H. J., Liao, H. C., Hung, K. P., & Ho, Y. H. (2012). Service guarantees in the hotel industry: Their effects on consumer risk and service quality perceptions. *International Journal of Hospitality Management*, 31(3), 757–763.

References

Bowen, D. E. (2016). The changing role of employees in service theory and practice: An interdisciplinary view. *Human Resource Management Review*, 26(1), 4–13.

Brownell, J. (2008). Building managers' skills to create listening environments. *Cornell hospitality tools*. Ithaca, NY: Cornell University Press and The Center for Hospitality Research, August.

Hogreve, J., & Gremler, D. (2009). Twenty years of service guarantee research. *Journal of Service Research*, 11(4), 322–343.

Kelley, S. W., Hoffman, D. K., & Davis, M. A. (1993). A typology of retail failures and recoveries. *Journal of Retailing*, 69(4), 429–452.

Voorhees, C. M., Brady, M. K., & Horowitz, D. M. (2006). A voice from the silent masses: An exploratory and comparative analysis of noncomplainers. *Journal of the Academy of Marketing Science*, 34(4), 514–527.

Chapter 8

Crafting a culture for service excellence

Study objectives

Having completed this chapter, readers should be able to:

- understand the important role of people in service organizations;
- recognize the value of human resource management and practices associated with it;
- understand the impact of internal service quality on external service quality and firm performance; and
- be familiar with the benefits of having committed and engaged employees.

The framework of this chapter

This chapter is set out as follows:

- Introduction
- Managing employees as customers
  - Employees are customers of top priority
  - Internal service to one another
  - Internal marketing
    - Compete for talent
    - Offer a vision
    - Prepare people to perform
- Human resource (or 'talent') management in service organizations
  - Important differences when managing service employees
- Important considerations for service employees
  - Emotional labor
  - Creating a service culture
  - Service climate
- Empowerment

DOI: 10.4324/9781003470373-9

- o The guiding philosophy of empowerment
- o Two essential dimensions of empowerment
  - The personal dimension
  - The organizational dimension
- o Benefits to management, employees, and customers
- Fueling firm performance
- o The service-profit chain
- o Internal service quality
- Summary of chapter
- Review questions
- Suggested readings
- References

Introduction

Chapter 7 concentrated on the distinctive nature of the service encounter and how managers can enhance the service interface with external customers. The chapter also introduced some approaches and strategies – namely, service recovery and guarantees – that leading service organizations employ successfully with the significant aid of frontline employees. We now move to concentrate on how the *internal management* of organizations is vitally important for achieving service excellence.

In the service sector, because employees create and render service to the customers, a firm's most important resource and core competency is its people. This has prompted leading organizations to regard their employees as 'internal customers', based on the understanding that, because employees determine the firm's success in the external marketplace, internal customer satisfaction is ultimately reflected in external customer satisfaction. Successful external marketing therefore starts with effective internal marketing.

This chapter discusses the topic of 'internal (or in-house) marketing' – a form of marketing especially suited to service industries – and outlines key strategies to overcome the fundamental challenges of managing human resources. Thus, much of the focus of this chapter has to do with workplace conditions, policies, and practices that are conducive to motivating workers to be service-oriented.

Ultimately, service managers and service organizations benefit from an awareness and understanding of the exceptional management of employees (referred to as human resources or talent). A service organization's workers, and how they are managed, can often determine the difference between success and failure in the market. We also introduce the concept of the service-profit chain, which draws a direct correlation between effective people management and firm performance.

Managing employees as customers

Employees are customers of top priority

The customers of first concern to a service firm must be its internal customers – its own employees. And the most important internal customers in this context are those who actually deliver the service to the external customers – the 'frontline' employees. This is because the service offered and received by internal customers invariably affects the service offered by the firm to its external customers.

Given the relationship between employee performance and the delivery of service quality, service-oriented organizations should treat frontline employees as individuals deserving treatment similar to that which management wants its external customers to receive. Similarly, service managers should adopt a philosophy of 'internal marketing', which means their primary task is to 'sell' the service concept to employees first, before attempting to sell it to external customers.

Internal service to one another

Within most service organizations, there are numerous departments and personnel performing various tasks, functions, and services – all of which are interdependent in the creation of the overall service experience. It is therefore essential that the various departments and personnel work collaboratively and cohesively to offer service commensurate with the customer's requirements.

As we touched on in Chapter 5, employees are both receivers and providers of service. In other words, everyone in a service firm *is* a customer and *has* customers. Essentially, this is the idea expressed by the concept of the 'internal customer' – it indicates the interdependency of every function within the organization.

The success of every service organization is thus dependent on collaboration between the internal customers (the employees) of every department. No service firm can give its external customers the quality they desire without the active participation of all of its employees, whether they are customer-facing or not. For example, it is difficult for a hotel receptionist to settle the accounts of a guest quickly if the accounting personnel have not entered charges in the customer's account in an appropriate fashion. Quality internal service and satisfied internal customers are essential if an organization is to establish an effective customer-oriented service culture. The founder of Marriott Hotels said it well: 'Take care of your employees, because if you take care of them, they'll take care of your customers, and the customers will keep coming back again and again'. This is a mantra that would suit nearly every organization well!

Internal marketing

In typical manufacturing contexts, marketing is devoted primarily to communicate and entice customers to purchase the products that the firm offers in the market. Therefore, 'sales' is often one of the primary functions of marketing in the product-focused industry. However, in a service context the primary focus of the firm is the customer, and therefore the appropriate 'use' or 'usability' of the service is important. For example, customers buy smartphones primarily to gain access to the mobile and/or Internet network. Therefore, it is the consistent use or usability of the network service that provides value to the customer. This means everyone within such a service organization who is responsible for rendering that network service to the customer assumes the most important role.

Hence, in service organizations, *the focus of marketing is very much on the service employees*, since they are the only people who can create and maintain external customers' trust in and loyalty to the organization. Some of the most successful companies such as Starbucks, Disney, and Southwest Airlines are well-known for recognizing their employees as their greatest assets. For example, at Southwest the common mantra is: 'Customers come second ... and still get great service'. When organizations associate value with their employees, those within the organization transform themselves into assets.

It is ultimately the service employees who have the opportunity, ability, and willingness to fulfill the service promise and should be empowered to provide customers with a superior experience. Employees, as internal customers, are thus critical to the success of service organizations because they can create and maintain trusting relationships between a service firm and its external customers. And these external relationships are largely dependent on satisfactory internal attitudes and relationships. It is indeed the internal customers who live the brand and reflect its core values to the external customers. Therefore, internal marketing recognizes the value of employees' contributions to the firm's success and aims to create a trustful relationship with them.

Many of the marketing processes applied to external relationships can be equally applied to internal relationships. The main aim of internal marketing must therefore be to ensure that employees share an understanding of the overall objectives of the organization and the service position that it seeks to adopt with regard to its *external customers*. The emphasis is thus on turning the well-honed communication techniques of marketing inward – such that they are directed toward the firms' employees (see Figure 8.1).

Internal marketing ensures that all employees at all levels of the organization understand and experience the business activities that support a customer-oriented approach, and ensures that all employees are motivated to act in a service-oriented manner. But these things do not happen without managerial planning and deliberate commitment. The concept of internal

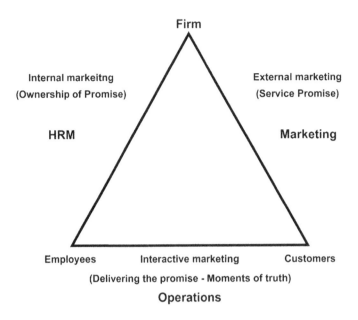

Figure 8.1 External, internal, and interactive marketing (Adapted and modified from Grönroos (2000))

marketing calls for ongoing, active engagement of employees, and redirects the focus of management to approach all activities in a strategic and systematic manner with a view to creating a customer-oriented service culture within the organization.

The overall objectives of internal marketing are thus twofold:

- to ensure that the employees are motivated toward customer-oriented and service-minded performance, and thus toward fulfilling their roles as 'part-time marketers' during the service encounter and
- to attract and retain service-minded employees.

To enhance the effectiveness of internal marketing in an organization, Berry (1995) proposed that the firms should:

- compete for talent;
- offer a vision; and
- prepare people to perform.

Each of these is considered below.

Compete for talent

Hiring the best possible people to perform the service is a key factor in the success of service firms. One of the principal causes of poor service quality is hiring the wrong people. Many firms fail to think and act like marketers when it comes to human resource issues.

Marketing is used by most firms to compete only for growing revenue. That is, they compete for customer market share in seeking revenue growth, but they do not compete for *talent* market share in attracting talented employees to build greater service capability. The service firms that turn their marketing powers to the labor market will fare best in the 'talent wars' that are pervasive across the globe now and are only likely to continue.

Offer a vision

A salary might keep a person on the job physically, but it will not keep a person on the job emotionally. Great companies stand for something worthwhile, and they communicate this vision to employees with passion. The key is to make employees believe in the value and meaningfulness of their work, which in turn makes them feel dignified.

The contribution that each employee makes to the satisfaction of external customers must be emphasized and re-emphasized. Employees work better when they understand the value of their contribution. The personal involvement of senior managers in such a vision is essential to preserving the company's culture.

Prepare people to perform

Service managers need to attract, develop, motivate, and retain service-minded employees. Learning should be an ongoing process, not a one-off event. Learning is a confidence builder, a motivating force, and a source of self-esteem. Better teachers should be promoted into middle management, and frontline service courses should first be offered to such middle managers, who can then pass this training on to frontline employees.

A key element of preparing employees to perform is also arming them with the necessary information to make customer-focused decisions and not have to ask permission to do so! This is an important management strategy and philosophy referred to as *empowerment*. Remember that Chapter 7 introduced the interrelationship among the strategies of service failure, recovery, and guarantees – and the vital importance of empowered employees to make this management approach successful (empowerment is covered in more detail later in this chapter).

Human resource (or 'talent') management in service organizations

Human resource management (or 'HRM') is concerned with the design of formal systems and continual proactive measures to ensure the effective and efficient use of a firm's people to accomplish organizational goals. Great service organizations pay very close attention to their human 'assets', leaving little to chance. The main activities of HR managers include sourcing, maintaining, and developing employees, which are often viewed as a 'bundle' of activities designed to enhance organizational performance.

Leading service organizations take a notably strategic approach to HRM, where employees are seen as valuable assets in the firm to be 'invited in' and 'developed' rather than 'hired' and 'trained'. Most successful firms compete in the market to attract talented employees ('compete for talent') in the same way they compete to attract customers. In many firms today, the HRM function is now seen as part of the 'executive team', with the senior HR manager sitting at the boardroom table and involved in major decisions. Many companies have also changed the title of the HR manager to reflect this more strategic and important role of managing people in the organization – for example, Chief Talent Officer, Talent Director, Employee Experience Manager, or People and Culture Manager. These new titles are vital as they convey the importance of the firm's human resources to organizational success, rather than using the HR function as an administrative process. This is an important distinction to consider as we proceed through this chapter.

It should also be noted that this chapter does not attempt to present a comprehensive or technical review of the 'principles' of HRM, but rather a summary of some of the critical concepts and measures that are vital to successful service organizations.

Important differences when managing service employees

Although much of the literature regarding HRM does not delineate service organizations from non-service organizations, there are some important differences when managing service employees. Bowen and Ford (2002) offer the following five reasons for these differences (many of which are covered in various sections of this book):

- *Co-production.* Because many service employee tasks include customer interactions, the employees must not only produce the service but also engage with it and involve customers in the process of service delivery through establishing trustworthy rapport and relationships with customers. This allows the employee to better understand the customers' wants and needs and to turn merely satisfied customers into loyal ambassadors.
- *Hiring for attitude.* The second difference is that employee selection and recruitment must focus on customer relationship skills. While

manufacturing organizations hire for technical skills and qualifications, service organizations hire for attitude first and can train for skills. Therefore, service organizations must place more emphasis on personality, energy, and attitude than on education, training, and experience.
- *Managing employee actions.* It is very difficult to manage every action an employee makes in a service organization. Rather, organizational norms and values are needed to guide behavior. A number of strategies are available to assist with managing the service employee, including the creation of a service culture and a service climate (discussed later in this chapter), which engenders an organizational-wide 'passion for service'.
- *Emotional labor.* The concept of emotional labor (see following section) relates to the management of emotions to create observable facial and body displays to produce the intended impressions in the minds of others. The required emotions for different service positions can vary. For example, a fast-food cashier would have a different requirement from a funeral director or a loan manager. The point is that service employees have to exert labor beyond just physical and mental labor.
- *Part-time marketers.* As discussed in Chapter 2, service employees are expected to perform a marketing function. Because they co-produce the service experience, employees are often expected to explain details about new products and services, and to attempt to get customers enthusiastic about the company and its offerings.

Important considerations for service employees

Emotional labor

The term *'emotional labor'* was coined by Hochschild (1983) to describe the work service employees perform that goes beyond their physical or mental duties and is when an employee is required to demonstrate an emotion such as care, enjoyment, concern, and happiness. We learned earlier (see Chapter 4) that customer perceptions of service quality rely on a number of important factors, including empathy (i.e., showing that you genuinely seem to care). Thus, service employees must frequently present demonstrative behaviors, like making eye contact, smiling, and showing genuine concern for customers' needs.

Emotional labor typically is difficult to manage, drawing as it does on frontline employees' feelings. Part of the challenge of emotional labor is that employees must often conceal their real emotions and they are expected to 'act' in a positive and welcoming way regardless of how the customer might be interacting with them.

Emotional dissonance occurs when an employee is asked to display a set of emotions that conflict with their current real feeling. For example, an employee coming to work feeling tired or in a bad mood has to then 'switch over' and become the warm, gracious, service-oriented host, with a genuine smile. This is not easy! Yet it is a requirement for service staff to come to work with their 'game faces' on.

Another critical consideration for managers is ensuring that employees feel that their organization is trustworthy. Many studies have highlighted the importance of trust in fostering positive work outcomes for individuals and organizations. In this context, trust is the belief that the employer is truthful, fair, has good intentions, and is predictable. For example, do employees feel that the firm really cares about their well-being? Or do they just say the right things to try to appear to be caring? Are HR practices perceived to be there to support the worker just as much as the organization?

Studies have shown that when employees attribute HR practices as an organizational benefit, job engagement and commitment will decrease, leading to lower levels of care and emotional labor, which in turn can impact service delivery. Trust can be a strong leverage point to improve the relationship with frontline employees. This makes sense if you think about it – if you trust your supervisor and your organization, you are surely more likely to try a bit harder, give a bit more effort, and strive to exceed customer expectations. So, service organizations must consider trust as a vital element in the way they build connections with employees.

Turning to key concepts to further an awareness of the internal organizational environment required to foster service excellence, the study of *culture* and *climate* seeks to better understand how individuals behave, or are likely to behave, in a work setting.

Creating a service culture

Every organization, whether intended or not, has a culture of some kind. Culture, from an organizational point of view, is often defined as the values and norms embedded in an organization. An organizational culture, particularly in a service business, has the ability to fill the gaps between:

- what the organization can anticipate and train its people to deal with and
- the opportunities and problems that arise in daily encounters with customers.

Since managers cannot supervise every interaction that takes place between employees and customers, it is important for service organizations to develop a predominating norm of behavior that is customer-centric and focused on service quality. Such an approach minimizes the gaps which unforeseen circumstances might cause in service delivery and also works to motivate unsupervised employees.

Simply put, organizational culture is a set of shared assumptions that guide interpretation and action in organizations by defining appropriate behavior for various situations. Successful businesses have strong cultures, which give signals to employees about what is important to that organization. Following this logic, service organizations need to create and foster a strong *service culture* with a particular focus on customer satisfaction and outstanding service.

Edgar Schein (1990), one of the preeminent experts on organizational culture, suggests that there are three basic levels that refer to the degree to which culture is 'visible' in an organization, including:

1. *Artifacts and behaviors* are attributes that can be seen, felt, and heard (e.g., buildings, furnishings, visible awards and recognition, the way that employees dress, and the like);
2. *Espoused values* are the professed culture of an organization's members (e.g., company slogans, mission statements, and other operational creeds that are often expressed); and
3. *Shared assumptions* are the deepest level and represent those attitudes and beliefs that are embedded, often tacit, unconscious assumptions. These are the elements of culture that are unseen and not cognitively identified – in other words, the 'unspoken rules' that exist without the conscious knowledge of the membership or the essence of the organization (e.g., in service culture, the shared assumptions might include taking care of another human being, and being helpful, generous, and respectful with others).

The diagram below (see Figure 8.2) is a visual representation of organizational culture as described by Schein (1990) above. The size of each circle is representative of the level of managerial control over each element. In other words, service managers can easily affect the physical elements of a service environment and can, to some extent, influence the stories of success that circulate, whereas managers have limited direct access to the unconscious knowledge of the organization's employees.

A strong culture is said to exist where staff respond to stimuli because of their clear and nonambiguous alignment with organizational values. Strong cultures help firms operate like well-oiled machines that may require only minor tweaking of existing procedures here and there. Conversely, in a weak culture there is little alignment with organizational values, and control must be exercised through extensive procedures and bureaucracy. A strong culture is especially beneficial to firms operating in the service sector since employees are responsible for delivering a high-quality experience and often must be trusted to do the right thing even unsupervised.

Service firms with a strong culture enjoy many benefits, including:

- higher employee motivation, engagement, and loyalty;
- increased team cohesiveness among the company's various departments and divisions; and
- shaping employee behavior at work and enabling the organization to be more efficient.

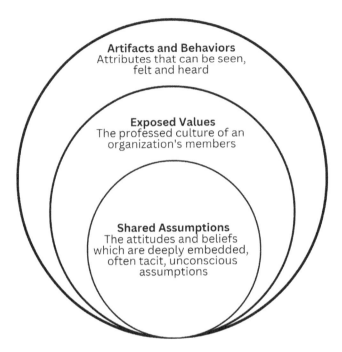

Figure 8.2 Levels of organizational culture (*authors' representation*)

Service climate

'Organizational climate', similar to culture, is defined as *employee perceptions* of the practices and procedures in the organization. It differs from culture in that it represents an assessment of how employees perceive various aspects of an organization, whereas culture represents the values and norms, and often the aspirations of management. Climate represents how well these aspirations are actually perceived by employees and those who come into contact with an organization. These aspirations are often communicated through artifacts, stories, and myths.

A *climate for service* represents the degree to which all of a firm's activities, policies, and practices are focused on *service quality*. Thus, a positive climate for service is said to exist when all of the aggregate conditions are present for excellent service to be provided to customers. Specifically, a positive service climate is likely to exist when employees perceive that they are rewarded for delivering quality service, when employees perceive that management devotes their time and energy to service quality, and when employees receive appropriate training.

Climate is usually measured by using a survey methodology. Many best-practice firms employ climate measures as part of their organizational learning process. With regular measures of an organizational climate, progressive-thinking companies use the results to improve employee perceptions, and then utilize improved employee perceptions as a key part of performance. Some of the questions that could be asked in a survey measuring service climate are listed below (adapted from Schneider (1998)):

1. Rate the job knowledge and skills of employees in your business to deliver superior quality service;
2. Rate efforts to measure and track the quality of service in your business;
3. Rate the recognition and rewards employees receive for the delivery of superior service;
4. Rate the overall quality of service provided by your business;
5. Rate the leadership shown by management in your business in supporting the service quality effort;
6. Rate the effectiveness of our communications efforts to both employees and customers; and
7. Rate the tools, technology, and other resources provided to employees to support the delivery of superior quality service.

It is always instructive and useful for service managers to ask these questions of their own organizations and how their own employees might answer them.

To ensure high service quality and customer loyalty, service businesses need to recognize the necessity of nurturing a service-oriented culture and climate. This also necessarily involves service managers inspiring, motivating, guiding, and supporting everyone around them. They must gain the trust and confidence of everyone and know how to encourage people to perform at their best. The following section examines in more detail the important concept of empowerment and why great service managers adopt a strategic HRM mindset that views the workforce as an appreciable asset requiring investment and ongoing attention, rather than just as a cost to be controlled.

Empowerment

In Chapter 7, we introduced *empowerment* as a complimentary strategy that supports effective service recovery and service guarantees, while also engendering a spirit of mutual trust between management and frontline employees. Successful managers understand the importance of a service workforce that is empowered to read situations, act as necessary in order to meet or exceed customer expectations, and also to address service failures on the spot so that appropriate service recovery can commence as soon as possible. Indeed, an empowered workforce is vital and a frequently found phenomenon in the world's great service organizations.

The traditional structures and work arrangements of many organizations can engender a feeling of disempowerment. In the past, the rigid policies, structures, and systems in many organizations have often presented barriers to individual talent and imagination. Service organizations that wish to instill a culture of empowerment must evolve systems and procedures, so as not to restrict employees and thus enable the organization to reap the full potential of its human resources. The concept of empowerment allows employees to utilize their personal resources in the workplace – to the benefit of employees, customers, and the organization (50%).

The guiding philosophy of empowerment

The guiding philosophy of empowerment is non-bureaucratic and worker-oriented. Empowerment fosters an environment of commitment and ownership, an environment in which employees utilize the information that they glean from their daily interactions with customers to improve services and contribute to management's understanding of customer requirements. Empowerment also provides employees with a sense of control that contributes to job satisfaction. Indeed, the management philosophy of empowerment has been found to have a direct effect on organizational performance, with positive results in such variables as cost and productivity, quality, speed in responding to customer requests, innovation, and employee morale.

The empowerment of service employees is also considered to be one of the best options available to service managers when dealing with the problems of customer complaints and operational bottlenecks. Employees who perceive that they have the right and the responsibility to solve problems themselves are more effective in handling all manner of day-to-day service difficulties.

Many leading service organizations – such as Tata Tele Business Services, outlined in the example below – utilize this philosophy successfully, seeking ways to encourage and reward their employees for exercising initiative in their day-to-day work. Such empowerment produces a state of mind (engendered by structures, practices, and policies) which assists employees to respond immediately and effectively to customers' difficulties.

Superior service does not result from employees undertaking systemized tasks according to set procedures with management adopting a training role. Rather, excellence in service comes from employees showing initiative in a trusting work environment in which management assumes a supporting role. Management must therefore ensure that it establishes appropriate strategies and systems whereby employees will be able to exercise trust.

Goal and strategy of empowerment

The goal of empowerment is, ultimately, to empower employees confidently and capably to address unique problems and opportunities as they occur.

This involves a company's commitment to:

- customizing and personalizing services;
- forming long-term relationships with customers;
- serving the unpredictable and nonroutine needs of customers;
- encouraging employees to make spontaneous decisions to assist customers; and
- seeking and retaining employees who have high aspirations, strong interpersonal skills, and a demonstrated ability to be intrinsically driven, passionate, and self-managed.

The 'Three Es' at Tata Tele Business Services: Employee Engagement, Empowerment, and Eudaimonia

By Dr. Rajneesh Choubisa, Birla Institute of Technology & Sciences

Tata Tele Business Services (TTBS) is a digital transformation enabler that belongs to the prestigious Tata Group, which has its headquarters in Mumbai, India. With services ranging from connectivity, collaboration, cloud, security, Internet of Things (IoT), and marketing solutions, TTBS offers the largest portfolio of ICT services for businesses in India. The brand has operations in over 60 cities with 1,200+ employees and 1,400+ partners and is thus well-positioned to cater to businesses of all sizes. Furthermore, a laser focus on its employees, customer centricity, and innovation has helped TTBS attract positive accolades and recognition.

TTBS provides an excellent work environment for its employees, which is grounded in the Tata Group's work ethic and code of conduct. The majority of TTBS employees enjoy this work culture, believe in the company's values and ethics, and have established a trusting relationship with their employer. Hence, employees consider TTBS as a favorable place to work, and feel empowered and engaged, because the company takes good care of them and their families. Some of the privileges that TTBS provides for their employees include medical insurance, flexi pay, on-time salary, and ethical rewards and recognition, to name a few. Additionally, the company has made the biometric attendance system voluntary, which saves staff the stress of having to punch the machine daily while demonstrating the two-way nature of trust between employer and employee. These benefits and strategies further enhance employees' commitment, loyalty, and happiness.

From a diversity and inclusion perspective, the company takes extra care of its physically challenged employees by providing wheelchair-enabled ramps, parking bays, tactile sensors, and voice synthesizers in the elevators. This allows disabled employees to adapt to their roles and

> give their best, while also helping to further empower and engage them. As a result, there is a general feeling of positivity among employees and an intention to maintain a long-term relationship with the company.
>
> As modern eudemonic philosophy suggests, a happy worker is a productive worker; thus, TTBS's employee-friendly and empowering approach has resulted in engaged and loyal workers who also keep their customers satisfied. In other words, the services and privileges enjoyed by the employees motivate them to work optimally and provide the best service to their customers. Therefore, TTBS is a prime example of how fostering employee engagement, empowerment, and well-being results in a culture of service excellence.

Two essential dimensions of empowerment

There are two essential dimensions of empowerment that are important in any organization:

- the personal dimension and
- the organizational dimension.

Each of these is discussed further below.

The personal dimension

The personal dimension relates to the enrichment of employees by providing appropriate knowledge and skills to prepare them to take up responsibility and act on behalf of the organization. The task of a service manager thus becomes that of a true leader – that is, someone who encourages and rewards employees for their initiatives, while tolerating their mistakes when well-intended efforts fail.

Empowerment enhances the personal well-being of employees because they feel trusted, and because they believe that their opinions matter. But personal empowerment has wider implications beyond that of personal satisfaction for the employee. Positive employee attitudes not only improve customer satisfaction but also substantially reduce employee turnover.

The organizational dimension

The second dimension, the organizational dimension, refers to the creation of an appropriate environment by removing barriers (that is, structures, systems, and policies) that prevent employees' creative self-expression. Empowerment becomes really effective if an organization's people, processes, and systems are designed to take on customer-oriented flexibility. That is, systems and processes in an organization should be designed to assist its people to serve customers better and should be flexible enough to adapt as required in accordance with the needs of the customer.

To be effective, empowerment should thus span across all functions and activities of the organization. It is a holistic concept that fosters a learning climate and a culture of knowledge-sharing in which individuals are encouraged to use initiative and judgment in providing superior personal service to customers.

Benefits to management, employees, and customers

Employee empowerment is an important HRM practice which, when combined with a strong service culture and service climate, can create a competitive advantage that is hard to replicate. An empowerment strategy provides benefits to management, employees, and customers.

For instance, the benefits of empowerment to *service managers* include:

- better relationships with employees and customers;
- increased number of loyal customers;
- reduction in costs and employee turnover;
- increased productivity;
- increased market share, sales, and profitability;
- opportunities for growth; and
- ultimately results in a competitive advantage.

Employees benefit from a strategy of empowerment by experiencing:

- increased self-esteem and confidence, when given the authority to decide;
- increased job satisfaction in an informal and friendly environment;
- a sense of ownership;
- increased motivation;
- personal autonomy in daily tasks;
- prevention of burnout;
- receiving management support, as opposed to management control; and
- the 'feel-good factor' of resolving customers' problems.

And finally, *external customers* benefit from empowerment in the following ways:

- their needs are readily satisfied;
- feeling valued and important when personal attention is given;
- receiving more than what is expected;
- a good relationship with the organization;

178 Crafting a culture for service excellence

- interacting with approachable employees;
- alleviation of stress and frustration in the long term; and
- reduced time delay.

Fueling firm performance

While sound people management practices in service organizations are indeed common sense, proactive and positive HRM strategies are supported by a strong conceptual argument and empirical evidence. The next section introduces a number of conceptual frameworks that help explain the important connection between creating positive employee attitudes and important organizational outcomes such as customer satisfaction, customer loyalty, and increased revenues and profit.

The service-profit chain

The service-profit chain is a frequently cited conceptual framework developed in the mid-1990s after many years of research and observation of the practices of successful service organizations. The authors (Heskett, 1997) found that a chain of related organizational occurrences existed, effectively linking the internal functioning of an organization ('internal' service, or the way employees feel) to employee loyalty and productivity, service value, customer satisfaction, and finally to revenue growth and profitability.

The service-profit chain (see Figure 8.3) proposes the following vital connections in a successful service organization:

1. profitability and revenue growth are caused primarily by customer loyalty;
2. customer loyalty comes from consistently satisfied customers;
3. satisfied customers are those who perceive value in purchasing from a firm;
4. value is created by satisfied, committed, and productive employees; and
5. satisfied and productive employees are created by sound internal organizational practices (internal service quality).

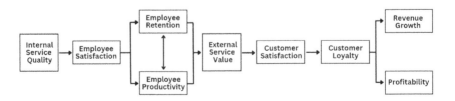

Figure 8.3 The service-profit chain (Adapted from Heskett & Sasser (2010))

The service-profit chain proposes that successful service firms place predominant effort inside the organization – creating the right workplace conditions to engender caring, committed, and engaged workers – rather than focusing directly on revenues and profits. This is not to say that service firms should not focus on the rest of the chain. Rather, successful service firms realize that many of the aspects of this chain are caused by a chain reaction, all starting with the way they manage the firm's human resources.

Service managers must thus strive to create a positive internal service environment to maximize the flow-on effects of the service-profit chain. Without strong leadership and support from service managers, the first link in the chain becomes weak, which in turn affects the rest of the elements.

More recent progressions from the original premise of the service-profit chain regarding employee and customer satisfaction include employee and customer commitment, engagement, and even 'ownership' as more effective predictors of profitability and organizational success. Despite these additional factors, management interventions aimed at profit and revenue growth must still begin internally with actions aimed at creating the most effective workplace conditions for service employees. There have been many studies on this topic with a range of results but generally aligned with the positive connections conveyed in the service-profit chain.

Internal service quality

The service-profit chain focuses firm attention on the quality of internal service that is given and received. *Internal service quality* is seen as the 'spark' that sets off a chain reaction, eventually creating increased revenue and profitability. It is viewed as a multidisciplinary concept drawing from marketing, operations, HRM, and management, with a shared belief that in organizations where service quality is important, meeting the needs of those who service the customers ('internal customers' or employees) is vital. Research suggests that internal service quality consists of a combination of (depending on context and service type) tools, policies and procedures, teamwork, management support, goal alignment, training, communication, and rewards and recognition (Hallowell et al., 1996).

Another aspect of perceived internal service is the way in which a firm cares for the well-being of its staff. Employees who feel that their employer cares for them tend to go the extra mile. *Fortune Magazine* offers one of the more accepted lists of 'great places to work' in their 'Hundred Best Companies to Work For' list each year (Great Place to Work Institute, 2014). From that list you can study various practices which companies use to attract, retain, and motivate employees. The example below of Haidilao also shows how a firm can achieve success and customer loyalty by, first and foremost, taking an interest in their employees' well-being.

Employee-centricity in Action: A Tale of Dignity, Respect, and Happiness

By Dr. Bin Wang (Peter), Dalian University of
Foreign Languages, China

Haidilao, one of the most successful hotpot restaurant chains in China, has over 1,597 outlets in over 20 countries (as of 2021). It started as a street food stall and has since developed into a popular restaurant group with operations across the globe.

Haidilao is reputed for its superior service and has won many service awards including the prestigious 'China Top 10 Best Service Company' and 'China's Most Innovative Service Practices Award'. Among many other factors that led to its success, building dignity, self-respect, and happiness for its employees is one of Haidilao's differentiating strategies that motivates its employees to deliver superior service to customers. 'Many of our employees are young, not well educated, and are from less well-off families. We treat them with dignity and respect them for who they are', says Haidilao CEO, Mr. Yong Zhang. The company's core philosophy of 'Treating employees as equals' has transformed Haidilao into a market leader and enabled the firm to uphold its service promise of 'Putting customers first and providing them with the best service'.

People in the foodservice industry are historically not valued in many countries and China is no exception. Migrant workers from rural areas who work in restaurants are less respected. The frequent frustrations and setbacks in building a life in cities have damaged their confidence and self-esteem. Haidilao endeavors to elevate employees' self-respect by treating them as rightful, equal urban citizens, and invariably, employees demonstrate their gratitude to the firm by delivering superior service.

To help employees feel a sense of belonging and to enhance their self-esteem, Haidilao provides its employees who are new to the city with fully furnished apartments and offers highly competitive salaries (over 20% higher than peer companies). Since many employees migrate to the cities to take up jobs at Haidilao and hence have to leave their families behind in remote rural villages, the company also provides assistance in the form of schooling for employees' children, medical support for family members, and even employment of relatives in the same establishment. All these efforts have greatly enhanced employees' commitment to Haidilao and to its customers, and allow employees to focus on providing superior service rather than being worried about their family's welfare.

Furthermore, Haidilao believes that job security and career growth boost employee self-esteem and happiness. The company values devotion and diligence, and promotes employees based on performance regardless of education, age, or gender. Haidilao also helps each person chart their career paths and develops employees" skills by sending them to 'Haidilao College' or to other educational institutions.

As a result of the firm's care, Haidilao employees have initiated many different service offerings to customers, which have provided a unique competitive advantage. Haidilao encourages such creativity each month by awarding 'golden points' to employees whose ideas are implemented throughout the firm. Employees thus feel truly empowered and committed to seeking out ways to improve their service to maintain their firm's leadership position in the market.

Haidilao is therefore a prime example of the service mantra; when you take care of your employees, your employees will take care of your customers. Just as the CEO of Haidilao said, 'Our success lies in our employees'.

Summary of chapter

Due to the highly competitive nature of today's marketplace, service organizations must seek all available points of differentiation possible. An organization's human resources represent a remarkable asset and can provide a company with a unique competitive advantage that cannot be copied by other firms. Given the nature of the service industry, service delivery and overall company performance is highly dependent on people. Therefore, service managers should invest in attracting talented employees that are ideally suited for service firms and then invest their time, resources, and effort to nurture, empower, and motivate customer-oriented employees to create trustful relationships with customers and the firm.

This chapter introduced a series of interrelated issues on people in service organizations and stressed the benefits of nurturing a service culture, service climate, and employee empowerment. The service-profit chain was introduced as a conceptual framework to understand the links between service employees (and how they feel cared for and important) with customer satisfaction and firm performance.

Emotional labor was also introduced as an important type of labor that service employees must perform, and that organizations must provide the right environment and HR practices to facilitate high levels of emotional labor from the workforce. Providing a trusting workplace where employees genuinely believe the organization cares about them and acts with integrity is another element covered in this chapter and vital for service organizational success.

Review questions

1. Why are service employees so critical to service marketing (and get to be called 'part-time marketers')?
2. Briefly describe the notion of 'internal customers'. How do internal customers affect a firm's marketing endeavors?
3. What is a service climate and how can service managers work to create this kind of climate?
4. Why is it so important that service employees trust their organizations and their motivations?
5. Explain the key ideas underpinning the service-profit chain and why this is particularly relevant for service organizations.

Suggested readings

Bowen, D. E. (1986). Managing customers as human resources in service organizations. *Human Resource Management*, 25(3), 371–383.

Heskett, J. L., Jones, T. O., Loveman, G. W., Sasser, Jr. W. E., & Schlesinger, L. A. (2008). Putting the service-profit chain to work. *Harvard Business Review*, 86(7–8), 118.

Solnet, D., Subramony, M., Ford, R. C., Golubovskaya, M., Kang, H. J. A., & Hancer, M. (2019). Leveraging human touch in service interactions: Lessons from hospitality. *International Journal of Service Industry Management*, 30(3), 392–409.

Subramony, M., Groth, M., Hu, X. J., & Wu, Y. (2021). Four decades of frontline service employee research: An integrative bibliometric review. *Journal of Service Research*, 24(2), 230–248.

Wirtz, J., & Jerger, C. (2016). Managing service employees: Literature review, expert opinions, and research directions. *The Service Industries Journal*, 36(15–16), 757–788.

References

Berry, L. L. (1995). *On great service: A framework for action*. New York, NY: Free Press.

Bowen, J., & Ford, R. C. (2002). Managing service organizations: Does having a "thing" make a difference? *Journal of Management*, 28(3), 447–469.

Great Place to Work Institute. (2014). Celebrating great workplace cultures: 2014 fortune's 100 best companies to work for. *Great Place to Work*. Retrieved from http://www.greatplacetowork.com/best-companies/100-best-companies-to-work-for

Grönroos, C. (2000). *Service management and marketing: A customer relationship management approach* (2nd ed.). West Sussex: John Wiley and Sons, Ltd.

Haidilao. (2022). *About Haidilao*. Retrieved from https://haidilao.com.cn

Hallowell, R., Schlesinger, L., & Zornitsky, J. (1996). Internal service quality, customer and job satisfaction: Linkages and implications for management. *Human Resource Planning*, 19(2), 20–32.

Heskett, J. L., & Sasser, Jr. W. E. (2010). The service profit chain. In P. P. Maglio, C. A. Kieliszewski, & J. C. Spohrer (Eds.), *Handbook of service science* (pp. 19–29). Springer.

Heskett, J. L., Sasser, Jr. W. E., & Schlesinger, L. A. (1997). *The service-profit chain*. New York, NY: Free Press.

Hochschild, A. (1983). *The managed heart*. Berkeley and Los Angeles, CA: University of California Press.

Schein, E. (1990). Organizational culture. *American Psychologist, 45*, 109–118.

Schneider, B., & White, S. (2004). *Service quality research perspectives*. Thousand Oaks, CA: Sage.

Schneider, B., White, S., & Paul, M. (1998). Linking service climate and customer perceptions of service quality: Test of a causal model. *Journal of Applied Psychology, 83*(2), 150–163.

Yu, K. (2020). The formative mechanism of brand ambassadors from the new-generation migrant workers: A case study of Haidilao. *Jiangxi Social Science, 6*, 205–215.

Chapter 9

Leveraging technology

Study objectives

Having completed this chapter, readers should be able to understand:

- how technology has redefined the service ecosystem and experience;
- the transformative role of technology in service marketing;
- the potential benefits technology brings to various aspects of service organizations; and
- the importance of leveraging technology to enhance the customer experience.

The framework of this chapter

This chapter is set out as follows:

- Introduction
- The growth of technology
- A new service ecosystem
  - 'High-touch' and 'high-tech'
  - The 'three realms' of service (servicescape)
  - Expectations of customers
  - The rise in popularity of online platforms
  - A new form of exchange
- Service marketing in the digital age
  - Digital marketing touchpoints
  - Utilizing data to enhance customer engagement
  - Utilizing data to empower employees
- Applications of technology in a service context
  - Key technological advancements
  - The roles of technology
  - The changing roles of customers and employees
  - Implications for the way organizations manage their frontline service

- Summary of chapter
- Review questions
- Suggested readings
- References

Introduction

The context in which service organizations operate today is fast-moving, global, and interconnected – largely due to rapid advancements in technology. There is a whole new set of rules around how customers and organizations connect and interact. The increasing awareness and expectations of customers for experience-oriented outcomes can also be attributed in part to how technology has lowered the barriers between organizations and customers – and between customers – all of whom can now communicate and transact instantaneously. Understanding this new service ecosystem and the role that technology plays in combination with people (both customers and employees) will be the key to achieving a competitive advantage.

Traditionally, technology has been viewed as primarily useful for productivity enhancements, particularly in manufacturing industries. Today, however, technology is used by firms to develop new service offerings and evolve ways of operating to add value to the customer experience.

There are numerous ways in which technology has revolutionized service organizations, including:

- enhancing service quality and convenience;
- improving accessibility and information;
- supporting service recovery;
- improving efficiency and productivity;
- augmenting the quality–value–loyalty chain;
- improving the skills of management and staff; and
- encouraging customer feedback.

Increased and ever-evolving technology has had a more profound effect on service in recent years than any other single external factor. Evolutions in technology have transformed service encounters (touchpoints), thus requiring managers and marketers to have updated perspectives on what used to be an exchange between persons. The 'Service Encounter 2.0' is characterized by changes in the roles and interdependencies between employees, customers, and technology. Interactions between human and nonhuman entities range from simple dyadic to complex multi-actor processes that occur through a variety of interfaces (see Figure 9.1). These facets offer additional complex implications for managing and marketing in service organizations.

186 Leveraging technology

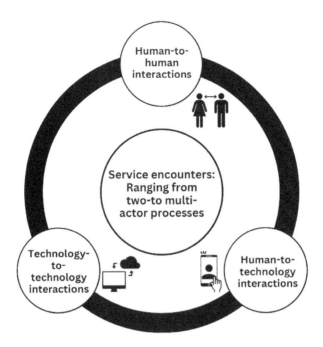

Figure 9.1 Different types of service encounters (*authors' representation*)

As a functional tool that can traverse departments, technology can also help to break-down organizational silos and enhance employees' ability to offer superior service and experiences to customers. For example, customer experience platforms such as Medallia are implemented across firms with data being used in many different ways. A large integrated resort company, for instance, may have customer experience feedback system kiosks installed throughout the hotel property that can provide nearly instant feedback about customer satisfaction across different parts of the customer journey (e.g., gaming floor, food, and beverage) and even about perceptions of certain marketing promotions and advertisements. This live information can be used by service managers to make instant decisions, changes, or even to counsel or praise employees.

When applied in a *holistic* way, technology can deliver improved results for both organizations and customers. There are numerous examples of leading service organizations that have creatively deployed technology to gain a competitive edge. One of the conclusions to be drawn from these examples is that technology does not, in itself, provide an advantage over competitors. Rather, it is the *innovative application* of technology, in conjunction with a firm's strategies focused on service orientation and human resources, which characterizes winning approaches.

An influential scholar in service management once remarked that, 'the service revolution and the information revolution are two sides of the same coin' (Rust, 2004, p. 24). In other words, these topics are inextricably interconnected, such that we cannot study one without an inherent understanding of the other. Further, the complexity of service today is that it occurs at many levels. Scholars argue that customer experience involves service and interactions across the physical, digital, and social realms (see, for example, Bolton et al., 2018), which are further explained below. Ultimately, service managers and marketers must keep abreast of technological advancements and proactively leverage relevant technologies to achieve and maintain market leadership in the future.

The growth of technology

The twenty-first century has seen exponential growth in the application of new technology to almost every aspect of businesses, alongside a rapid increase in the number of online customers and service providers representing both business-to-business ('B2B') and business-to-consumer ('B2C') services. The online marketplace is now valued in the trillions of dollars, and any estimate of the number of online users is likely to be outdated as soon as it is made. Hence, businesses without a presence on the Internet will lose vital opportunities and jeopardize their market position.

The World Economic Forum suggests that we have entered a 'Fourth Industrial Revolution' characterized by the mass adoption of digital technologies and innovations in every sector. This revolution follows other transformative periods in the development of the world: the first industrial revolution was mobilized through water and steam-powered devices, the second through electric powered mass production, and the third through electronics and information technology powered automation. While we may still be in the early stages of this age of digital transformation (DX), the effects are already evident, with just over half of Fortune 500 companies disappearing due to new digital business models since 2000.

Despite these trends, there are barriers to the adoption of new technologies and digital literacy in organizations today. It is estimated that less than 5% of businesses are 'digitally mature', with common reasons for most firms lagging being cost pressures and difficulties in keeping pace with an ever-changing technology landscape.

In service contexts, there is a range of technological advancements that have disrupted the way firms operate and engage with their customers and suppliers – such as artificial intelligence (AI), robotics, and virtual reality (VR) – which will be touched on later in this chapter. What is important to note at this stage is that while DX may be occurring at a frenetic pace, it is essential that service managers and marketers embrace this reality in order to remain competitive.

A new service ecosystem

In an increasingly hybrid world, technological and digital interfaces are no longer just a 'nice to have' in service contexts. Firms striving to compete in the twenty-first century are viewing the integration of technology into the service encounter as a strategic imperative.

Leading businesses are recognizing the value of digital technologies to provide highly personalized and immersive contexts that allow customers to co-create value and interact with the organization in a meaningful way. In turn, digital technologies have impacted customers' expectations and behaviors, as well as the role of 'humans' in service firms. This last point is important, and the changes associated with technology integration are further discussed below.

'High-touch' and 'high-tech'

As mentioned above, the rapid growth of technology has fundamentally altered the way service firms and customers interact. Technology is playing an increasingly important role in customer-centric service firms – to identify, communicate with, and evaluate customers and their needs. The service industry has been transformed from a traditional 'hands-on, low-tech' context into one that combines 'high-touch' and 'high-tech' – providing benefits to customers, employees, and firms. It is nearly impossible to think of a service firm today that does not rely on technology to either offer customers greater convenience (e.g., food ordering kiosks rather than cashiers and mobile platforms for your favorite food delivery) or as a way to enhance efficiencies (e.g., through online accounting and dynamic pricing apps and programs).

The service interface that customers interact with is now a complex, multidimensional system – encompassing people (i.e., employees and other customers), the physical servicescape, and technology. Importantly, the service interface is becoming technology-dominant (rather than human-driven), and this trend is only expected to continue as companies seek to engage with customers who are becoming ever more technologically savvy.

Despite this shift, customer-centric firms understand that there is a delicate balance to strike between human and digital service interfaces. For instance, banks have made significant investments in IT to automate and standardize numerous transactions, yet many are now finding that by doing so they have unknowingly created distance from customers and lost human interaction and trust, making banking merely transactional. ING Direct, a Dutch multinational banking and financial services corporation, identified this challenge and set up 'cafes' where customers could visit a physical space to have a coffee while interacting with staff and learning more about the company's offers.

Hence, service managers should remember that the personal touch will always be basic to quality service, but modern technology, deployed strategically, can make that personal touch all the more effective. In support of the growing nature of technology in service organizations, one of the authors of this book developed a model that offered a roadmap to how human touch could be leveraged depending on the type of service and the expectations of customers, highlighting the many variables that must be taken into account to determine the degree to which human touch is considered necessary or important (see Solnet et al., 2019).

The 'three realms' of service (servicescape)

As technology becomes increasingly infused in service contexts, managers' consideration of the 'servicescape' must broaden to encompass not only the physical elements but also the digital and social elements (see Figure 9.2). It is imperative for service managers to *integrate all three* realms to facilitate a better customer experience. For instance, in today's interconnected service contexts a customer might interact with a service robot in a physical setting, a mobile app, and a human all at the same time. Thus, the digital realm cannot be considered in isolation or separate from the social or physical realms – it is very much part of the *whole* servicescape and should be *blended seamlessly*.

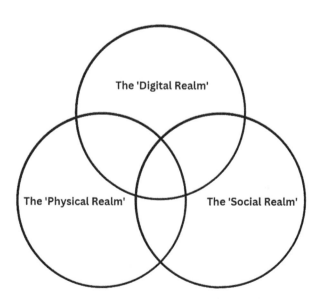

Figure 9.2 The 'three realms' of today's integrated servicescape (*authors' representation*)

Expectations of customers

As we know from previous chapters, customer perceptions and expectations are ever-changing – and technology has only magnified this! Customers today are becoming increasingly aware of new and emerging technologies, and understandably expect higher levels of service.

To take a simple example of a hotel or restaurant, customers know that online reservation systems are available and should work seamlessly. Thus, they are less likely to tolerate double-bookings, lost or forgotten bookings, and similar errors that might have been accepted in the past as 'human error'. While this may be a basic example, it illustrates the way in which technology has 'raised the bar' in terms of customer expectations.

Due to the application of machine learning and AI in many service contexts, customers have come to expect higher levels of personalization and intuition from service providers to better meet their needs. It has therefore become imperative for all firms to respond to these changes in customers' expectations and demands by seeking ways in which they can provide better value to their customers through the use of technology – within the physical, social, and digital realms. In addition, as competitors become more digitally savvy and employ new technologies to attract customers, even the most loyal customers become aware of what is available in the market and can be tempted to switch.

Similarly, firms' expectations of the role of customers have also evolved. The widespread use of technology and social media has led firms to view customers as 'co-owners' of their brand equity and, as such, expect them to be active co-producers of value. By adopting this perception, firms are more inclined to harness the creativity of customers – often through social media or some other technological channel – to uncover new ideas and innovations (see Chapter 10 for a more detailed discussion on how firms can foster co-innovation).

Technology thus presents significant challenges as well as opportunities for service managers and marketers wanting to engage and build valuable relationships with their customers.

The bar has been lifted

A recurrent theme of this book has been that firms today compete on the basis of *service*, and not so much on the basis of *physical products*. For example, there is often no apparent difference between the accommodation and other physical facilities provided by two international hotel chains. Rather, it is the *service* offered by a hotel that provides true value to the customer.

> The rapid advances in technology complicate this basic issue. Modern technology makes superior service easier to achieve, but it also makes it more expected. And customers who are otherwise loyal are very much aware of what is on offer elsewhere from competitors who advertise widely through online channels.
>
> The 'bar has been lifted' by modern technology, and successful service providers must rise to the challenge.

The rise in popularity of online platforms

Many firms today compete globally by using online platforms such as Amazon and eBay as key distribution channels – and while these firms often sell 'products', the process of ordering and delivery (in other words, the service and experience elements) is a critical part of the way their organization, product, or service is perceived by customers. Through these digital networks, firms are able to establish strategic alliances and partnerships that enhance value for both their customers and the organization.

Leveraging online platforms and strategic alliances can provide numerous benefits to service firms, including:

- enhancing service capabilities;
- reducing cost outputs; and
- maximizing personalization and customization, which enhances the customer experience and builds deeper relationships.

Online platforms (of various types as depicted in Figure 9.3) are growing in popularity as an effective way to compete on a global scale and reach significantly more customers. For example, the sharing economy platforms, such as Ola and MakeMyTrip, have experienced unprecedented demand in the past decade. These online businesses are able to better meet customers' needs by offering a heterogeneous range of services, assets, or resources to choose from. However, it is also worth noting that online platform business models have also created new challenges, such as potential friction that can arise for customers if the platform reaches a level of capacity that results in information or choice overload (i.e., high 'search costs').

Indeed, the increasing popularity of online platforms and the growth of the sharing economy have disrupted the service ecosystem and customers' consumption patterns, the impacts of which we are only just beginning to see.

192 Leveraging technology

Figure 9.3 Types of online platforms (*Adapted from Wirtz et al. (2019)*)

A new form of exchange

Alongside the growth of online platforms, 'collaborative consumption' has emerged as a new form of exchange in many markets. This term describes the way products or services are used or shared in exchange for a fee, yet there is no transfer of ownership. This exchange can take place locally or globally, and has been fueled by the widespread availability of the Internet, the popularity of mobile apps, and the increasing sophistication of analytics and AI.

In this context, the service encounter triad (a 'triadic exchange') consists of three core actors:

- *platform providers* – who play the key role of 'matchmaker' (e.g., Airbnb website linking customers to accommodation);
- *peer service providers* – who are both the 'customer contact employees' and 'brand ambassadors', acting as representatives of the platform and providing a valuable personal touch for customers (e.g., the Airbnb Host); and
- *customers* – who are the end users of the product or service (e.g., the individual or family who rents the Airbnb accommodation).

The main difference here, compared to the 'traditional' service triad, is that customers are being served by two different service providers. Furthermore, platform providers must consider two different customer groups – the peer service providers and the end users. This has implications for service managers and marketers alike.

It is worth remembering that technology alone is not a competitive differentiator, but rather it is the *actual service experience* (involving both technological and human resources) that creates the biggest impact on customer loyalty and brand equity. Hence, we now turn our attention to how service managers and marketers can utilize technology to create more personalized experiences, increase customer engagement, and support employees to better meet customers' needs.

Service marketing in the digital age

Advancements in technology have led to considerable changes in how service firms approach marketing, communication, and relationship building. Service marketers not only need to understand how to leverage new technologies to create value but also how customers' expectations and behaviors have changed as a result of digital disruption.

For instance, across the customer journey, during the *pre-purchase stage*, the Internet and application of CRM (customer relationship management) systems (or 'database marketing') have given service firms the ability to communicate with prospective customers all around the world. In turn, customers have significantly more information easily accessible at their fingertips when searching and evaluating alternatives.

During the *consumption stage* (the 'service encounter' or 'touchpoint'), digital technologies have accelerated the trend of customer-firm value co-creation and have created new 'experiencescapes' that can also elevate service offerings. For example, museums often have an audio feature for visitors that not only narrates the visit but also provides deeper levels of authenticity by using the voices of famous archaeologists talking about the experience they had in uncovering some kind of historical artifact, thereby enhancing the visitor experience.

Post-encounter, satisfaction and repurchase intentions may be higher if the application of technology has resulted in lower pricing and easier use of a service. Online reviews are also important during the post-consumption stage for building brand trust and can heavily influence other customers' adoption of a service. Thus, while service marketers have long recognized the value of positive word-of-mouth (WOM), digital technologies and social media have heightened its impact.

Ultimately, technology has provided new tools that firms can use to engage people (both customers and employees) in more meaningful relationships and enhance the co-creation of value. Some of the more important marketing implications of this digital revolution are discussed below.

Digital marketing touchpoints

The growth of technology has led to a dramatic increase in the number and type of communication channels, which means there are now many more 'touchpoints' between an organization and its customers. Think about your favorite restaurant, for example – your interactions with that business are no longer limited to simply visiting the physical space, since it is likely you can also visit their website, engage with their posts on social media, and order takeaway from them via a food delivery app. In this context, service managers and marketers thus need to ensure they are managing the *whole* experience and harnessing the power of digital to create customer delight and loyalty.

Research has shown that attention to 'small touches' regarding the following key areas has a significant influence on the overall customer experience:

- the ease of interacting with a service firm (e.g., taking the restaurant example above, your experience as a customer may be poorly impacted if you find their website is slow to load or hard to navigate);
- the consistency of the message across all communication channels (e.g., it would be confusing to find a different menu listed on the restaurant's website and social media pages);
- the provision of multiple channels to interact and shop (e.g., if you want to purchase take-away, you may be able to visit the physical restaurant, make a phone call, or place an order via an app); and
- the firm's responsiveness to customer needs (e.g., if your food delivery is incorrect and you make a complaint, the restaurant should have a service recovery strategy in place to resolve the failure).

The digital channels that service marketers have at their disposal include websites, blogs, social media, search engines, emails, text messages, mobile apps, podcasts, television, radio, and many more! To leverage these channels, new digital marketing strategies have also emerged, such as content marketing, search engine optimization (SEO), search engine marketing (SEM), social media marketing (SMM), and digital advertising or 'pay-per-click', to name a few.

While this list of marketing channels and strategies is by no means exhaustive, it gives you an idea of the complex and dynamic digital landscape that service marketers now have to navigate. The type of digital channel and strategy adopted will depend on each firm's unique context and target market; however, in most cases a multichannel approach will be taken whereby a mix of digital mediums and strategies will be used to reach the right customers, in the right place, at the right time.

It is not within the scope of this chapter to provide a detailed description of each of these digital marketing channels or strategies, but one area that deserves particular mention is social media, which is attracting growing attention from service researchers and practitioners alike. Social media is most popular among Generation Y customers and, across all industries, the majority of businesses are utilizing this channel to generate buzz around their brand. Platforms like Facebook and Instagram can be credited in part to driving demand for experiences, because people enjoy posting about these memorable moments and sharing them with their online network of friends and family. This trend has also led to the emergence of a new role for customers as paid 'influencers' – a relationship that formalizes firm-customer co-creation and elevates customers as brand ambassadors.

However, the exponential adoption of social media has meant that many firms struggle to keep up with the latest trends, and have to think about how to leverage this channel to create value, and how to best harness the vast amount of data and information available. Firms that measure success on social media by narrow metrics such as the number of 'likes' can miss the opportunity for meaningful relationship building or lose sight of a customer's *holistic experience with the brand*. What is useful for marketers to remember is that social media is meant to be social – in other words, success involves listening, collaborating, and interacting. Indeed, research has shown that social media does not directly impact a firm's performance, but rather plays the important role of customer engagement in the value creation process.

Overall, some of the key benefits of utilizing a range of digital marketing channels include:

- the potential for wide and targeted reach;
- cost-effective and flexible advertising;
- the ability to gain feedback and ideas from customers and employees (see Chapter 10 for a discussion on co-innovation);
- the opportunity to engage both customers and employees in new ways that develop deeper relationships and more loyal brand advocates; and
- the ability to collect, monitor, and optimize metrics that are important to gain insight into customers' needs, wants, and behaviors, which can be used to improve customer engagement and enhance value co-creation.

Utilizing data to enhance customer engagement

Almost every service organization today utilizes a form of database marketing or CRM system. These tools give service managers the ability to learn more about their customers and can be used to build customer loyalty and enhance engagement. Database marketing can thus provide a firm with a critical edge in customer service, while the strategic use of CRM systems has produced profitable marketing programs for many types of customer-focused businesses.

In its simplest form, database marketing involves collecting, storing, and analyzing information regarding the unique expectations and behaviors of individual customers. Customer records can then be sorted to produce useful information on target markets and ever-evolving customer trends. The case below of REDTAG highlights how firms can successfully utilize digital data to identify demographic patterns among their best customers, which in turn can build customer loyalty and reduce the cost of marketing by increasing its precision.

A key benefit of utilizing digital data is a better understanding of customers' behavior in order to personalize service and ultimately enhance customer experience. A key challenge, however, is the sheer volume and the need to accurately merge data regarding multichannel customers into a central system in order to capture a 'complete' picture of the customer. There are also ethical considerations (particularly regarding the use of neurophysiological tools, machine learning, and AI) and security concerns around the storage of personal information, which firms need to navigate. This topic is emerging and changing at a fast pace, and while it is outside the scope of this textbook, there are excellent ways to enhance your knowledge of this topic, and we encourage our readers to pursue this area more deeply (see, for example, Breidbach & Maglio, 2020).

> **Enhancing Customer Experience through Data-driven Decision-making: The Case of REDTAG**
>
> By Dr. Madhavi Ayyagari, Mindsbourg Consulting, Dubai, UAE
> Dr. Sanjai Parahoo, Hamdan Bin Mohammed Smart University, UAE
> Dr. Ravi Chatterjee, IMT Business School, Dubai, UAE
>
> REDTAG is a chain of value fashion and home stores operating in more than 160 locations across the Middle East and Africa. The company claims to be one of the first adopters of a loyalty program and currently operates one of the largest programs under a single brand in the region. Known as RT Rewards, REDTAG's loyalty program has been successful in attracting more than 11 million members to date and averaging 40,000 new registrations every week.
>
> An analysis of data from the loyalty program has helped the company to identify its customer segments, understand their buying behaviors, and hence be in a position to serve each segment better. In this regard, REDTAG identified six customer segments and developed targeted strategies for each one, as outlined in Table 1.
>
> REDTAG's data-driven approach to decision-making and customer experience has been embedded throughout its operations. For instance, using propensity modeling, the company analyzes customer purchase

data to identify the needs of each segment and tailor their approach accordingly. The company's content marketing strategy also ensures customers only receive specific promotional messages that are likely to be of relevance and value to them. This strategy helps to maintain customer attention and interest by reducing the clutter of mobile mass marketing used by competing fashion retailers. In addition, the most loyal customers of REDTAG are awarded special benefits like additional discounts and a preview of new collections before these are launched in the stores. This special recognition given to loyal customers makes them feel privileged and hence strengthens their brand loyalty.

Overall, data-driven decision-making and relationship marketing have enabled REDTAG to provide a positive customer experience, nurture long-term relationships, and ensure they receive tailored communications that add value. The success of this mutually beneficial loyalty program is evident in its strong membership base and the company's annual growth rate of 20 percent. For over a decade, REDTAG has established itself as a leader in value fashion and demonstrates how data and technology can be leveraged to enhance the customer experience.

Utilizing data to empower employees

While robust databases can be utilized to build stronger, more customized relationships with customers, such data can also be leveraged to empower employees. This is equally important for service managers and marketers to understand, since ultimately it is the frontline employees who provide a competitive differentiation and create the personal touchpoints and memorable experiences for customers (see Chapter 8).

CRM systems can support employees by assisting with the sharing of important information across different departments, thus enabling better and faster decision-making throughout the organization. For instance, a hotel reservations officer who interacts with a guest via a phone call can make a note about that guest's preferences on their digital profile, which can then be accessed by staff across the front office, food and beverage, and room service departments, all of whom can use that data to tailor the guest's experience while staying at the hotel. Hence, making customer data easily accessible (while ensuring it is securely and accurately stored!) enables frontline staff to better meet customers' unique needs and expectations or resolve a service failure without delay.

Digital data can also enable junior members of staff to assume responsibility for making on-the-spot decisions (without the need to consult senior management) based on a customer's profile in the system. Research suggests that allowing Generation Y and Z employees (who are generally digitally savvy) to use technologies and social media in carrying out their roles, can increase their productivity and motivation, which results in customers receiving better service (remember the service-profit chain!). Firms looking to harness the power of CRM systems thus need to ensure employees are encouraged and trained to access relevant data, and empowered to make use of this data in ways that add value to both customers and the organization.

Overall, data, in itself, is of no value. Rather, value comes from the insights gained from customer information collection and the translation of these insights into effective service strategies. When applied well, CRM systems can foster an environment characterized by access to knowledge, a narrowing of management hierarchy, and enhanced employee empowerment. Digital technologies can thus support customer-focused organizations to achieve enhanced customer service.

Applications of technology in a service context

As mentioned above, the growth of technology has led to the creation of many more 'touchpoints' between an organization and its customers, and increasingly, technology is stepping in to 'represent' the organization at these touchpoints. For example, a stay at many hotels can now be done virtually without any interaction with people. Like other hotel companies, Hilton enables you to book a room from your mobile app, use that app as your room key to check into your room, to charge food and beverage, and for check out. The quality of that technology interface and experience (alongside the actual quality of the hotel room and amenities, of course) will be the major factor in repeat visits. Indeed, technology represents more and more touchpoints!

What was once the primary domain of employees is now enhanced or sometimes replaced by innovations such as self-service technology, AI, and interactive voice response, with countless more being developed! Since every touchpoint is an opportunity to create a moment-of-truth, it is important for service managers and marketers to have at least a basic understanding of the types of technology currently available and how it can be applied in a service context.

Key technological advancements

Any list of available technologies would be outdated almost as soon as it is published! However, this section draws attention to a few key technologies that have impacted service firms and customers' expectations, and which are predicted to continue disrupting the service landscape as innovations evolve and advance.

Examples of key technological advancements that have impacted how service firms operate and interact with their various stakeholders include:

- Smartphones, mobile devices, and mobile applications (apps) – now the dominant form of Internet access, smartphones can become a 'digital concierge' to enhance the customer experience;
- Artificial intelligence (AI) – by observing and learning customers' consumption patterns, AI can be an active contributor to the co-creation process;
- Virtual reality, augmented reality, and extended reality (VR, AR, and XR) – service brands can utilize such technologies to provide immersive experiences and overcome the barrier of physical distance from their customers; and
- Autonomous devices and conversational agents – for instance, virtual assistants (VAs), chatbots, robots, and drones are increasingly being used to support customer service, provide standardization in service delivery, and gather data from servicescapes.

Other technological innovations such as robotics, radio frequency identification (RFID) sensors, the Internet of Things (IoT), cryptocurrency, blockchain, and location-based services – to name a few! – have also significantly changed firms' service offerings and customers' experience. While it is not within the scope of this section to explain these technologies in detail, readers who are interested in learning more are encouraged to consult the suggested readings and references at the end of this chapter (see, for example, Buhalis et al., 2019; Grewal et al., 2020 Kabadayi et al., 2019).

Another example of how technologies have disrupted service contexts is the use of 'gamification' to engage customers and employees. For instance, many service firms now apply game elements in customer rewards programs by integrating leaderboards and achievement badges or points, which can lead to higher levels of customer loyalty. The below case example of CRED illustrates how gamification can be utilized to transform customers' experience with credit card payments.

How Gamification Helped CRED to Transform Customer Experience

By Yupal Shukla, University of Bologna, Italy

CRED is an innovative Indian fintech startup that has transformed customers' experience with credit card payments. In the past, credit card payments used to be challenging for customers (especially those who own multiple credit cards) because they had to remember their credit card numbers, expiry dates, bill amounts, and due dates, and always carry the physical cards with them to make purchases. In 2018, CRED developed a simplified credit card payment solution by keeping user experience and convenience as top priorities. Essentially, CRED helped to aggregate multiple credit cards owned by customers on one mobile app, which allows users to see real-time transactions, keep track of payment due dates, check their credit score see real-time, and access promotional offers available on each credit card. CRED's core value propositions and service promises include the convenience of managing multiple credit cards on a single platform, timely reminders for payment of credit card bills, a seamless bill payment experience, protection of users' funds by exposing hidden charges on credit cards, and an innovative way of earning rewards for each transaction (Thanwal, 2021).

CRED has turned the hassle of paying credit card bills into a fun activity for users, since it offers rewards such as access to events, experiences, and exciting gift vouchers. The mobile app includes two innovative reward features: 'CRED coins' and 'gamified guaranteed cashback'. For every credit card bill payment, customers can earn 'CRED coins' that they can use to purchase a range of products and access curated experiences, while the 'gamified guaranteed cashback' leverages gaming elements that allow customers to enjoy rewards with every transaction with the possibility to win additional prizes in the form of cashback. These features represent CRED's service philosophy, which they call 'Feel special more often'.

CRED's mobile app functions on an artificial intelligence-backed support system that ensures the smoothness of users' credit card payment journey and provides every detail of their spending patterns and statistics. Importantly, CRED prioritizes the security of customers' credit card details, which helps gain the long-term trust of their customers. Beyond the technology elements of the app, the company has also successfully developed an ecosystem of collaboration with leading brands who offer discounts to users; this not only benefits customers when they make credit card payment, but also provides partners with access to additional channels to sell their products and services.

In 2022, CRED was valued at $6.4 billion (Singh, 2022), making it India's most successful startup. So, how has CRED become so successful? The answer lies in its ability to leverage gamified technology to offer a personalized, seamless customer experience.

While the range of technologies available may seem overwhelming, service firms that are able to effectively integrate relevant innovations into their servicescape can unlock new ways to engage customers and co-create value. But

Leveraging technology 201

how do service firms determine the best way to utilize these technologies? And what implications do these new technologies have on the role of humans in service firms? The answers to these questions are explored in the sections that follow.

The roles of technology

In the Service Encounter 2.0, technology generally plays one of three key roles, depending on the service firm's business model:

1. *Augmentation* – where technology functions to assist or support the work of humans, in other words, technology and humans work in tandem (e.g., CRM systems, as described above) ;
2. *Substitution* – where technology replaces humans in the service encounter, due largely to advances in robots and smart devices (e.g., the use of chatbots on websites to help answer customer questions); or
3. *Network facilitation* – where technology enables connections and relationships to facilitate the service encounter (e.g., as is the case with online platforms like Ola and MakeMyTrip).

It is thus important for service managers and marketers to understand the distinction between technology as *the central service* (i.e., where it takes on the role of substitution) and technology as a valuable tool that *compliments* the primary service actor(s) (i.e., where it functions in an augmentation role). By knowing the different roles that technology can play, organizations can strategically infuse technological elements throughout the service process to deliver enhanced quality and experiences to their customers.

The changing roles of customers and employees

With technology filling one of the three core roles outlined above, in turn, employees and customers have also taken on distinct roles in the Service Encounter 2.0, as described in Table 9.1. While these changing roles present opportunities for firms to develop new innovations and achieve higher service quality, the positive outcomes rely on both employees and customers having a level of *role clarity* regarding what is expected of them, the *ability* to perform as expected, and the *motivation* to do so. Thus, service firms need to invest in systems and processes to ensure that employees and customers are sufficiently trained and prepared on how they can successfully interact with other human and nonhuman actors in the service encounter.

Furthermore, as AI capabilities have advanced, a 'feeling economy' is emerging whereby AI is able to do many of the 'thinking' tasks (such as responding to frequently asked questions that accrue so that the AI system continues to learn from itself) and employees are finding their niche in more

Table 9.1 REDTAG's data-driven approach to customer experience

Segment	Buying behavior	Decisions informed by CRM data
'Hidden mothers'	Mothers who buy for their children but not for themselves	REDTAG sent offers such as a 30% discount on women's wear to encourage mothers to purchase products for themselves
'Explorers'	Customers whose present spend is low but have the potential to buy more	The company focused on cross-selling opportunities and targeted promotions to increase the conversion rate of this segment
'Need-based buyers'	Customers who buy for specific needs and occasions only	These customers received specific promotions such as warm clothing in the winter season, festival offers, and so on
'Family buyers'	Customers who purchase for all family members, including clothing and accessories for children, men's wear, women's wear, household products and accessories	Strategies were developed to increase retention as this segment was found to be very profitable
'High-value customers'	Customers who purchase high-margin products	This segment was also identified as very important and one that needs to be retained and encouraged to buy more, hence they received promotions of premium products to increase their frequency of visits and purchases
'Sale chasers'	Customers who always come during the sale period and less frequently at other times	Being the source of additional sales during the promotion period, this segment was specially targeted with discounts and other offers

people-focused or empathetic tasks. Many service firms now have very effective AI-driven chat features and an automatic routing to a person when questions go beyond the capability. While empathy has always been an important element of employees' roles, the rapid developments in technology are heightening the emphasis here (Table 9.2).

Implications for the way organizations manage their frontline service

These rapid technological advancements and changing roles of actors in the service encounter have redefined the face of the organizational frontline. In particular, the development of AI and its application in smart and connected objects, digital assistants, and humanoid robots has altered how service is delivered by frontline employees and experienced by customers.

Table 9.2 The changing roles of customers and employees in the Service Encounter 2.0

Role	Employees	Customers
'Enabler'	Employees can help customers and technology interact as needed, or handle service failures that result from either customers or technology not functioning well	Customers are increasingly seen as valuable brand partners and active co-creators of value who support employees and/or technology in performing their roles (particularly on social media!)
'Innovator'	Employees can provide an irreplaceable source of creativity and perceptiveness in meeting customers' needs, beyond what technology can currently provide	Customers can collaborate with and provide valuable ideas to firms in the development of new service innovations, often mediated by technological interfaces
'Coordinator'	As service systems become more complex and comprise of multiple network partners, employees can take a leading role in managing the interdependencies	Customers can be involved with bringing together multiple actors in the service encounter to build communities or solve problems
'Differentiator'	While technology can be easily copied, employees remain unique sources of competitive advantage and can provide an authentic human touch in an increasingly digital world	As active co-creators, customers can directly influence the service encounter and contribute to customization, thereby increasing the likelihood of satisfaction and loyalty

Source: Adapted from Bowen (2016)

Generally, frontline service technology (FST) is being utilized by service firms to reduce staff costs, improve service delivery through personalization, and enhance value creation. While basic applications still exist (e.g., ATMs and self-service technologies), FSTs have advanced to incorporate more a sophisticated *support* role (e.g., by simplifying digital payment processes, as in the case of Apple Pay) and an *actor* role, whereby a smart device exerts a level of agency without human intervention (e.g., Nest's self-regulating thermostat) (De Keyser et al., 2019).

Another key technology that has had – and will continue to have – a disruptive impact on the organizational frontline and service industry more broadly is service robots. While robots present exciting opportunities for new service innovations and productivity gains, it is important for firms to first consider how they can be best deployed to meet customers' needs and add value to both the customer and organization. Readers who are interested to learn more about this evolving area of research are encouraged to read further (see, for example, Wirtz et al., 2018).

Summary of chapter

The pervasive role of technology in modern society has had significant implications for business organizations of all types. In the service industry, which is traditionally viewed as a 'high-touch' sector, technology is fast becoming a critical element in the competitive strategies of firms. In a 'high-tech' competitive environment, firms are forced to update the technological aspects of their service offerings on a continuous basis if they are to satisfy their increasingly demanding customers. And as competitors continue to improve their technological capabilities, this increases customer expectations and effectively produces new industry norms and standards.

The increasing integration of technology in all areas of a firm's functions means that the traditional perception of service as a 'low-tech' industry no longer holds true. As such, technological capability is becoming an imperative for employees at all levels of an organization. And if leveraged effectively, technology can empower employees and support them in providing superior customer service.

Ultimately, service firms that carefully curate each touchpoint and consider all three realms (digital, social, and physical) can establish a leading position in the market. And those that harness technology to gain a faster and more accurate understanding of their customers' needs, expectations, and behaviors will be better placed to provide personalized service and enhance value. In turn, these firms are likely to enjoy higher levels of customer engagement, satisfaction, and loyalty – a result of achieving customer experience excellence.

Review questions

1. In which ways does the increasing use of technology revolutionize service organizations?
2. Why do technology-savvy service firms have to carefully leverage both high-touch and high-tech strategies?
3. How does technology shape the servicescape and customer expectations?
4. Explain the implications of digitization for service marketing.
5. How can data and CRM systems be used directly by employees to make immediate impacts on customer experience?
6. Describe the changing nature of the role of service employees with the rise of technology impacting service organizations.

Suggested readings

Brougham, D., & Haar, J. (2017). Smart Technology, Artificial Intelligence, Robotics, and Algorithms (STARA): Employees' perceptions of our future workplace. *Journal of Management & Organization,* 24(2), 239–257.

Flavián, C., Ibáñez-Sánchez, S., & Orús, C. (2019). The impact of virtual, augmented and mixed reality technologies on the customer experience. *Journal of Business Research, 100*, 547–560.

Shankar, V., Kalyanam, K., Setia, P., Golmohammadi, A., Tirunillai, S., Douglass, T., Hennessey, J., Bull, J. S., & Waddoups, R. (2021). How technology is changing retail. *Journal of Retailing, 97*(1), 13–27.

Wiggins, M. W., Auton, J., Bayl-Smith, P., & Carrigan, A. (2020). Optimising the future of technology in organisations: A human factors perspective. *Australian Journal of Management, 45*(3), 449–467.

References

Benoit, S., Baker, T. L., Bolton, R. N., Gruber, T., & Kandampully, J. (2017). A triadic framework for collaborative consumption (CC): Motives, activities and resources & capabilities of actors. *Journal of Business Research, 79*, 219–227.

Bolton, R. N., McColl-Kennedy, J. R., Cheung, L., Gallan, A., Orsingher, C., Witell, L., & Zaki, M. (2018). Customer experience challenges: Bringing together digital, physical and social realms. *Journal of Service Management, 29*(5), 776–808.

Bowen, D. E. (2016). The changing role of employees in service theory and practice: An interdisciplinary view. *Human Resource Management Review, 26*(1), 4–13.

Breidbach, C. F., & Maglio, P. (2020). Accountable algorithms? The ethical implications of data-driven business models. *Journal of Service Management, 31*(2), 163–185.

Buhalis, D., Harwood, T., Bogicevic, V., Viglia, G., Beldona, S., & Hofacker, C. (2019). Technological disruptions in services: Lessons from tourism and hospitality. *Journal of Service Management, 30*(4), 484–506.

De Keyser, A., Köcher, S., Alkire, L., Verbeeck, C., & Kandampully, J. (2019). Frontline service technology infusion: Conceptual archetypes and future research directions. *Journal of Service Management, 30*(1), 156–183.

Garrido-Moreno, A., García-Morales, V., King, S., & Lockett, N. (2020). Social media use and value creation in the digital landscape: A dynamic-capabilities perspective. *Journal of Service Management, 31*(3), 313–343.

Grewal, D., Hulland, J., Kopalle, P. K., & Karahanna, E. (2020). The future of technology and marketing: A multidisciplinary perspective. *Journal of the Academy of Marketing Science, 48*, 1–8.

Huang, M.-H., Rust, R., & Maksimovic, V. (2019). The feeling economy: Managing in the next generation of artificial intelligence (AI). *California Management Review, 61*(4), 43–65.

Kabadayi, S., Ali, F., Choi, H., Joosten, H., & Lu, C. (2019). Smart service experience in hospitality and tourism services. *Journal of Service Management, 30*(3), 326–348.

Kandampully, J., Bilgihan, A., & Zhang, T. (2016). Developing a people-technology hybrids model to unleash innovation and creativity: The new hospitality frontier. *Journal of Hospitality and Tourism Management, 29*, 154–164.

Kumar, V., Chattaraman, V., Neghina, C., Skiera, B., Aksoy, L., Buoye, A., & Henseler, J. (2013). Data-driven services marketing in a connected world. *Journal of Service Management, 24*(3), 330–352.

Larivière, B., Bowen, D., Andreassen, T. W., Kunz, W., Sirianni, N. J., Voss, C., Wünderlich, V. N., & Keyser, A. D. (2017). "Service encounter 2.0": An investigation into the roles of technology, employees and customers. *Journal of Business Research*, *79*, 238–246.

Luri Minami, A., Ramos, C., & Bruscato Bortoluzzo, A. (2021). Sharing economy versus collaborative consumption: What drives consumers in the new forms of exchange? *Journal of Business Research*, *128*, 124–137.

Nanterme, P. (2016). Digital disruption has only just begun. *World Economic Forum*, January 17. Retrieved from https://www.weforum.org/agenda/2016/01/digital-disruption-has-only-just-begun/

Rogers, B., Maguire, E., & Nishi, A. (2017). *Digital transformation: Using data-driven insights for exceptional customer engagement*. Jersey City, NJ: Forbes Insights.

Rust, R. T. (2004). If everything is service, why is this happening now, and what difference does it make? Invited commentaries on 'evolving to a new dominant logic for marketing'. *Journal of Marketing*, *68*, 23–24.

Singh, M. (2022). India's CRED valued at $6.4 billion in new funding. *Tech Crunch*. Retrieved from https://techcrunch.com/2022/06/09/india-cred-valued-at-6-5-billion-in-new-funding/

Solnet, D., Subramony, M., Ford, R. C., Golubovskaya, M., Kang, H. J. A., & Hancer, M. (2019). Leveraging human touch in service interactions: Lessons from hospitality. *Journal of Service Management*, *30*(3), 392–409.

Thanwal, H. (2021). The pros and cons of paying credit card bills through third-party mobile apps. *Money Control*. Retrieved from https://www.moneycontrol.com/news/business/personal-finance/the-pros-and-cons-of-paying-credit-card-bills-through-third-party-mobile-apps-5897711.html

Wirtz, J., Patterson, P. G., Kunz, W. H., Gruber, T., Lu, V. N., Paluch, S., & Martins, A. (2018). Brave new world: Service robots in the frontline. *Journal of Service Management*, *29*(5), 907–931.

Wirtz, J., So, K. K. F., Mody, M. A., Liu, S. Q., & Chun, H. H. (2019). Platforms in the peer-to-peer sharing economy. *Journal of Service Management*, *30*(4), 452–483.

Chapter 10

Fostering service innovation

Study objectives

Having completed this chapter, readers should be able to understand:

- the different types of innovation in a service context;
- why adopting a strategic approach to innovation is essential to remain competitive;
- how to foster a culture for service innovation and embed innovation across the entire organization; and
- how to leverage innovation to enhance the customer experience.

The framework of this chapter

This chapter is set out as follows:

- Introduction
  - Importance of innovation for service organizations
  - The evolution of service innovation
- Understanding service innovation
  - Types of service innovation
  - Innovation as a process
- Embedding service innovation across the organization
  - Fostering a culture of innovation
- Opportunities for service organizations to innovate
  - New service business models
  - Artificial Intelligence (AI) and service innovation
  - Imposed service innovation
- An integrated approach
  - Blended (hybrid) innovation
  - Co-innovation with key stakeholders
- Beyond innovation to service transformation
- Summary of chapter

DOI: 10.4324/9781003470373-11

- Review questions
- Suggested readings
- References

Introduction

One of the 'gurus' of modern management, Peter Drucker, argued that since the purpose of a business is to create a customer, its primary functions are twofold – marketing and innovation. There are innumerable books and articles that translate Drucker's message to businesses as: *innovate, or else!*

Innovation helps organizations to create a unique customer experience, so it's important for service managers to adopt a strategic approach to innovation to build a competitive advantage. The increasing interest in innovation by business leaders across a variety of industries has led to a vast amount of research into the concept and has resulted in 'innovation' becoming a management buzzword.

There are many definitions of innovation. For instance, Keiningham et al. (2019) describe it as 'a departure from the past' (p.

370) and suggest that 'innovativeness may be regarded as the perceived change of various tangible and intangible elements of the product or service (as compared to already existing ones)' (p. 374). Thus, innovation is about *doing* and *using* new things, which is distinct from the concepts of creativity and invention that are about *finding* new things.

In the context of service management, the concept of innovation is still broad and requires further research. Yet for the purposes of this chapter we adopt the definition of service innovation as a process aiming at developing new services or improving existing ones.

Importantly, innovation is not just about having new ideas! It also needs to lead to the creation of *value* – either economic, social, and/or environmental. This is more vital than ever in today's competitive environment, as change and innovation occur at a rapid pace – and it is easy to fall behind and become irrelevant very quickly (think about video movie rental stores, so popular in the 1990s!).

Importance of innovation for service organizations

There is strong evidence that service innovation and innovativeness have a positive impact on firm performance, value, and customer satisfaction. Furthermore, research has found that highly innovative firms also have a happier workforce, better financial performance and profitability, greater resilience during turbulent times, and higher growth and efficiency (among many other positive outcomes!) when compared to similar but less innovative firms. The key is to innovate in multiple different ways; successful firms aren't just innovating their products or services – they are usually also innovating their internal systems and processes to enhance the customer experience.

Service firm innovativeness is also important from a customer's perspective, as this can influence their brand attitude, preferences, and loyalty. Additionally, customers generally consider new innovations as offering more value and being better able to meet their need for exclusivity, which can positively influence buying intentions. Thus, innovation is important for both the attraction and retention of customers.

Domino's Pizza is a good example of how innovation can transform a service business. Facing increased competition, Domino's then-CEO Patrick Doyle challenged his company to develop a system that could make it as easy and efficient as possible for any customer with a smartphone to order a pizza in 17 seconds – leading to their 'build and order your own pizza' app. Domino's now considers itself a *technology service* company selling pizzas, with over 15,000 stores across nearly 90 countries. They continue to innovate with driverless cars and e-bikes, among the many other innovations, ensuring that this 'pizza' company stays ahead of its competition!

The Domino's example also illustrates how many firms engage their frontline employees to identify and implement innovations that can improve operations, efficiency, and customer experience. We will discuss this important issue of building an innovation culture and climate later in this chapter.

The evolution of service innovation

In order to successfully compete in an ever-evolving marketplace and effectively cater to customers' changing needs and expectations, business leaders in almost every sector have embraced innovation as a strategic imperative. Over the past two decades, 'innovation management' has also received a lot of academic attention, yet most of the early research in this area has its roots in the manufacturing industry. Such studies provided a fairly narrow perspective, being focused on how technology can be adopted to make processes more efficient and reduce costs, primarily for the benefit of the firm. However, as we know from Chapters 1 and 2, applying a manufacturing lens is inadequate in today's experience economy, and leading firms are transferring their earlier product focus to a customer-centric focus instead.

Technological and digital innovations can indeed provide benefits to service firms in the form of efficiency, productivity, and cost reductions (see Chapter 9), however recent studies highlight the need to focus on the 'human' element of the service encounter and strive for innovations that enhance the customer experience in a positive, memorable, and distinctive way. This is particularly relevant for service firms in the hospitality sector, where studies have shown that innovations in human-related elements of the service encounter (e.g., the way employees are engaged and build relationships with customers) are more important to create a sustainable competitive advantage than technological innovations.

While traditional manufacturing firms would invest heavily in research and development (R&D) activities to develop innovative products, successful service businesses today are innovating the customer experience. Service leaders also recognize that rather than developing new ideas entirely 'in-house', the best service innovations emerge from a collaborative process of *co-creation of value* with key stakeholders (employees, customers, and society).

As the field of innovation continues to evolve, it is important for service managers and marketers to embrace an innovative mindset while staying abreast of developments and trends. Hence, this chapter offers a foundational understanding of what service innovation is, why it is so vital for service organizations, and some of the important considerations for service managers and marketers. Readers who are interested in learning more about this topic are encouraged to consult the suggested readings and reference list at the end of this chapter.

Understanding service innovation

Types of service innovation

The two key types of service innovation include: incremental innovation (creatively applying existing ideas), and radical innovation (introducing a new idea). Radical service innovations in particular have the potential to disrupt business models and industries – think of the transformations we've seen in the transport and accommodation industries after the launch of Uber and Airbnb!

There are four main areas across which firms can reimagine their service offering and customer experience. Key dimensions of service innovativeness, from the perspective of the customer, include:

- *New value proposition* – the newness and usefulness of the service compared to existing offerings (i.e., products and services that provide more benefits to the consumer than already existing offerings and that better match the needs and wants of the consumer than current products and services, are perceived as more innovative by consumers);
- *New service delivery* – the newness and convenience of the service delivery process compared to existing processes;
- *New ways to treat customers, or new ways that customer relationships are cemented* – the newness of the interaction between the customer and the firm (i.e., developing new approaches to involving customers by training employees to interact with them in different ways to create more rapport); and
- *New interaction space* – the newness of the servicescape, which can be digital, physical, or social (see Chapter 9) (Keiningham et al., 2019).

Firms need not innovate across all four dimensions; for instance, a service may still be perceived as 'new' if the delivery process is more efficient or of a higher quality, despite the value proposition remaining the same (illustrated in the example below of Reliance Retail). Thus, service managers and marketers can choose to address the dimensions that best match their organization's strategy and resources.

What is important to remember is that in a true co-creation sense, customers can – and must – be engaged in the process of creating and executing innovations! Hence, service firms aspiring for innovation should maintain an unwavering customer orientation (or an 'outside–in' approach). A following section of this chapter also addresses another critical element in service innovation – the use of technology and artificial intelligence.

One of India's Most Innovative Companies: Reliance Retail

Every year, Fast Company releases a list of the 'World's Most Innovative Companies', which showcases businesses that are disrupting services, products, industries, and cultures. In 2022, the Indian telecom giant Reliance Retail made the list for rethinking the way they engage with customers and deliver service.

The company launched a partnership between their network of superstores, JioMart, and the global messaging app, WhatsApp, which enabled users of the app to purchase products from the stores. This simple, convenient service is offered for free and allows customers to choose their delivery and payment preferences. By leveraging WhatsApp, the company also aims to attract more local corner stores to join their network, which would increase the diversity of choice for customers (Gagne, 2022, Online).

Overall, this example highlights how a company has recognized a trend among its stakeholders (i.e., the growing use of WhatsApp by customers and suppliers) and has innovated its delivery process to offer a new and useful service.

Innovation as a process

As mentioned above, innovation is more than just a new idea. Too many organizations stop once they've simply had a great idea, but that's only the first part of the service innovation process. There are three main stages, including:

- generating new ideas (either incremental or radical);
- selecting which ideas to pursue (based on a firm's strategy and resources); and
- implementing and diffusing new ideas (to create value).

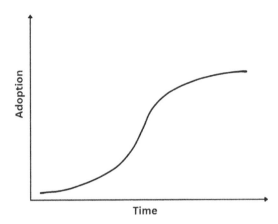

Figure 10.1 The innovation S-curve (*authors' illustration*)

In most cases, new innovations are never adopted instantly; instead, they tend to follow an S-curve where growth is slow at the start until it hits a tipping point and then starts to spread more broadly (see Figure 10.1). During the implementation and diffusion phase, it is important for service managers and marketers to make it clear to customers and other external stakeholders how the new idea meets their needs and creates value. Meanwhile, internal stakeholders also need to be kept positively engaged to ensure the idea can be brought fully to life (for instance, the finance department may be eager to see a return on investment, so service managers need to offer reassurance that the innovation process takes time).

As the environment in which service firms operate has evolved, so too has the way in which innovations are developed changed, with the process now involving many more contributors. In the past, innovations would generally be developed in-house and then launched to see if anyone would buy them, yet nowadays service innovation is about engagement and co-creation with key stakeholders (employees, customers, and suppliers). This means that service managers and marketers need to adopt a collaborative, flexible, and responsive approach at each stage of the innovation process.

Throughout the entire process, service managers should also encourage an approach that is characterized by experimenting and learning. This demands strategic agility, creativity, and co-creation with a variety of stakeholders to ensure value is created. For example, when a restaurant known for its lunch and dinner excellence tries to move into the breakfast segment, this can take some time and be an interactive process for the market to adjust and for the product and service to develop. Bretts Wharf Restaurant in Australia was in this position some years back; however, the owners and management team did not fully commit to the idea. After a few months of frustration, there were no alternative ideas offered, no experimenting, and no commitment to the concept. The restaurant did not pursue the new idea with the aim of learning and adjusting. As a result, the idea was abandoned with much hard work wasted. Had a more systematic approach been taken to this new idea, it could have worked out much differently! Indeed, innovation requires commitment, agility, and a plan!

Embedding service innovation across the organization

A feature of successful innovation cultures is that the goal and value of innovativeness are sensed throughout the entire organization. Earlier chapters have discussed the importance of breaking down internal silos and encouraging an environment of collaboration, and when it comes to bringing new ideas to life this is particularly important!

Service leaders can facilitate innovation by designing systems and processes, and fostering a positive culture, that encourages agility, collaboration, and co-learning. By rallying the entire firm around the goal of innovation, service managers can harness value from every employee and create an environment that encourages and enables new ideas to thrive. However, this is easier said than done!

Fostering a culture of innovation

Unlike the earlier industrial era when investments in innovation were largely focused on product development, in the new service era – which demands agility and adaptability in the face of constant change – the focus is much more on human capital. This means service managers need to make sure they have employees with the right blend of expertise, organized in the right way, and with the right culture (see Chapter 8 for further discussion on service culture and climate).

Researchers have undertaken substantial work seeking to better understand how to measure an innovation culture. Some suggest that there are four dimensions that capture the main areas needed for an innovation culture to be strong, including:

- the need for the firm to have a clearly stated intention to be innovative;
- the infrastructure available to support innovation;
- the knowledge and orientation of employees to support thoughts and actions necessary for innovation; and
- an environment to support implementation which balances risk and reward trade-offs (Dobni, 2008).

Furthermore, Thomke (2020) offers guidance for creating a culture that supports innovation while also deepening organizational engagement. He highlights a number of commonly shared traits or mindsets among innovators, including:

- a passion for new ideas;
- a disciplined pursuit of new ideas;
- the ability to strategically weigh up options;
- a focus on adaptability during the execution phase; and
- the ability to foster engagement and collaboration among a team.

Importantly, Thomke identifies one vital trait that is the driving force behind innovation: *curiosity*. Hence, service managers looking to create a culture of experimentation need to engage the people around them to express their curiosity – to imagine new ways of delivering value and enhancing the customer experience.

Innovation thus requires strategy, people, and culture – but what kind of culture spurs innovation in a firm where there are many frontline employees? A service culture that encourages innovation is characterized by a clear and well-defined vision that specifies the aim of the organization and the importance of continual attempts to innovate. This is enabled by a trusting work environment where positive relationships between supervisors can help employees be more willing to contribute to decision-making. In addition, employees will contribute their creativity and innovative ideas when they perceive approval and realistic support when they present those ideas (even if they are opposing views!) to those more senior in the organization. Employees should be encouraged to communicate openly in the work environment, and to listen and collect information from various sources, such as customers, which can result in a rich source of ideas for service innovation. The case below of The Bombay Canteen illustrates how service firms can foster innovation by building a culture based on employee empowerment, respect, and engagement.

Innovation and Empowerment: The Bombay Canteen – Local Food with Love

By Dr. Vidya Patwardhan, Dr. Thirugnanasambantham K, and Dr. Senthil Kumaran P, Welcome Graduate School of Hospitality Administration, Manipal

Diners in this digital era are hyper-connected with a wealth of information about food. In order to attract customers and compete effectively, restaurants must thus focus on continuous innovation in their menus and service excellence as key points of differentiation. Known for its 'local food with love' approach and creative cocktails, The Bombay

Canteen (TBC) serves India's diverse regional dishes by blending age-old Indian traditions with a twist of the West. TBC has established itself in a competitive market by combining an innovative menu with a strong people-oriented service culture. With regard to their employees, the core philosophy at TBC is to learn, care for each other, have fun, and put a smile on the face of every guest. This tone is set by the restaurant's managers, who consider their employees as valuable assets and the core reason for TBC's success.

Since its establishment, TBC has fostered a people-oriented culture where managers want new recruits to pursue a long-term career with the company. The foundation built through a robust orientation program helps employees to familiarize themselves with the ethos of the company, the management processes and practices, and the relationship between cross-functional departments. Regardless of their role, employees are empowered through specific training modules and cross-training, which develops their skills and helps them to obtain a holistic sense of how the organization functions. This also shapes their attitudes and approach to work that fits with TBC's culture.

The accommodating workplace culture at TBC is intended to make employees feel happy and comfortable. Respect for others at every level is supremely important, and TBC creates an engaging environment by encouraging equal opportunities for all in key business decisions. For instance, the menus are chosen by the whole team, from butchers to bartenders, which helps to create a sense of community and trust. To reward exceptional employees, TBC has introduced different types of transparent, growth-based programs that recognize people who have overcome challenges and provided excellent service. For instance, 'Canteen Superstar' is an initiative where employees attain stars from their colleagues for their distinctive contribution and for helping to create a positive team spirit. Another unique feature of TBC's culture is a 'fair and just' method of sharing service charges, which rightfully belong to employees, thus reiterating the organization's people-oriented approach.

The secret to TBC's high level of talent retention lies in their efforts toward training and development, offering higher than industry average pay scales, rewards, and recognition; creating a friendly and nurturing environment; and fostering positive attitudes among managers and employees alike. TBC's human resources philosophy is grounded in an understanding that an empowered and engaged employee will serve customers better. The restaurant's founders know that the success of TBC depends on many factors, but perhaps most important is the positive relationships forged between its internal and external customers. Ultimately, the success of TBC's people-oriented approach is evident in

> their accolades, including receiving the Great Place to Work award and being recognized by Condé Nast Traveler magazine through their 'Top Restaurant Awards' and 'Where in the World to Eat' list.

Opportunities for service organizations to innovate
New service business models

In response to today's ever-changing environment, service leaders are discovering new ways of structuring firms to better facilitate innovation – which ultimately helps to better serve their customers, create value, and establish competitive differentiation in the marketplace. For organizations trying to innovate, traditional or hierarchical business structures may hinder the introduction of new ideas and prevent employees from progressing innovations, as rigid systems and processes can slow the pace of change. Instead, research has found that more organic structures provide the flexibility to innovate and are more suitable in today's dynamic business context. Hence, firms that innovate their business model can unleash a powerful form of value creation and competitive advantage. The example below of iGrab Café provides an interesting insight into an innovative café business model designed to differentiate in a saturated market.

> ### iGrab Café: An Innovative Business Model to Compete in a Congested Market
>
> By Dr. Sanjai k Parahoo, HBMSU,
> Dr. Madhavi Ayyagari, Wollongong University, and
> Dr. Ardhendu Shekhar Singh, Symbiosis International
> (Deemed University)
>
> The tea and coffee market in the United Arab Emirates (UAE) stood at USD 180 million in 2019. This country of 10 million people has the highest number of food and beverage outlets per capita in the world. The UAE café market has a dense network of global brand franchises as well as numerous local independent specialty coffee shops, all fiercely competing. Such an environment makes it very challenging for a small startup to enter the market and sustain itself.
>
> This was the dilemma faced by two Emirati entrepreneurs, Fahad AL Shehhi and Mohammed AL Hosani, when they decided to launch a café in 2016. They recognized that they did not have the resources to

compete with the branding and communications budgets of the global coffee chains like Starbucks, Costa, Tim Hortons, and Gloria Jeans. While brainstorming about their business concept, the two entrepreneurs took inspiration from the Emirati cultural values, especially generosity and giving back to others, which is considered to be a form of blessing. These values formed the basis of their core business model, which focused on creating shared value for all key stakeholders in the supply chain and not just their own profitability and success.

Fahad and Mohammed named their startup, iGrab café (the 'i' in iGrab pronounced as in 'it'), which is an Arabic term that means 'Welcome, Come in'. They identified over 40 local micro entrepreneurs (mainly women), who operated their own specialty home food businesses using social media to market their products. With the aim of creating a value network, each iGrab outlet provided shelf space and ample storage space (ambient and refrigerated) to these entrepreneurs. iGrab thus offered the opportunity to rent space at a physical sales outlet, which the local businesses would not have been able to establish on their own. Furthermore, iGrab also mentors each local entrepreneur and educates them on the market, packaging, branding, and so on. The business model embodies a transformative and sustainable service since it enables the micro entrepreneurs to expand and grow their businesses through omnichannel marketing with iGrab absorbing the major share of the associated risk.

In turn, iGrab enhanced its image as a social enterprise besides being able to offer a wider variety of local snacks and pastries. The customers also have access to a variety of home foods and specialty coffee, while enjoying the satisfaction of supporting local entrepreneurs. Further, the one-stop shop provided by iGrab is much more convenient than ordering from multiple vendors online and saves the cost associated with multiple deliveries.

iGrab's innovative business model proved to be a winning proposition. They launched successive outlets in Sharjah in 2017, and in Dubai and Abu Dhabi in 2019, followed by a fifth outlet in Ras Al Khaimah in October 2020. Fahad's idea and creative thinking in creating a mutually beneficial sustainable partnership enabled iGrab to create a blue ocean that fostered local micro businesses to succeed. The more branches iGrab launches, the more families it supports. Furthermore, the innovative business model has been copied and replicated by 30 people in the market. Yet Fahad does not mind as it underlines the success of his idea, and supports his dream to benefit women entrepreneurs.

Other business model innovations can be very simple, yet successfully meet market conditions and challenges. In Australia, like many other parts of the world where the COVID-19 pandemic has impacted people and businesses, there is a severe labor and skill shortage. In addition, there is a growing demand for more healthy fresh food options. David's Noodle and Hotpot addresses both issues. Customers choose their raw ingredients and place them in a bowl (charged by weight), then hand these to a chef who cooks them quickly. This reduces the need for service staff and provides fresh food with customers literally involved in the service process. A simple yet effective service business model innovation is shown in Figure 10.2.

Artificial I ntelligence (AI) and service innovation

As we know from Chapter 9, rapid advancements in technology have disrupted the service landscape and presented rich opportunities for innovation. In particular, Artificial Intelligence (or AI) is being used by an increasing number of service organizations to create value for their stakeholders. For instance, many readers have likely used streaming services like Netflix to watch movies or Spotify to listen to music – both platforms are powered by AI to recommend similar content or playlists that match users' preferences.

Another recent innovation that utilizes AI is the at-home digital assistant (for example, the Amazon Echo or the Google Home). These objects are primarily built to provide a service and the ultimate value received by users is convenience (like turning the lights off or controlling a smart thermostat). As well as being beneficiaries of a service, customers are also involved in co-creating the intelligence in AI systems, since every time they use the device they are contributing to the underlying data sets and helping to make the algorithms smarter. This is a good example of how customers do not simply buy a 'product', but rather the service or experience that it renders – and AI and technology open up enormous opportunities for service organizations to innovate and continue to surprise and delight their customers.

It is important to remember here that even when we speak of technology and innovation, it is the *improved service or experience* that creates added value – not the technology or innovation alone. Innovation occurs when service firms get the right combination of business model, culture, and technology that delivers value for all stakeholders.

Imposed service innovation

While a proactive rather than reactive approach to innovation is preferable, it is worth noting that social, environmental, and economic crises can force businesses to reassess and reconfigure their service offering. Such a scenario has been described as 'imposed service innovation' by Heinonen and

Fostering service innovation 219

Figure 10.2 David's Noodle and Hotpot *(Photos taken by Author)*

Strandvik (2021) in their study of how the COVID-19 pandemic sparked new ideas to emerge as managers looked beyond their existing strategies. Indeed, in disruptive contexts like this, service innovation is accelerated and elevated to a strategic imperative to ensure a firm's survival.

The COVID-19 pandemic also highlighted the importance of embracing new technologies, since those companies that had already been investing in online and digital innovations generally fared better than those that did not already have those capabilities. For instance, many schools and universities reverted to virtual classrooms throughout the pandemic – a switch that was made more seamless for those institutions that had previously been exploring online learning and already had the internal systems and capabilities in place to pivot quickly. Innovation and digitization can thus be considered a useful strategy for firms to become more flexible and resilient in the face of unexpected changes.

While such crises are largely unpredictable, service managers and marketers should nonetheless be aware of and ready to leverage the opportunity for innovation when they do arise.

An integrated approach

Blended (hybrid) innovation

Leading service firms like Disney and Starwood recognize that combining two distinct and required components – people and technology – produces a 'hybrid organization' that benefits from new technology while still providing an appropriate climate and culture that supports employees to facilitate new ideas and ways to innovate. While technology-based innovations can provide efficiency and cost reductions, successful service managers remember that it is the human elements (e.g., the way employees interact with customers) that often have the greatest impact on creating memorable moments-of-truth. Thus, by blending the unique powers of people and technology, service firms can unlock the creative potential of both employees and customers in conjunction with technology, to stimulate innovation and build a competitive advantage.

In the past, technology was seen as the primary source of innovation. In the new hybrid approach, however, technology is now considered a fundamental enabler, with the primary focus for innovation being co-creation with both internal and external stakeholders. Online communities and virtual platforms, for example, allow firms to engage employees and customers to harness their creativity, and offer a relatively accessible, low-cost way to link technology and people. Since people (both internal and external) are seen as core drivers of innovation in hybrid organizations, much research has been dedicated to determining the ideal environment to nurture their creativity (see earlier section in this chapter regarding fostering a culture for innovation, as well as Chapter 8).

Overall, while technologies and digital tools certainly have a role to play, innovation is now much more focused on human and intellectual capital. By using technology to augment human intelligence, service firms can harness the creativity of their stakeholders to co-create value. Therefore, it is important for service managers and marketers to be able to establish trusting and supportive relationships with both employees and customers to encourage co-innovation and continuous value creation.

Co-innovation with key stakeholders

The authors of this textbook published a research paper that identified common practices among ten exemplar firms that have become part of 'service excellence folklore' (Solnet & Kandampully, 2008). The findings of their study revealed that these highly customer-centered organizations seem to share a number of traits, among them being an *active engagement of customers in developing new ideas*. Successful organizations are those that are most attuned to market demands and needs – and the best way to understand what customers want and need is to *work with* them (often through frontline employees). Service managers and marketers should thus utilize the range of technologies available to co-create innovation and value with their key stakeholders.

As mentioned in the previous chapter, the 'Service Encounter 2.0' is characterized by changes in the roles of employees and customers. One of the four new roles that Bowen (2016) identified for both groups of stakeholders is that of an *Innovator*, since people remain a non-substitutable source of creativity despite the growing sophistication of AI and machine learning. Involving frontline employees more in the service innovation process can lead to greater volumes of innovation, while customers take part in the process by acting as 'free' consultants and providing feedback or ideas through either direct or digital interactions. Examples of customers as innovators can be found in Starbucks' online platform 'My Starbucks Idea' and Nike's website that allows customers to customize the color and style of their shoes. Such initiatives produce value for both the customer and the organization, by providing a personalized experience and revealing valuable information about consumers' preferences and desires.

Ultimately, the creation of new innovations is significantly enhanced when service managers and marketers are able to get diverse inputs from a range of key stakeholders. Furthermore, it may seem counterintuitive, but service firms should not focus too much on existing customers and instead talk to those who feel they are not currently being well catered to by existing services (i.e., a firm's potential customers), as this can also help to uncover innovative ideas. Service firms that are most effective in engaging a broad network in the co-innovation process – including employees, customers (existing and potential), suppliers, and even competitors – will be better able to leverage innovation to enhance the customer experience and establish a competitive advantage.

Beyond innovation to service transformation

To round out readers' understanding of service innovation, it is worth noting an emerging area of interest that goes beyond the concept of innovation – that is, *service transformation*. This growing field of study builds on the concepts of incremental and radical innovation, and sees service transformation as critical to ongoing success in a highly competitive and ever-changing environment.

While service transformation stems from the innovation literature, there are key differences between the two concepts. As discussed earlier in this chapter, service innovation occurs when firms reimagine their service offering and/or customer experience to help a firm achieve its service vision (or 'end goal'). On the other hand, scholars argue that service transformation should be *the visionary goal* that firms aim for to enhance performance and market position. In this context, innovation and technology are seen as key drivers or tools that guide and support firms toward their revolutionary goals. Hence, service transformation is not a destination, but rather an *aspiration and strategic orientation* that keeps pushing firms to evolve based on changing market dynamics.

Service firms that pursue transformation embark on a continuing cycle of not only improving existing functions but also removing redundant functions to make way for new services to be created. Kandampully et al. (2021) describe three key pathways that firms can take to achieve service transformation (what the authors call the '3Rs of Service Transformation') that occur on a continuum, including:

- *Reformation* – characterized by incremental or gradual changes; usually pursued by firms operating in a steady environment or that have limited financial and/or human resources, so new technologies are adopted over time (e.g., a local boutique that decides to add an online store to their website);
- *Renovation* – involves sequential stages of re-engineering outdated services, structures, processes, and practices to improve them in a way that better meets internal or external needs and enhances value for the customer (e.g., Netflix evolved multiple times from when it launched in 1997 as a DVD mail-order service to the global streaming giant it is today a transformation driven by the firm's ability to identify and adapt to changing consumer demands and technological advancements); and–
- *Reincarnation* – when firms take a completely new direction that was not previously part of their service vision or mission (i.e., a 'business

mutation'); usually pursued by firms at risk of becoming irrelevant due to operating in challenging environments that are changing radically (e.g., Fujifilm reimagined its original core business model of generating revenue through selling film for cameras and has reinvented itself into a diversified company that now offers medical imaging solutions and other electronics operations).

While the idea of completely destroying existing services or business models through the process of 'reincarnation' may sound daunting to some service managers, it is worth drawing a parallel here to the three Hindu deities (the 'Trimurti'), which reminds us that creation, preservation, and ultimate destruction are important elements for all things that exist.

There are various internal and external factors that influence the success of a firm's service transformation, yet arguably the most important of these factors is the adoption by service managers of a revolutionary strategic mindset. Service managers who are able to embrace this mindset and accept the importance of continuous change can spark positive impacts such as improved customer experience, profitability, and corporate social responsibility. Ultimately, firms that focus on service transformation – rather than just innovation or digitalization – will experience an internal revolution that impacts every element of their business and an enhanced ability to maintain a competitive edge.

Summary of chapter

In today's rapidly changing business environment, service innovation is a core driver of competitiveness. Thus, service managers and marketers need to understand how to foster innovation in a way that enhances the customer experience and delivers exceptional service. As the world has shifted from a product-based to an experience-based economy, a focus on service innovation is crucial now more than ever.

Service leaders must approach innovation both from an external perspective, by adopting a customer orientation that focuses on value co-creation, and from an internal perspective, by intentionally creating a culture of continuous experimentation and learning. Most importantly, it is vital for organizations to not lose sight of the overall vision and organizational strategy, as they continue in the race for innovation and service excellence in an ever-changing environment.

Review questions

1. Describe how the concept of innovation has evolved.
2. What are the four key types of service innovation? Provide examples of each.

3. How can service managers foster a culture of service innovation?
4. Why is it important for service firms to take a blended or 'hybrid' approach to innovation?
5. Explain the difference between each of the 3Rs of service transformation.

Suggested readings

Berry, L. L., Shankar, V., Parish, J. T., Cadwallader, S., & Dotzel, T. (2006). Creating new markets through service innovation. *MIT Sloan Management Review, 47*(2), 56–63.

Boudreau, K. J., & Lakhani, K. R. (2013). Using the crowd as an innovation partner. *Harvard Business Review, 91*(4), 60–140.

Carlborg, P., Kindström, D., & Kowalkowski, C. (2014). The evolution of service innovation research: A critical review and synthesis. *The Service Industries Journal, 34*(5), 373–398.

Chandler, J. D., Danatzis, I., Wernicke, C., Akaka, M. A., & Reynolds, D. (2019). How does innovation emerge in a service ecosystem? *Journal of Service Research, 22*(1), 75–89.

Ford, R. C., Edvardsson, B., Dickson, D., & Enquist, B. (2012). Managing the innovation co-creation challenge: Lessons from service exemplars Disney and IKEA. *Organizational Dynamics, 41*(4), 281–290.

den Hertog, P., van der Aa, W., & de Jong, M. W. (2010). Capabilities for managing service innovation: Towards a conceptual framework. *Journal of Service Management, 21*(4), 490–514.

Hsieh, J.-K., Chiu, H.-C., Wei, C.-P., Rebecca Yen, H., & Cheng, Y.-C. (2013). A practical perspective on the classification of service innovations. *The Journal of Services Marketing, 27*(5), 371–384.

Kandampully, J., Bilgihan, A., Van Riel, A. C. R., & Sharma, A. (2022). Toward holistic experience-oriented service innovation: Co-creating sustainable value with customers and society. *Cornell Hospitality Quarterly 64*(2), 161–183.

Kandampully, J., Bilgihan, A., & Zhang, T. (2016). Developing a people-technology hybrids model to unleash innovation and creativity: The new hospitality frontier. *Journal of Hospitality and Tourism Management, 29*, 154–164.

Melton, H., & Hartline, M. D. (2015). Customer and employee co-creation of radical service innovations. *The Journal of Services Marketing, 29*(2), 112–123.

Sudbury-Riley, L., Hunter-Jones, P., Al-Abdin, A., Lewin, D., & Naraine, M. V. (2020). The trajectory touchpoint technique: A deep dive methodology for service innovation. *Journal of Service Research, 23*(2), 229–251.

References

Bowen, D. E. (2016). The changing role of employees in service theory and practice: An interdisciplinary view. *Human Resource Management Review, 26*(1), 4–13.

Cadwallader, S., Jarvis, C. B., Bitner, M. J., & Ostrom, A. L. (2009). Frontline employee motivation to participate in service innovation implementation. *Journal of the Academy of Marketing Science, 38*(2), 219–239.

Conde Nast Traveler. (2018). *The Bombay canteen voted India's best restaurant.* Retrieved from https://www.cntraveller.in/story/bombay-canteen-voted-indias-best-restaurant-indian-accent-second/

Dobni, C. B. (2008). Measuring innovation culture in organizations. *European Journal of Innovation Management, 11*(4), 539–559.

Dotzel, T., Shankar, V., & Berry, L. L. (2013). Service innovativeness and firm value. *Journal of Marketing Research, 50*(2), 259–276.

Feng, C., Ma, R., & Jiang, L. (2021). The impact of service innovation on firm performance: A meta-analysis. *Journal of Service Management, 32*(3), 289–314.

Gagne, Y. (2022). The 10 most innovative Asia-Pacific companies of 2022. *Fast Company*. Retrieved from https://www.fastcompany.com/90724356/most-innovative-companies-asia-pacific-2022

Heinonen, K., & Strandvik, T. (2021). Reframing service innovation: COVID-19 as a catalyst for imposed service innovation. *Journal of Service Management, 32*(1), 101–112.

Jain, S., Basu, S., Dwivedi, Y. K., & Kaur, S. (2022). Interactive voice assistants – Does brand credibility assuage privacy risks? *Journal of Business Research, 139*, 701–717.

Kandampully, J., Bilgihan, A., Bujisic, M., Kaplan, A., Jarvis, C. B., & Shukla, Y. S. (2021). Service transformation: How can it be achieved? *Journal of Business Research, 136*, 219–228.

Karlsson, J., & Skålén, P. (2015). Exploring front-line employee contributions to service innovation. *European Journal of Marketing, 49*(9/10), 1346–1365.

Keiningham, T. L., He, Z., Hillebrand, B., Jang, J., Seuss, C., & Wu, L. (2019). Creating innovation that drives authenticity. *Journal of Service Management, 30*(3), 369–391.

NCR Corporation. (2021). *The digital innovations that took Domino's from pizza place to tech titan.* Retrieved from https://www.ncr.com/blogs/restaurants/digital-innovations-dominos

Sawhney, V. (2020). What makes the Bombay canteen India's most beloved restaurant. *Harvard Business Review*, February. Retrieved from https://hbr.org/2020/02/what-makes-the-bombay-canteen-indias-most-beloved-restaurant

Solnet, D., & Kandampully, J. (2008). How some service firms have become part of "service excellence" folklore: An exploratory study. *Managing Service Quality, 18*(2), 179–193.

Thomke, S. (2020). Building a culture of experimentation. *Harvard Business Review*, March–April. Retrieved from https://hbr.org/2020/03/building-a-culture-of-experimentation

Index

**Page numbers in bold reference tables.
**Page numbers in italics reference figures.

Adidas 4
adoption of service vision 115–116
Airbnb 46
AI *see* artificial intelligence
Al Ghurair, Rashid 60
aligning service vision, strategy, process and systems 121–124
Apple products, corporate image 76–77
artifacts, service culture 171
artificial intelligence (AI) 199, 201–202, 221; fuel-on-demand 60–61; service innovation 218
Asia, quality management 65–66
assessing the quality of service before consumption 30–31
augmentation 201
autonomous devices 199

BAIF Development Research Foundation, Nahari 118–119
balancing service quality and financial performance **143**
behaviors, service culture 171
blended (hybrid) innovation 220–221
The Bombay Canteen (TBC) 214–216
brand communities, creating 108–109
branded differentiation 31–32
brand image 77
brands, variability 33
Bretts Wharf Restaurant 212–213
Burner India 73–75
BYJU, The Learning App 16–17

CAFU, fuel-on-demand 60–61
capacity: maximum capacity 53; online platforms 53–54; optimum capacity 53; and quality 52–53; sharing economy 53–54; *see also* service capacity
Carlzon, Jan 129
cascade in moments-of-truth 127–129
categories: of customers 88; of service failures 149–150
Caterpillar 4
central service 201
challenges: associated with service capacity *see* service capacity; to customer centricity 93; in managing and marketing services 22–29
chase-and-level strategy 57
chase demand strategies 48
CIT *see* critical-incident technique
CLV *see* customer lifetime value
Co-create IKEA 36
co-creating value 146–147
co-creation 35–36, 210
co-innovation with stakeholders 221–222
collaboration: between internal customers 164; service encounter triad 141; total quality management (TQM) 67
communication, customer-to-customer 103–104
company mindset, transforming 7
competitor's customers 88
complaining, lack of 150–151
complaint analysis 101–102
confirmation/disconfirmation paradigm, service quality 69–70
consumption stage 193
continuous improvement in systems, total quality management (TQM) 66

control of service output 26
conversational agents 199
coordinated benefits, interdependency of service providers 13–14
Coordinators 145, 203
co-ownership 146
co-production 168
'Core' elements, service quality 82
core services 11–12
corporate image 76–77
Costco 159
COVID-19 220
CRED 199–200
Crimson Cup Coffee & Tea 147–149
critical-incident technique (CIT) 100–101
CRM *see* customer relationship management
Crown Resorts, Medallia 40–41
culture, fostering a culture of innovation 213–216; *see also* service culture
curiosity, fostering a culture of innovation 214
current external customers 88
custom-centered vision 116–117
customer advocates, employees as 107
customer-centric approaches 90
customer centricity: complaint analysis 101–102; creating brand communities 108–109; critical-incident technique (CIT) 100–101; customer-to-customer communication 103–104; defined 89–90; focus-group interviews 98; in-depth interviews with 97–98; at Indian Coffee House (ICH) 107–108; in-house customer satisfaction surveys 99; market surveys 98–99; mystery shoppers 102; Net Promoter Score (NPS) 99–100; path to 92–93; PayTm Gold 90–92; responding to customer feedback 104; *see also* listening to customers
customer centric organizations, characteristics of 94–95
customer-contact person 129–130
customer delight 73
customer deviance 143
customer-driven, total quality management (TQM) 66
customer engagement 146–147; enhancing utilizing data 195–197
customer expectations 59; new service ecosystem 190

customer experience (CX) 6, 136–138; Adidas 4; Caterpillar 4; consumption 139; employee-customer interface/touchpoint 142; evolution of 39–40; optimizing 130–133; post-consumption 139–140; pre-consumption 139; service encounter triad 140–142; service guarantees 156–158
customer experience platforms 186
customer feedback 140
customer journey 127–129, 138; *see also* customer experience
customer journey mapping 131–133
customer lifetime value (CLV) 72
customer management system 125
customer relationship management (CRM) 193, 195–197
customer relationship skills 168–169
customers 87, 192; assessing the quality of service before consumption 30–31; categories of 88; discriminating between one service offering from another 29; listening to external customers 95–97; perceptions of 96; personal interaction 12; quality control 34; risk perceptions with service purchases 29; role of technology 201–202; seeking personal information regarding reliability of services 30
customer satisfaction 40; linking to loyalty 72–75; loyalty 71–72; *see also* customer experience
customer-to-customer communication 103–104
customer variability 143
customer voice 140

data, utilizing: to empower employees 197–198; to enhance customer engagement 195–197
database marketing 193
Dave's Noodle and Hotpot 218–219
demand for services 46; balancing capacity and demand 48–52; managing 54–59; pricing and revenue 58–59; reliability and timing 47–48
demand pricing 58–59
Deming, W. Edwards 65
differentiation from other companies, service vision 115
Differentiators 145, 203

digital age, service quality 81–82
digital marketing touchpoints 194–195
digital networks 191
digital transformation (DX) 187
disconfirmation, service quality 69–70
discriminating between one service offering from another 29
disempowerment 173
Disney 88
distinctive characteristics of service, implications of **28**
diversity 24–25
Domino's Pizza 209
DX *see* digital transformation
dynamic pricing strategies 58–59

'E' service quality 81–82
education/training, total quality management (TQM) 67
emotional dissonance 169
emotional labor 169–170
emotions **143**
employee actions 169
employee centricity, Haidilao 180–181
employee-customer interface/touchpoint 126, 142; challenges with managing **143**; moments-of-truth 126–129
employee deviance **143**
employee empowerment 155–156; data 197–198
employee management system 125
employees: creating brand communities 108–109; as customer advocates 107; employee-centricity 180–181; empowerment 173–174, 176–178; encouraging feedback 106; frontline service employees (part-time marketers) 144–145; inseparability 105; interdependency 105–106; internal customers 87–88; as internal customers 87–88; as listening posts 105; managing as customers 164–166; role of technology 201–202; *see also* firm performance
employee stress **143**
empowerment 167, 173–178; organizational dimension 176–177; personal dimension 176; Tata Tele Business Services 174–176; total quality management (TQM) 67; utilizing data to empower employees 197–198
Enablers 145, **203**

engaging: customers 146–147; internal customers 104–105
espoused values 171
E-S-QUAL (electronic service quality) 81–82
exceeding expectations, service quality 70
ex-customers 88
expectations: gaps model 79; service quality 70
experience 4 *see also* customer experience
experience economy 76
experience management 6
'Extended Marketing Mix' 10
external customers 87–88, 165; listening to 95–97

failure *see* service failures
Fast Company 211
Federal Express (FedEx) 115
feedback: encouraging from employees 106; responding to 104; TripAdvisor.com 103
firm performance 178; internal service quality 179; service-profit chain 178–179
fluctuations in demand 54–55
focus-group interviews 98
forms of exchange, new service ecosystem 192–193
fostering a culture of innovation 213–216
four Ps of the 'Marketing Mix' 10, 37–38
Fourth Industrial Revolution 187
frontline employees, role of 144–145; *see also* employees
frontline service employees (part-time marketers) 136, 164; customer experience 138; technology 202
Frontline Service Technology (FST) 15, 203
fuel-on-demand 60–61
functional quality 75–76
funding mechanism, service design 125

gamification 199–200
gaps model, service quality 78–79
gaps principle 77
global economies, evolution of 7–8
goods-dominant logic 41
Google 5

Google India, Internet Saathi 50–51
growth: of service sector 8–9; technology 187

Haidilao 180–181
Harley Davidson 109
harmony between organizations, employees, and customers 140–142
Heavenly Bed 31
heterogeneity **28**; challenges in managing and marketing services 24–25; 'high-touch' and 'high-tech' 188–189; managing 32–33
Hilton Hotels 116–117
holistic view of relationships 147–149
hotels, branded differentiation 31–32
HRM *see* human resources management
human interaction 188
human resources management (HRM) **144**, 168–169
human touch 12
hybrid innovation 220–221

IBM 4, 13
ICH *see* Indian Coffee House
identifying service failures 150–151
iGrab Café 216–217
IHIP (intangibility, heterogeneity, inseparability and perishability) 22, 37, 41, 46
IKEA 36
implications of distinctive characteristics of service **28**
imposed service innovation 218–220
impression management **144**
in-depth interviews with individual customers 97–98
Indian Coffee House (ICH) 107–108
influencers 195
ING Direct 188
in-house customer satisfaction surveys 99
innovation 208; blended (hybrid) innovation 220–221; co-innovation with stakeholders 221–222; importance of 208–209; integrated approach to 220–222; as a process 211–213; S-curve *212*; *see also* service innovation; technology
innovation management 209
innovativeness 208–209
Innovators 145, **203**

inseparability 26, **28**; employees 105; managing 33–36
intangibility **28**; branded differentiation 31–32; challenges in managing and marketing services 23–24; managing 29–32
integrated approach to innovation 220–222
interdependency: of employees 105–106; of service providers 13–16
internal customers 87–88; internal marketing 104, 165–167; *see also* employees; listening to 104–105
internal marketing 165–167
internal service quality 179
Internet of Things (IoT) 60–61
Internet Saathi 50–51
internet *see* online platforms
interviews with individual customers 97–98
IoT *see* Internet of Things

Japan: moments-of-truth 127; quality control 65–66
JioMart 211

knowledge graph, The Learning App (BYJU) 17

leadership: Narayana Health 122–124; total quality management (TQM) 67
The Learning App (BYJU) 16–17
leveraging place 59
linking satisfaction and loyalty 72–75
listening posts, employees as 105
listening skills **144**
listening to: customers, internal customers 104–107; external customers 95–99; internal customers 104–105
long-term relationships, building 145–146
loyalty 145–146; customer satisfaction 71–72; linking to satisfaction 72–75
loyalty programs, REDTAG 196–197

machine learning 60–61, 221
management 5; philosophy on quality 65–66; *see also* quality management
managing employees: as customers 164–166; human resources management (HRM) 168–169; service climate

Index

172–173; service culture, creating 170–172
managing service capacity 52–54
managing service demand 54–59
managing services: challenges to 22–27; heterogeneity 32–33; inseparability 33–36; intangibility 29–32; perishability 36–37; supply and demand 48–52
marketing 5; challenges to 22–27; internal marketing 165–167; purpose of 36; service strategy 117–118; *see also* service marketing
Marketing Mix: four Ps of 10, 37; seven Ps 37–39, 57–58
market surveys 98–99
Marriott International 31–32, 164
maximum capacity 53
Medallia, Crown Resorts 40–41
mindset, transforming 7
moments-of-truth 126–130
multiple consumption 34–35
MyStarbucksIdea.com 146
mystery shoppers 102

Nahari 118–119
Narayana Health 122–124
Net Promoter Score (NPS) 99–100
network facilitation 201
new service business models 216–218
new service ecosystem: customer expectations 190; 'high-touch' and 'high-tech' 188–189; forms of exchange 192–193; online platforms 191–192; realms of service (servicescape) 189
Nike 35, 221
Nordic approach 75–77
Nordstrom 94–95
NPS *see* Net Promoter Score

objectivity, total quality management (TQM) 67
offering, service design 125
on-demand service models 59
online banking services 59
online platforms 191–192; capacity 53–54; interdependency of service providers 15–16
Online Reputation Management (ORM) 154
optimism **144**

optimizing customer experience 130–133
optimum capacity 53
organizational climate 172–173
organizational culture 171; levels of *172*
ORM *see* Online Reputation Management

part-time marketers 136, 169; *see also* frontline service employees
PayTm Gold 90–92
peer service providers 192
people, Marketing Mix **38**, 57
perception: of customers 96–97; of quality 35, 121, 145, 149
peripheral services 11–12
perishability **28**; challenges in managing and marketing services 27–28; managing 36–37
personal interaction 12
personalization 190
personal touch 188–189
physical evidence, Marketing Mix **39**, 58
place, Marketing Mix **38**, 57, 59
platform providers 192
post-encounters 193
potential future customers 88
price, Marketing Mix **38**, 57
pricing, service capacity 58–59
process, Marketing Mix **39**, 58
process dimensions, zone of tolerance 80–81
product, Marketing Mix **38**, 57
product-centric approaches 90
product centricity 89–90
product differentiation, quality 71
product-experience continuum *24*
product variation 57
promotion, Marketing Mix **38**, 57
Ps of Marketing Mix 10, 37–39, 57–58
psychology of waiting 56

quality 45; assessing services before consumption 30–31; and capacity 52–53; importance of 71–72; internal service quality 179; perception of 121; relationship with demand 55–56; service process 120; waiting 56; *see also* service quality
quality control 34, 65–66, 71; customers' role in 34

quality management 64; in Asia 65–66; early days of 65; as philosophy 65–66; service quality movement 68; total quality management (TQM) 66–67
quality of service performance 25
queuing strategies 56–57

Raveendran, Byju 16–17
readjusting service strategy 118
realms of service (servicescape) 189
Recovery' elements, service quality 82
REDTAG 196–197, 202
reduction in capacity 49
reformation 222
reincarnation 222–223
relationship chains 147–149
relationships: building long-term relationships 145–146; holistic view of 147–149
reliability of services: seeking personal information regarding 30; service capacity 47–48
Reliance Retail 211
renovation 222
responding to customer feedback 104
revenue, service capacity 58–59
risk perceptions with service purchases 29
robots 203

SAS *see* Scandinavian Airlines
satisfaction, linking to loyalty 72–75
Scandinavian Airlines (SAS) 128–129
search engine marketing (SEM) 194
search engine optimization (SEO) 194
seeking personal information regarding reliability of services 30
SEM *see* search engine marketing
SEO *see* search engine optimization
service 4–5; defined 10–11; as a unified force 6; *see also* experience
service blueprints 130–131
service capacity 46–47; balancing capacity and demand 48–52; managing 52–54; managing service demand 54–59; pricing and revenue 58–59; reliability of services 47–48; timing 47–48
service climate 172–173
service consumption, stages of *138*
service culture, creating 170–172
service design 124–126
service differentiation 147

service dimensions, importance of *80*
service-dominant logic 41–42
Service Encounter 2.0 185, 201, **203**, 221
service encounters 126, *186*; building long-term relationships 145–146; customer-contact person 129–130; identifying challenges 142; moments-of-truth 126–129; overcoming challenges 142–144; role of frontline employees 144–145; *see also* customer experience
service encounter triad 140–142
service excellence, commitment to 159
service failures 149; categorizing 149–150; identifying failures 150–151; service recovery 152–153; *see also* service recovery
service guarantees 137, 155–159
service imperative 1
service innovation: artificial intelligence (AI) 218; evolution of 209–210; fostering a culture of innovation 213–216; imposed service innovation 218–220; new service business models 216–218; types of 210–211; *see also* innovation
service interrelationships 14–15
service managers 2; challenges for 28–32; *see also* managing services
service marketing 193; defined 9; digital marketing touchpoints 194–195; utilizing data 195–198
service networks (ecosystems) 14
service-oriented activities 8
service output, control of 26
service packages/bundles 11–12
service performance, quality of 25
service process 114, 120–124, 150
service products 14
service-profit chain, firm performance 178–179
service providers, interdependency of 13–14
service quality 64, 129; Burner India 73–75; confirmation/disconfirmation paradigm 69–70; customer delight 72–75; defined 68–69; in digital age 81–82; exceeding expectations 70; expectations 70; gaps model 78–79; gaps principle 77; loyalty 72–75; Nordic approach 75–77; organizational climate 172–173;

SERVQUAL 79–80; zone of tolerance 80–81; *see also* quality
service quality movement 68
service recovery 151–152; benefits of 155; implementing recovery strategies 155–156; Zomato 153–155
service recovery strategies 137, 152–153; implementing 155–156
services 21; core services 11–12; peripheral services 11–12; tangible-intangible continuum 12
servicescape 189
service scripting **144**
service sector 7; GDP composition 9; growth of 8–9
service strategy 114, 117–119, 121–124
service systems 113–114, 120–124
service transformation 222–223
service vision 113–117, 121–124
service vision statements 115
servitization 12–13
SERVQUAL 77, 79–80
seven Ps 10, 37–39, 57–58
shared assumptions 171
shared vision, total quality management (TQM) 67
sharing economy 15–16; capacity 53–54
Shetty, Devi Prasad 122–124
The Silent Masses 150
Singapore Airlines 33, 140–141
smiling **144**
social media marketing (SMM) 194–195
solution orientation 1, 4
Southwest Airlines 118
stakeholders, co-innovation with 221–222
Starbucks 146, 221
substitution, technology 201
successful service organizations 113; service-profit chain 178–179
supply and demand *see* service capacity
surveys: in-house customer satisfaction surveys 99; market surveys 98–99

talent management 168–169
talent retention 215–216
tangible-intangible continuum of services 12
Tata Tele Business Services, (TTBS) 174–176

Tata Trusts, Internet Saathi 50–51
teamwork, total quality management (TQM) 67
technical quality 75
technological advancements 198–199
technology 185–186; application of 198–203; changing roles of customers and employees 201–202; engaging customers 146; growth of 187; new service ecosystem 188–193; robots 203; role of 201; service touchpoints 145; *see also* innovation
technology-led interrelationships 15–17
time-and-location variation 57
timing 47–48
total organizational approach, importance of 40–41
total quality management (TQM) 66–67
touchpoints 7, 142; digital marketing touchpoints 194–195; employee-customer interface/touchpoint 126; moments-of-truth 126–129
TQM *see* total quality management
transforming: company mindset 7; from products to services/experiences 7–8
TripAdvisor.com 103
trust 5, 170
TTBS *see* Tata Tele Business Services

Uber 46, 140
Udaan 124

value 5, 21–22, 30–31; co-creation 35–36, 146–147
value-experience continuum *138*
variability 24, 32–33
variations in demand 54–55
virtual queues 56
virtual reality 199

waiting 56; queuing strategies 56–57
Westin hotel group 31
WhatsApp 211
word-of-mouth (WOM) 139, 193

yield management 57–59

Zomato 153–155
zone of tolerance (ZOT) 80–81

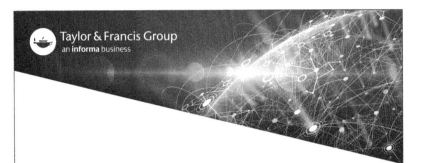

Printed and bound by CPI Group (UK) Ltd, Croydon, CR0 4YY
01/12/2024
01797780-0009